THE
EXECUTIVE
BRANCH OF THE FEDERAL GOVERNMENT

PURPOSE, PROCESS, AND PEOPLE

THE EXECUTIVE

BRANCH OF THE FEDERAL GOVERNMENT

PURPOSE, PROCESS, AND PEOPLE

EDITED BY BRIAN DUIGNAN, SENIOR EDITOR, RELIGION AND PHILOSOPHY

Educational Publishing

IN ASSOCIATION WITH

EDUCATIONAL SERVICES

Published in 2010 by Britannica Educational Publishing
(a trademark of Encyclopædia Britannica, Inc.)
in association with Rosen Educational Services, LLC
29 East 21st Street, New York, NY 10010.

Distributed exclusively by Rosen Educational Services.
For a listing of additional Britannica Educational Publishing titles, call toll free (800) 237-9932.

First Edition

Britannica Educational Publishing
Michael I. Levy: Executive Editor
Marilyn L. Barton: Senior Coordinator, Production Control
Steven Bosco: Director, Editorial Technologies
Lisa S. Braucher: Senior Producer and Data Editor
Yvette Charboneau: Senior Copy Editor
Kathy Nakamura: Manager, Media Acquisition
Brian Duignan: Senior Editor, Religion and Philosophy

Rosen Educational Services
Hope Lourie Killcoyne: Senior Editor and Project Manager
Nelson Sá: Art Director
Matthew Cauli: Designer
Introduction by Richard Worth

Library of Congress Cataloging-in-Publication Data

The executive branch of the federal government: purpose, process, and people / edited by
Brian Duignan.
    p. cm. — (U.S. government: the separation of powers)
"In association with Britannica Educational Publishing, Rosen Educational Services."
ISBN 978-1-61530-023-5 (library binding)
1. Presidents—United States—History. 2. Presidents—United States—Biography.
3. Executive departments—United States. 4. United States—Politics and government.
I. Duignan, Brian.
JK511.E94 2010
351.73—dc22

2009037873

CONTENTS

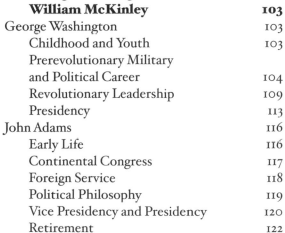

267

282

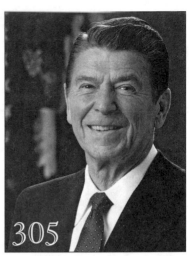

305

324

344

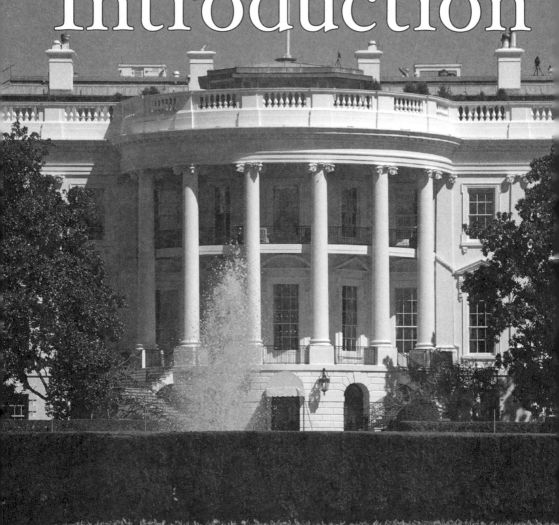

Introduction

During the hot summer months of 1787, delegates from the American states met in Philadelphia and created a new framework of government, called the United States Constitution. While the delegates recognized the need for a strong executive to govern the United States, they did not want an all-powerful monarch who might become a tyrant. Instead they created three branches of government—the executive, the legislature and the judiciary—each with specific powers, and each with the power to check and balance the other.

In Article II, the Constitution spells out the powers of the president, the chief executive of the United States. They include the power to make treaties with foreign governments and to appoint ambassadors, federal judges, and other officials—but only with the consent of the U.S. Senate. The president is also commander in chief of the nation's armed forces, but only Congress has the power to declare war. In 1789, as a result of the first presidential election, George Washington became president of the United States and John Adams vice president. Washington named a small group of political leaders to his cabinet, including Alexander Hamilton, Secretary of the Treasury; Thomas Jefferson, Secretary of State; and Henry Knox, Secretary of War. The Constitution specified that the president's term of office should be four years, although it did not state how many times a president could run for reelection. Washington chose to run in 1792 for a second four-year term. After serving his second term, he declined to run for a third, setting a precedent followed by other presidents until the 20th century.

The president and vice president are not elected directly by the American voters. Rather, they are elected by electors, who are selected, under the Constitution, by a method determined by each state legislature (today, voters choose electors, who in turn elect America's top two executives).

According to the Constitution as it was written in 1787, the electors voted for two people. The one who received the most votes became president, and the individual who came in second became vice president. But in the presidential election of 1800, as electors began to vote along party lines, there was a tie vote between Thomas Jefferson and Aaron Burr, who ostensibly ran as a ticket. The House of Representatives, under the terms of the Constitution, was required to break the tie, and Jefferson was elected. To avoid a similar problem in the future, Congress proposed the Twelfth Amendment in 1803. According to that Amendment, ratified in 1804, electors could cast only one vote specifically for president and one vote specifically for vice president. A year later the Amendment was approved by a majority of the states and became part of the Constitution.

Meanwhile, the power of the executive branch was growing in America's foreign affairs. In his Farewell Address to the United States, President George Washington had warned against the United States becoming involved in the affairs of other nations. But in 1812, at the request of James Madison, the House of Representatives approved a declaration of war against Great Britain. This bloody conflict finally came to a conclusion in 1815. Madison's successor, James Monroe, proclaimed the Monroe Doctrine—warning European powers that the Americas were no longer to be considered areas for further expansion of colonial empires and pledging that the United States would not interfere in the internal affairs of or the wars between European powers.

Andrew Jackson, elected in 1828, has been considered by historians to be one of America's strongest chief executives. Under the Constitution, the president has the right to veto legislation passed by Congress, which can override his veto only by a two-thirds majority. Jackson vetoed a bill to re-charter a national bank that had been established decades earlier. President Jackson felt that the national bank favoured the interests of the wealthy. In his conflict with the bank, President Jackson invoked a president's right to executive privilege and refused to turn over certain records to the U.S. Senate. Proponents of executive privilege maintain that the executive branch should have the right to keep confidential certain documents and internal communications whose release might adversely affect the operation of the federal government. Many presidents since Jackson have invoked a similar right, believing it the only way to ensure candor among top advisors — otherwise, they might be afraid to say something controversial for fear that it might eventually leak out to the press and be used against them.

The power of the presidency grew after the election of President Abraham Lincoln in 1861, as the new president tried to respond to the secession of eleven southern states from the Union. Lincoln called up the militia in the North, although the Constitution stated that this act required congressional approval. He increased the size of the army and navy and spent money to arm them without the consent of Congress. And finally, he suspended the writ of habeas corpus, a foundation stone of the American judicial system stipulating that anyone who is arrested must be charged under the law or released. While the Constitution stated that the writ of habeas corpus could be suspended during a period of rebellion, it was unclear whether Congress or the president had the right to suspend it.

Near the end of the Civil War, President Lincoln was assassinated and succeeded in office by his vice president, Andrew Johnson. The U.S. Constitution specifies that upon the president's death, resignation, or removal from office by impeachment, the vice president shall assume all of the presidential duties. (However, until the Twenty-fifth Amendment to the Constitution, ratified in 1967, the

office of vice president would remain vacant after the vice
president succeeded to the presidency.) Johnson was the
third vice president to take over the presidency. In 1867,
however, following a series of conflicts with Congress,
Johnson was charged with "high Crimes and Misdemeanors,"
and impeached by the House of Representatives. He was
tried in the U.S. Senate, as specified in the Constitution,
but was acquitted by one vote (conviction requires a two-
thirds vote) and continued to serve until 1869, when a new
president took office.

A central feature in the history of the U.S. Government
has been the changing balance between the executive and
legislative branches. Congress reasserted its power during
the impeachment of President Johnson and continued to
do so over the next several decades. By the early 20th century, however, the balance had shifted again. In 1901, Vice
President Theodore Roosevelt became chief executive
after the assassination of President William McKinley.
Among other departures from the past, Roosevelt led the
United States to a much stronger role in international
affairs. In one of his speeches, President Roosevelt said
that the foreign policy of the United States should be
"Speak softly and carry a big stick." As part of his "Big
Stick Diplomacy," Roosevelt doubled the size of the
U.S. Navy. In 1903, he supported a rebellion in Panama—
part of Colombia—and sent the Navy to prevent the
Colombian government from putting down the revolt.
The new Panamanian government soon agreed to allow
the United States to build a canal across the Isthmus of
Panama, connecting the Caribbean and the Pacific Ocean.

The role of the president in world affairs grew larger
after the election of President Woodrow Wilson in 1912.
Two years later, World War I broke out in Europe, pitting
the Allies—Great Britain, France, and Russia—against the
Central Powers—Germany, Austria-Hungary, and the

Ottoman Empire. Although Wilson had campaigned in 1916 on the slogan "He Kept Us Out of War," in 1917 he secured a Congressional declaration of war to join the Allies in their struggle. As America prepared to enter the war, President Wilson formulated a program called the Fourteen Points as the foundation of a peace agreement after the war had ended. Perhaps the most important part of the program was Point Fourteen—a League of Nations that would try to prevent future wars from breaking out. Following the defeat of the Central Powers a year later, President Wilson traveled to a peace conference in Versailles, France, to persuade the Allies to abide by his Fourteen Point program. Although Wilson failed, the Allies did agree to establish a League of Nations as part of the Treaty of Versailles. However, the president was unable to persuade the U.S. Senate—which had to approve all foreign treaties—to agree to the treaty, and the United States never joined the League. It was a stinging defeat for Wilson and a shifting of the balance of power from the executive branch to the U.S. Congress.

In 1929, the United States and the rest of the world sank into a severe economic downturn known as the Great Depression. An estimated 25 percent or more of the American labour force was thrown out of work. In 1932, Americans elected as president Democrat Franklin Roosevelt who promised to fight the depression with an array of federal programs known as the New Deal. After the U.S. Supreme Court invalidated many of these measures, Roosevelt proposed a reorganization plan that would have enabled him to appoint one new Supreme Court justice for each sitting justice aged 70 or over, thereby decreasing the chance that the court would strike down future reform legislation. This "court-packing" scheme, which would have greatly enhanced the power of the executive, was eventually voted down in Congress.

The New Deal created agencies that financed construction and environmental-cleanup projects, established new parks, and built dams to provide hydroelectric power, all of which created jobs for thousands of unemployed workers. In 1935, the Social Security Administration became part of the executive branch, administering a program of benefits for the unemployed and a retirement program for the aged.

In 1940, President Roosevelt broke the precedent established by George Washington and ran for a third term in office. He became the first president elected three times and successfully ran for a fourth term in 1944. After his death the following year, Roosevelt was succeeded by his vice president, Harry Truman. During Truman's tenure in office, Congress proposed an amendment stating that no individual could be elected president more than twice. The Twenty-second Amendment was approved by the states in 1951.

Nevertheless, the growth of the executive branch continued, as more and more agencies and departments were added. By 1950, there were already seven departments: Department of State (1789), Department of the Treasury (1789), Department of Interior (1849), Department of Agriculture (1862), Department of Justice (1870), Department of Commerce (1913), Department of Labor (1913), and Department of Defense (1947, the new name for the War Department, which had been established in 1789).

Since then seven more departments have been created: Department of Housing and Urban Development (1965), Department of Transportation (1967), Department of Energy (1977), Department of Health and Human Services (1979), Department of Education (1980), Department of Veterans Affairs (1989), and Department of Homeland Security (2003).

During the 1960s, President Lyndon Johnson initiated a series of reforms known as the Great Society, which expanded the domestic programs directed by the executive branch. These included a retirement health-care program called Medicare. Meanwhile, Johnson had also persuaded Congress to pass the Gulf of Tonkin Resolution following an alleged conflict off the coast of North Vietnam between U.S. destroyers and North Vietnamese torpedo boats. This resolution enabled the president to use military power to assist nations in Southeast Asia that were threatened by invasion. As a result, President Johnson greatly expanded the U.S. commitment to the war in Vietnam without ever going to Congress for a declaration of war.

Like Lyndon Johnson, Republican President Richard Nixon, Johnson's successor, tried to assert the power of the executive over the other branches of government. Following the break-in at Democratic headquarters in Washington's Watergate office-apartment-hotel complex in 1972, President Nixon asserted that tape recordings of conversations made in his office regarding Watergate were protected by executive privilege. Therefore, he asserted, they should not be turned over to the Congressional committees investigating the break-in. However, the Supreme Court ruled against Nixon, which led eventually to his resignation in 1974—the first president to resign his office.

More recently, the issue of presidential power arose after the terrorist attacks in America on September 11, 2001, that killed nearly 3,000 people. President George W. Bush responded by declaring a War on Terror. Arguing that wartime conditions existed in the United States, the Bush administration claimed that the president could suspend the writ of habeas corpus by placing "enemy combatants," including American citizens, in indefinite

military custody without charge and without legal representation. The Bush administration also sanctioned the
torture of captured enemy combatants to extract information from them regarding potential terrorist attacks—a
violation of international law. At the centre of these controversies was not only President Bush but his vice
president, Dick Cheney. Most vice presidents in the past
have remained in the background, exercising very little
power. But Cheney played a key role in making decisions
during the Bush administration. Both Bush and Cheney
strongly believed in enhanced powers for the executive
branch of government.

Barack Obama, the first African American to serve as
U.S. President, took the oath of office in January 2009.
Hailed by many abroad and at home as the best hope for
America's future, he was simultaneously beset by critics
who questioned both the depth of his background and his
legislative agenda. Obama is the latest in a line of presidents to take the office and reshape it, and in so doing,
reshape the nation he represents.

The Role of the Executive

I n his *Politics*, the ancient Greek philosopher Aristotle
distinguished among three kinds of governmental
activity: the decisions of leaders or other officials, the
deliberations of citizens concerning their common affairs,
and the legal rulings of the courts. This threefold classification is not precisely the same as the modern distinction
among the executive, legislative, and judicial functions of
government. In modern states, the executive functions
include formulating and directing the domestic and foreign policies of the government; the legislative functions
include creating laws and (in many countries) selecting
government leaders, appropriating funds, and ratifying
treaties and appointments; and the judicial functions
include deciding controversies over the application of the
law and (in many countries) issuing authoritative interpre-
tations of the law and determining whether existing laws
or the acts of government institutions are constitutionally
valid. Another difference between Aristotle's classification
and the practice of modern states is that Aristotle intended
to make only a theoretical distinction among governmental functions—he stopped short of recommending that
they be assigned as powers to separate institutions or
branches of government. The first person to advocate the
separation of governmental powers among executive,
legislative, and judicial branches was the 17th-century
French political theorist Montesquieu. After Montesquieu,
the concept of separation of powers became one of the
principal doctrines of modern constitutionalism. Nearly
all modern constitutions, from the U.S. Constitution (1787)

through the French Declaration of the Rights of Man and of the Citizen (1789) up to the constitutions of the post-colonial states founded in Africa and Asia in the mid-20th century provide for the separate establishment of an executive, a legislature, and a judiciary.

An important feature of constitutional government is that the functions assigned to the different branches ensure that political power is shared among them. In the U.S. system, for example, the different branches share some of the same powers insofar as each branch is able to prevent certain actions by the others—e.g., the president (the chief executive) may veto, or reject, legislation passed by Congress, the legislative branch of the federal government; the Senate (one of the two chambers of Congress, the other being the House of Representatives) may reject treaties and certain appointments made by the president; and the courts may invalidate laws passed by Congress or certain acts by the president or by executive agencies. In parliamentary forms of government such as that of the United Kingdom, power is shared through an even greater integration of the functions and even the personnel of the executive and the legislature. In the nonconstitutional systems of totalitarian or dictatorial countries, in contrast, although there may be separate institutions such as legislatures, executives, and judiciaries, power is not shared but rather concentrated in a single institution. Because this body is not subject to the checks of shared power, the exercise of political power is uncontrolled or absolute.

THE POLITICAL EXECUTIVE

Political executives are government officials who participate in the formulation and direction of government policy. They include not only heads of state and government leaders—presidents, prime ministers, premiers, chancellors, and other chief executives—but also many secondary figures, such as cabinet members and ministers, councillors, and agency heads. In the United States and other large industrialized countries there are several thousand political executives, including the president, dozens of political appointees in the cabinet departments, in the agencies, in the commissions, and in the White House staff, and hundreds of senior civil servants.

The crucial element in the organization of a national executive is the role assigned to the chief executive. In presidential systems, such as in the United States, the president is both the political head of the government and also the ceremonial head of state. In parliamentary systems, such as that of the United Kingdom, the prime minister is the national political leader, but another figure, a monarch or elected president, serves as the head of state. In mixed presidential–parliamentary systems, such as that established in France under the Fifth Republic's constitution of 1958, the president serves as head of state but also wields important political powers, including the appointment of a prime minister and cabinet to serve as the government.

The manner in which the chief executive is elected or selected is often decisive in shaping his role in the political system. Thus, although he receives his seals of office from the monarch, the effective election of a British prime minister usually occurs in a private conclave of the leading members of his party in Parliament. Elected to Parliament from only one of nearly 650 constituencies, he is tied to the fortunes of the legislative majority that he leads. In contrast, the American president is elected by a nationwide electorate, and, although he leads his party's ticket, his fortunes are independent of his party. Even when the opposition party controls the Congress, his fixed term and his independent base of power allow him considerable

freedom to manoeuvre. These contrasts explain many of
the differences in the roles of the two chief executives.
The British prime minister invariably has served for many
years in Parliament and has developed skills in debate and
in political negotiation. His major political tasks are the
designation of the other members of the cabinet, the
direction of parliamentary strategy, and the retention of
the loyalty of a substantial majority of his legislative party.
The presidential chief executive, on the other hand, often
lacks prior legislative and even national-governmental
experience, and his main concern is with the cultivation of
a majority in the electorate through the leadership of public opinion. Of course, since the president must have a
legislative program and often cannot depend on the support of a congressional majority, he may also need the skills
of a legislative strategist and negotiator.

Another important area of contrast between different
national executives concerns their role in executing and
administering the law. In the U.S. presidential system, the
personnel of the executive branch are constitutionally
separated from the personnel of Congress: no executive
officeholder may seek election to either house of Congress,
and no member of Congress may hold executive office. In
parliamentary systems the political management of government ministries is placed in the hands of the party
leadership in parliament. In the U.S. system the president
often appoints to cabinet positions persons who have had
little prior experience in politics, and may even appoint
members of the opposition party. In the British system,
cabinet appointments are made to consolidate the prime
minister's personal ascendancy within the parliamentary
party or to placate its different factions. Thus in the U.S.
system the cabinet is responsible to the president, whereas
in the British system it is responsible to the majority or

governing party in Parliament. These differences extend even further into the character of the two systems of administration and the role played by civil servants. In the U.S. system a change in administration is accompanied by the exodus of a very large number of top government executives—the political appointees who play the vital part in shaping day-to-day policy in all the departments and agencies of the national government. In Britain, when political control of the House of Commons changes, only the ministers, their parliamentary secretaries, and one or two other top political aids are replaced. For all practical purposes, the ministries remain intact and continue under the supervision of permanent civil servants.

PRESIDENTIAL SYSTEMS OF GOVERNMENT

The basic features of the U.S. presidency noted above are part of what distinguishes presidential systems of government from other systems. By definition, in a presidential system the president must originate from outside the legislative authority. In most countries such presidents are elected directly by the citizens, though separation of origin can also be ensured through an electoral college (as in the United States), provided that legislators cannot also serve as electors. Second, the president serves simultaneously as head of government and head of state; he is empowered to select cabinet ministers, who are responsible to him and not to the legislative majority. And third, the president has some constitutionally guaranteed legislative authority: for example, the U.S. president signs into law or vetoes bills passed by Congress, though Congress may override a presidential veto with a two-thirds majority vote in both houses.

In presidential systems the president holds power for a fixed term of office, and his authority does not depend on the strength of his party in the legislature. In many such systems the president may be removed from office only through impeachment—in the United States this requires a vote of impeachment by a majority of the House of Representatives followed by conviction by a two-thirds majority vote of the Senate. Government officials may also be impeached in the British system; in Britain the House of Commons acts as prosecutor and the House of Lords as judge in an impeachment proceeding. Whereas in Britain conviction on an impeachment has resulted in fines, imprisonment, and even execution, in the United States the penalties extend no further than removal and disqualification from office. In the United States the impeachment process has rarely been employed, largely because it is so cumbersome. It can occupy Congress for a lengthy period of time and involve conflicting and troublesome political pressures. Repeated attempts by Congress to amend the procedure, however, have been unsuccessful, partly because impeachment is regarded as an integral part of the system of checks and balances in the U.S. government.

Presidential systems may differ in important respects from the U.S. model. In terms of constitutional provisions, the most important variation is in the powers that the constitution delegates to the president. In contrast to the requirement that Congress needs a supermajority to override a presidential veto in the United States, for example, in some countries (e.g., Brazil and Colombia) a presidential veto may be overridden by a simple majority. Many presidential constitutions (e.g., those in Argentina, Brazil, Colombia, and Russia) explicitly give the president the authority to introduce new laws by decree, thereby bypassing the legislature, though typically the legislature can rescind such laws after the fact.

THE PRESIDENCY OF THE UNITED STATES

DUTIES OF THE OFFICE

The presidency is the chief executive office of the United States. The president is vested with great authority and is arguably the most powerful elected official in the world.

The Constitution succinctly defines presidential functions, powers, and responsibilities. The president's chief duty is to make sure that the laws are faithfully executed, and this duty is performed through an elaborate system of executive agencies that includes cabinet-level departments. Presidents appoint all cabinet heads and most other high-ranking officials of the executive branch of the federal government. They also nominate all judges of the federal judiciary, including the members of the Supreme Court. Their appointments to executive and judicial posts must be approved by a majority of the Senate. The Senate usually confirms these appointments, though it occasionally rejects a nominee to whom a majority of members have strong objections. The president is also the commander in chief of the country's military and has unlimited authority to direct the movements of land, sea, and air forces. The president has the power to make treaties with foreign governments, though the Senate must approve such treaties by a two-thirds majority. The president has the power to sign into law or veto bills passed by Congress, though Congress can override the president's veto by summoning a two-thirds majority in favour of the measure. In practice, presidential powers have expanded to include drafting legislation, formulating foreign policy, conducting personal diplomacy, and leading the president's political party. By virtue of the Twenty-second Amendment (1951), the president is elected to two terms of office.

PRIMARY DOCUMENT: THE CONSTITUTION OF THE UNITED STATES: ARTICLE II

Section 1. The executive power shall be vested in a President of the United States of America. He shall hold his office during the term of four years, and, together with the vice-president, chosen for the same term, be elected as follows:

Each state shall appoint, in such manner as the legislature thereof may direct, a number of electors, equal to the whole number of senators and representatives to which the state may be entitled in the Congress.

The electors shall meet in their respective states and vote by ballot for two persons. And they shall make a list of all the persons voted for and of the number of votes for each; which list they shall sign and certify, and transmit sealed to the seat of the government of the United States, directed to the president of the Senate. The president of the Senate shall, in the presence of the Senate and House of Representatives, open all the certificates, and the votes shall then be counted. The person having the greatest number of votes shall be the President, if such number be a majority of the whole number of electors appointed; and if there be more than one who have such majority, and have an equal number of votes, then the House of Representatives shall immediately choose by ballot one of them for President; and if no person have a majority, then from the five highest on the list the said house shall in like manner choose the President. In every case, after the choice of the President, the person having the greatest number of votes of the electors shall be the vice-president.

No person except a natural-born citizen, or a citizen of the United States at the time of the adoption of this Constitution, shall be eligible to the office of President; neither shall any person be eligible to that office who shall not have attained to the age of thirty-five years.

Section 2. The President shall be commander in chief of the Army and Navy of the United States. He may require the opinion, in writing, of the principal officer in each of the executive departments upon any subject relating to the duties of their respective offices. And he shall have power to grant reprieves and pardons for offenses against the United States, except in cases of impeachment.

He shall have power, by and with the advice and consent of the Senate, to make treaties, provided two-thirds of the senators present concur; and he shall nominate, and by and with the advice and consent of the Senate, shall appoint ambassadors, other public ministers and consuls, judges of the Supreme Court, and all other officers of the United States whose appointments are not herein otherwise provided for, and which shall be established by law.

Section 3. He shall from time to time give to the Congress information of the state of the Union, and recommend to their consideration such measures as he shall judge necessary and expedient.

Section 4. The President, vice-president, and all civil officers of the United States shall be removed from office on impeachment for, and conviction of, treason, bribery, or other high crimes and misdemeanors.

HISTORICAL DEVELOPMENT OF THE PRESIDENCY

In North America the title of president was first used for the chief magistrate of some of the British colonies. These colonial presidents were always associated with a colonial council to which they were elected, and the title of president carried over to the heads of some of the state governments (e.g., Delaware and Pennsylvania) that were organized after the start of the American Revolution in 1776. The title "President of the United States" was originally applied to the officer who presided over sessions of the Continental Congress and of the Congress established under the Articles of Confederation (1781–89). In 1787–88 the framers of the new country's Constitution created the vastly more powerful office of the presidency of the United States. The president was vested with a variety of duties and powers, including negotiating treaties with foreign governments, signing into law or vetoing legislation passed by Congress, appointing high-ranking members of the executive branch and all judges of the federal judiciary, and serving as commander in chief of the armed forces.

The nation's founders originally intended the presidency to be a narrowly restricted institution. They distrusted executive authority because their experience with colonial governors had led them to believe that executive power was inimical to liberty and that a strong executive was incompatible with the republicanism embraced in the Declaration of Independence (1776). And of course, they felt betrayed by the actions of George III, the king of Great Britain and Ireland. Accordingly, their revolutionary state constitutions provided for only nominal executive branches, and the Articles of Confederation (1781–89), the first "national" constitution, established no executive branch.

Until agreement on the electoral college, most executive powers, including the conduct of foreign relations, were held by the Senate. The delegates hastily shifted powers to the executive, and the result was ambiguous. Article II, Section 1, of the Constitution of the United States begins with a simple declarative statement: "The executive Power shall be vested in a President of the United States of America." The phrasing can be read as a blanket grant of power, an interpretation that is buttressed when the language is compared with the qualified language of Article I: "All legislative Powers herein granted shall be vested in a Congress of the United States."

This loose construction, however, is mitigated in two important ways. First, Article II itemizes, in sections 2 and 3, certain presidential powers, including those of commander in chief of the armed forces, appointment making, treaty making, receiving ambassadors, and calling Congress into special session. Had the first article's section been intended as an open-ended authorization, such subsequent specifications would have made no sense. Second, a sizable array of powers traditionally associated with the executive, including the power to declare war, issue letters of marque and reprisal, and coin and borrow money, were given to Congress, not the president, and the power to make appointments and treaties was shared between the president and the Senate.

The delegates could leave the subject ambiguous because of their understanding that George Washington (1789–97) would be selected as the first president. They deliberately left blanks in Article II, trusting that Washington would fill in the details in a satisfactory manner. Indeed, it is safe to assert that had Washington not been available, the office might never have been created.

POSTREVOLUTIONARY PERIOD

Scarcely had Washington been inaugurated when an extra-constitutional attribute of the presidency became apparent. Inherently, the presidency is dual in character. The president serves as both head of government (the nation's chief administrator) and head of state (the symbolic embodiment of the nation). Through centuries of constitutional struggle between the crown and Parliament, England had separated the two offices, vesting the prime minister with the function of running the government and leaving the ceremonial responsibilities of leadership to the monarch. The American people idolized Washington, and he played his part artfully, striking a balance between "too free an intercourse and too much familiarity," which would reduce the dignity of the office, and "an ostentatious show" of aloofness, which would be improper in a republic.

But the problems posed by the dual nature of the office remained unsolved. A few presidents, notably Thomas Jefferson (1801–09) and Franklin D. Roosevelt (1933–45), proved able to perform both roles. More common were the examples of John F. Kennedy (1961–63) and Lyndon B. Johnson (1963–69). Although Kennedy was superb as the symbol of a vigorous nation—Americans were entranced by the image of his presidency as Camelot—he was ineffectual in getting legislation enacted. Johnson, by contrast, pushed through Congress a legislative program of major proportions, including the Civil Rights Act of 1964, but such was his failure as a king surrogate that he chose not to run for a second term.

Washington's administration was most important for the precedents it set. For example, he retired after two terms, establishing a tradition maintained until 1940. During his first term he made the presidency a full-fledged branch of government instead of a mere office. As commander in chief during the American Revolutionary War, he had been accustomed to surrounding himself with trusted aides and generals and soliciting their opinions. Gathering the department heads together seemed a logical extension of that practice, but the Constitution authorized him only to "require the Opinion, in writing" of the department heads. Taking the document literally would have precluded converting them into an advisory council. When the Supreme Court refused Washington's request for an advisory opinion on the matter of a neutrality proclamation in response to the French revolutionary and Napoleonic wars—on the ground that the court could decide only cases and not controversies—he turned at last to assembling his department heads. Cabinet meetings, as they came to be called, remained the principal instrument for conducting executive business until the late 20th century, though some early presidents, such as Andrew Jackson (1829–37), made little use of the cabinet.

The Constitution also authorized the president to make treaties "by and with the Advice and Consent of the

Senate," and many thought that this clause would turn the Senate into an executive council. But when Washington appeared on the floor of the Senate to seek advice about pending negotiations with American Indian tribes, the surprised senators proved themselves to be a contentious deliberative assembly, not an advisory board. Washington was furious, and thereafter neither he nor his successors took the "advice" portion of the clause seriously. At about the same time, it was established by an act of Congress that though the president had to seek the approval of the Senate for his major appointments, he could remove his appointees unilaterally. This power remained a subject of controversy and was central to the impeachment of Andrew Johnson (1865–69) in 1868.

Washington set other important precedents, especially in foreign policy. In his farewell address (1796) he cautioned his successors to "steer clear of permanent alliances with any portion of the foreign world" and not to "entangle our peace and prosperity in the toils of European ambition, rivalship, interest, humor, or caprice." His warnings laid the foundation for America's isolationist foreign policy, which lasted through most of the country's history before World War II, as well as for the Monroe Doctrine.

Perils accompanying the French revolutionary wars occupied Washington's attention, as well as that of his three immediate successors. Americans were bitterly divided over the wars, some favouring Britain and its allies and others France. Political factions had already arisen over the financial policies of Washington's secretary of the treasury, Alexander Hamilton, and from 1793 onward animosities stemming from the French Revolution hardened these factions into a system of political parties, which the framers of the Constitution had not contemplated.

The emergence of the party system also created unanticipated problems with the method for electing the president. In 1796 John Adams (1797–1801), the candidate of the Federalist Party, won the presidency, and Thomas Jefferson (1801–09), the candidate of the Democratic-Republican Party, won the vice presidency; rather than working with Adams, however, Jefferson sought to undermine the administration. In 1800, to forestall the possibility of yet another divided executive, the Federalists and the Democratic-Republicans, the two leading parties of the early republic, each nominated presidential and vice presidential candidates. Because of party-line voting and the fact that electors could not indicate a presidential or vice presidential preference between the two candidates for whom they voted, the Democratic-Republican candidates, Jefferson and Aaron Burr, received an equal number of votes. The election was thrown to the House of Representatives, and a constitutional crisis nearly ensued as the House became deadlocked. Had it remained so until the end of Adams's term on March 4, 1801, Supreme Court Chief Justice John Marshall would have become president (in keeping with the existing presidential succession act). On Feb. 17, 1801, Jefferson was finally chosen president by the House, and with the ratification of the Twelfth Amendment, beginning in 1804, electors were required to cast separate ballots for president and vice president.

THE PRESIDENCY IN THE 19TH CENTURY

Jefferson shaped the presidency almost as much as did Washington. He altered the style of the office, departing from Washington's austere dignity so far as to receive foreign ministers in run-down slippers and frayed jackets. He shunned display, protocol, and pomp; he gave no public balls or celebrations on his birthday. By completing the transition to republicanism, he humanized the presidency and made it a symbol not of the nation but of the people. He talked persuasively about the virtue of limiting government—his first inaugural address was a masterpiece on the subject—and he made gestures in that direction. He slashed the army and navy, reduced the public debt, and ended what he regarded as the "monarchical" practice of addressing Congress in person. But he also stretched the powers of the presidency in a variety of ways. While maintaining a posture of deference toward Congress, he managed legislation more effectively than any other president of the 19th century. He approved the Louisiana Purchase despite his private conviction that it was unconstitutional. He conducted a lengthy and successful war against the Barbary pirates of North Africa without seeking a formal declaration of war from Congress. He used the army against the interests of the American people in his efforts to enforce an embargo that was intended to compel Britain and France to respect America's rights as a neutral during the Napoleonic wars, the ultimate goal being to bring those two countries to the peace table. In 1810 Jefferson wrote in a letter that circumstances "sometimes occur" when "officers of high trust" must "assume authorities beyond the law" in keeping with the "*salus populi* . . . , the laws of necessity, of self-preservation, of saving our country when in danger." On those occasions "a scrupulous adherence to written law, would be to lose the law itself . . . thus absurdly sacrificing the end to the means." As he wrote,

> *When, in the battle of Germantown, General Washington's army was annoyed from Chew's house, he did not hesitate to plant his cannon against it, although the property of a citizen. When he besieged Yorktown, he leveled the suburbs, feeling*

that the laws of property must be postponed to the safety of the
nation. While the army was before Yorktown, the governor of
Virginia took horses, carriages, provisions, and even men by
force, to enable that army to stay together till it could master
the public enemy; and he was justified. A ship at sea in distress
for provisions meets another having abundance, yet refusing a
supply; the law of self-preservation authorizes the distressed to
take a supply by force. In all these cases, the unwritten laws of
necessity, of self-preservation, and of the public safety control
the written laws of meum and tuum.

From Jefferson's departure until the end of the century,
the presidency was perceived as an essentially passive institution. Only three presidents during that long span acted
with great energy, and each elicited a vehement congressional reaction. Andrew Jackson exercised the veto
flamboyantly; attempted, in the so-called Bank War, to
undermine the Bank of the United States by removing federal deposits; and sought to mobilize the army against
South Carolina when that state adopted an Ordinance of
Nullification declaring the federal tariffs of 1828 and 1832 to
be null and void within its boundaries. By the time his term
ended, the Senate had censured him and refused to receive
his messages. (When Democrats regained control of the
Senate from the Whigs, Jackson's censure was expunged.)

James K. Polk (1845–49) maneuvered the United
States into the Mexican War and only later sought a formal congressional declaration. When he asserted that "a
state of war exists" with Mexico, Sen. John C. Calhoun of
South Carolina launched a tirade against him, insisting
that a state of war could not exist unless Congress declared
one. The third strong president during the period,
Abraham Lincoln (1861–65), defending the *salus populi* in
Jeffersonian fashion, ran roughshod over the Constitution

during the American Civil War. Radical Republican congressmen were, at the time of his assassination, sharpening their knives in opposition to his plans for reconstructing the rebellious Southern states, and they wielded them to devastating effect against his successor, Andrew Johnson. They reduced the presidency to a cipher, demonstrating that Congress can be more powerful than the president if it acts with complete unity. Johnson was impeached on several grounds, including his violation of the Tenure of Office Act, which forbade the president from removing civil officers without the consent of the Senate. Although Johnson was not convicted, he and the presidency were weakened.

Contributing to the weakness of the presidency after 1824 was the use of national conventions rather than congressional caucuses to nominate presidential candidates. The new system existed primarily as a means of winning national elections and dividing the spoils of victory, and the principal function of the president became the distribution of government jobs.

CHANGES IN THE 20TH CENTURY

In the 20th century the powers and responsibilities of the presidency were transformed. Pres. Theodore Roosevelt (1901–09) regarded the presidency as a "bully pulpit" from which to preach morality and rally his fellow citizens against "malefactors of great wealth." (And by extracting from Congress a generous fund for railroad travel, he managed to put his pulpit on wheels.) Other presidents followed Roosevelt's example, with varying results. Woodrow Wilson (1913–21) led the United States into World War I to make the world "safe for democracy," though he failed to win congressional approval for American membership in the League of Nations. Franklin D. Roosevelt was the first president to use the medium of radio effectively, and he raised the country's morale dramatically during the Great Depression. Ronald Reagan (1981–89), known as the "Great Communicator," employed televised addresses and other appearances to restore the nation's self-confidence and commit it to struggling against the Soviet Union, which he referred to as an "evil empire."

Theodore Roosevelt also introduced the practice of issuing substantive executive orders. Although the Supreme Court ruled that such orders had the force of law only if they were justified by the Constitution or authorized by Congress, in practice they covered a wide range of regulatory activity. By the early 21st century some 50,000 executive orders had been issued. Roosevelt also used executive agreements—agreements between the United States and a foreign government that are made directly by the president and are not subject to constitutional ratification by the Senate—as an alternative to treaties. The Supreme Court's ruling in *U.S. v. Belmont* (1937) that such agreements had the constitutional force of a treaty greatly enhanced the president's power in the conduct of foreign relations. The use of executive agreements increased significantly after 1939; whereas U.S. presidents had made 1,200 executive agreements before 1940, from that year to 1989 they made more than 13,000.

Woodrow Wilson (1913–21) introduced the notion of the president as legislator in chief. Although he thought of himself as a Jeffersonian advocate of limited government, he considered the British parliamentary system to be superior to the American system, and he abandoned Jefferson's precedent by addressing Congress in person, drafting and introducing legislation, and employing pressure to bring about its enactment.

Franklin D. Roosevelt (1933–45) completed the transformation of the presidency. Congress granted him unprecedented powers as part of his New Deal domestic program to raise the country out of the Great Depression; after 1937 the Supreme Court acquiesced to the changes. Through the New Deal Roosevelt aimed at bringing about immediate economic relief as well as reforms in industry, agriculture, finance, waterpower, labour, and housing, all of which vastly increased the scope of the federal government's activities. Opposed to the traditional American political philosophy of laissez-faire, Roosevelt embraced the concept of a government-regulated economy aimed at achieving a balance between conflicting economic interests.

During the administration of Roosevelt's successor, Harry S. Truman (1945–53), the United States established itself as a military superpower and the U.S. presidency became the most powerful elected office in the world. In his capacity as "leader of the free world," Truman declared in 1947 that the United States would oppose communist aggression against Greece and Turkey with both economic and military aid. This policy, known as the Truman Doctrine, was followed 10 years later by the Eisenhower Doctrine, declared by Pres. Dwight D. Eisenhower (1953–61), which extended a similar guarantee of assistance to the countries of the Middle East. Yet, although he used the country's military might to defend democracy, in his farewell address, Eisenhower also warned that democracy in the United States could be undermined by the growing "military-industrial complex," which included government officials and private companies whose power or profits would be enhanced through ever-increasing military spending.

John F. Kennedy (1961–63) renewed the country's commitment to defend freedom and democracy around the world in his inaugural address (1961), declaring that "we shall pay any price, bear any burden, meet any hardship, support any friend, oppose any foe, in order to assure the survival and the success of liberty." Calling also for an end to injustice and poverty at home, he enjoined his fellow Americans: "Ask not what your country can do for you— ask what you can do for your country." Although the promise of his administration went largely unfulfilled because of his assassination in 1963, Kennedy remained an inspiring figure, especially for young people, through the 1960s and beyond. During his administration the Twenty-third Amendment to the Constitution, which granted residents of the District of Columbia representation in the electoral college, was passed (1961).

The limits of U.S. military power and indeed the wisdom of opposing the spread of communism in all parts of the globe were severely tested during the administration of Lyndon B. Johnson (1963–69), during which the country fully committed itself to what would be a long and

PRIMARY DOCUMENT: THE CONSTITUTION OF THE UNITED STATES: TWENTY-THIRD AMENDMENT

Section 1—The District constituting the seat of Government of the United States shall appoint in such manner as the Congress may direct:

A number of electors of President and Vice President equal to the whole number of Senators and Representatives in Congress to which the District would be entitled if it were a State, but in no event more than the least populous State; they shall be in addition to those appointed by the States, but they shall be considered, for the purposes of the election of President and Vice President, to be electors appointed by a State; and they shall meet in the District and perform such duties as provided by the twelfth article of amendment.

Section 2—The Congress shall have power to enforce this article by appropriate legislation.

bloody war in Southeast Asia, the Vietnam War. Johnson arguably acquired for the executive branch the power to commit U.S. military forces to major hostilities abroad without a formal declaration of war by Congress. (Truman had earlier involved U.S. troops in the Korean War without consulting Congress, but in doing so he was at least technically acting under the authority of the United Nations.) The Gulf of Tonkin resolution, passed overwhelmingly by Congress in August 1964 after dubious reports of unprovoked attacks on U.S. warships by North Vietnamese forces, declared support for the president's determination to take all necessary measures to repel armed attacks against the forces of the United States. It was later seen as giving the president blanket authority to wage war and was repealed in 1970. Nevertheless, no subsequent U.S. military action against a foreign country has been preceded by a declaration of war, though some have occasioned congressional declarations quite similar to the Gulf of Tonkin resolution.

Partly in reaction to the experience of the Vietnam War, Congress enacted in 1973—over a veto by Pres. Richard Nixon—the War Powers Act, which required the executive branch to consult with and report to Congress before involving U.S. forces in foreign hostilities. The act was nonetheless resisted or ignored by subsequent presidents, most of whom regarded it as an unconstitutional usurpation of their executive authority.

Presidential power remained at unprecedented levels until the mid-1970s, when Richard Nixon (1969–74) was forced to resign the office because of his role in the Watergate scandal. The Watergate affair greatly increased public cynicism about politics and elected officials, and in the 1970s and '80s it inspired legislative attempts, ultimately short-lived, to curb executive power.

IN FOCUS: THE WATERGATE SCANDAL

The Watergate Scandal concerned the revelation of illegal activities on the part of the incumbent Republican administration of Pres. Richard M. Nixon during and after the 1972 presidential election campaign. The matter was first brought to public attention by the arrest of five men who, on June 17, 1972, broke into the headquarters of the Democratic National Committee at the Watergate office complex in Washington, D.C. Charges of burglary and wiretapping were brought against the five and against E. Howard Hunt, Jr., a former White House aide, and G. Gordon Liddy, general counsel for the Committee for the Re-election of the President. Of the seven, five pleaded guilty and two were convicted by a jury. One of the defendants, James W. McCord, Jr., charged in a letter to the court that the White House had been conducting a cover-up to conceal its connection with the break-in.

In February 1973 the Senate Select Committee on Presidential Campaign Activities, under the chairmanship of Democratic Sen. Sam J. Ervin, Jr., began televised public hearings on the Watergate affair, during which former White House counsel John Dean accused Nixon of direct involvement in the cover-up. Other witnesses testified to acts of spying and burglary committed by a group known as the "plumbers" (because they investigated news leaks) and the use of federal agencies to harass prominent politicians, journalists, academics, and others who had been placed on Nixon's "enemies" list.

On July 16, 1973, Alexander P. Butterfield, formerly of the White House staff, disclosed that conversations in the president's offices had secretly been recorded on tape. Both Archibald Cox, the Watergate special prosecutor, and the Ervin Committee promptly subpoenaed the tapes, but Nixon refused to comply on the grounds of executive privilege and national security. Nixon eventually offered to provide written summaries of the tapes instead. After Cox rejected the proposal, Nixon ordered Attorney General Elliot L. Richardson to fire the special prosecutor. Both Richardson and William D. Ruckelshaus, deputy attorney general, resigned rather than carry out the order, and Cox was finally dismissed by a compliant solicitor general, Robert Bork.

A storm of public protest pressured Nixon into releasing seven of the nine of the subpoenaed tapes; one of the seven contained an

18-minute gap that, according to a later report by a panel of experts, could not have been made accidentally.

In May 1974 the House Judiciary Committee initiated a formal impeachment inquiry. On July 24 the Supreme Court ruled unanimously that Nixon must provide transcripts of additional tapes to Cox's successor as special prosecutor, Leon Jaworski. Between July 27 and 30 the House Judiciary Committee passed three articles of impeachment. On August 5 Nixon supplied transcripts of three tapes that clearly implicated him in the cover-up, and on August 8 he announced his resignation. He left office at 11:35 AM the following day, August 9. He was spared punishment when his successor, Gerald R. Ford, granted him an unconditional pardon on Sept. 8, 1974.

Pres. Ronald Reagan (1981–89) revived the notion that the United States must stop the spread of communism, particularly in the developing world, by extending military and economic assistance to threatened governments. During his administration military spending increased dramatically, a policy that led to huge budget deficits, but which was generally credited with hastening the collapse of the Soviet Union and the demise of eastern European communism in 1990–91.

The end of the Cold War shattered the long-standing bipartisan consensus on foreign policy and revived tensions between the executive and legislative branches over the extent of executive war-making power. The presidency also had become vulnerable again as a result of scandals and impeachment during the second term of Bill Clinton (1993–2001), and it seemed to be weakened even further by the bitter controversy surrounding the 2000 presidential election, in which Republican George W. Bush (2001–09) lost the popular vote but narrowly defeated the Democratic candidate, Vice Pres. Al Gore, in the electoral college after the U.S. Supreme Court

ordered a halt to the manual recounting of disputed ballots in Florida.

Events during the first year of Bush's presidency pre-
cipitated a vigorous resurgence of executive power.
Following the terrorist September 11 attacks on the United
States, Bush unilaterally declared an open-ended "global
war on terror." In 2002 the administration announced
what would become known as the Bush Doctrine: that the
United States reserved the right to attack any foreign
country or group it deemed a threat to its security, even
without immediate provocation by the enemy. A majority
of Americans supported the subsequent U.S. attack on
Afghanistan, whose Taliban regime had been accused of
harbouring al-Qaeda, the terrorist organization responsible for the September 11 attacks. The United States soon
began transferring suspected terrorists captured in
Afghanistan and elsewhere to a special prison at the U.S.
naval base at Guantánamo Bay, Cuba, where some were
subjected to interrogation techniques considered torturous under international law. The indefinite detention of
the prisoners without charge led to several habeas corpus
suits on their behalf in the federal courts.

In 2002 Bush shifted his attention to Iraq, charging
the government of Ṣaddām Ḥussein with possessing and
actively developing weapons of mass destruction (WMD)
and with having ties to terrorist groups, including al-
Qaeda. On Bush's order the United States led an invasion
of Iraq in 2003 that quickly toppled Ṣaddām but failed to
uncover any WMD, prompting critics to charge that Bush
had misled the country into war.

Declaring his intention to put the treatment of detainees on a sound legal footing, Bush's successor, Barack
Obama (2009–), the first African American president
of the United States, immediately prohibited the use of

torturous interrogation techniques. However, he resisted calls for a national commission to investigate whether the treatment of detainees during the Bush administration violated U.S. and international laws.

SELECTING A PRESIDENT

THE ELECTORAL COLLEGE

The Articles of Confederation (1781–89), the first constitution of the United States, vested the selection of the president in the legislature. Near the end of the Constitutional Convention (1787), at which a new constitution was written, the electoral college was proposed to provide a system that would select the most qualified

Presidents (left to right) *George Bush, Ronald Reagan, Jimmy Carter, Gerald Ford, and Richard Nixon attend the opening of the Ronald Reagan Presidential Library, Simi Valley, Calif., 1991.* Marcy Nighswander—Associated Press/U.S. Department of Defense

president and vice president. Historians have suggested a variety of reasons for the adoption of the electoral college, including concerns about the separation of powers and the relationship between the executive and legislative branches, the balance between small and large states, slavery, and the perceived dangers of direct democracy.

Article II, Section 1, of the Constitution stipulated that states could select electors in any manner they desired and in a number equal to their congressional representation (senators plus representatives). (As stated earlier, the Twenty-third Amendment, adopted in 1961, provided electoral college representation for Washington, D.C.) The electors would then meet and vote for two people, at least one of whom could not be an inhabitant of their state. Under the original plan, the person receiving the largest number of votes, provided it was a majority of the number of electors, would be elected president, and the person with the second largest number of votes would become vice president. If no one received a majority, the presidency of the United States would be decided by the House of Representatives, voting by states and choosing from among the top five candidates in the electoral vote. A tie for vice president would be broken by the Senate.

Although the framers of the Constitution thus established a system for electing the president, they did not devise a method for nominating presidential candidates or even for choosing electors. They assumed that the selection process as a whole would be nonpartisan and devoid of factions (or political parties), which they believed were always a corrupting influence in politics. The original process worked well in the early years of the republic, when George Washington, who was not affiliated closely with any faction, was the unanimous choice of electors in both 1789 and 1792. However, the rapid development of political parties soon presented a major challenge, one leading to changes that would make presidential elections more partisan but ultimately more democratic as well.

Beginning in 1796, the last year of Washington's second term, congressional caucuses, organized along party lines, met informally to select presidential and vice presidential nominees. Electors, chosen by state legislatures mostly on the basis of partisan inclination, were not expected to exercise independent judgment when voting. So strong were partisan loyalties in 1800 that all the Democratic-Republican electors voted for their party's candidates, Thomas Jefferson and Aaron Burr. Since the framers had not anticipated party-line voting and there was no mechanism for indicating a separate choice for president and vice president, the tie had to be broken by the Federalist-controlled House of Representatives. The election of Jefferson after 36 ballots led to the adoption of the Twelfth Amendment in 1804, which specified separate ballots for president and vice president and reduced the number of candidates from which the House could choose from five to three.

The development of political parties coincided with the expansion of popular choice. By 1836 all states selected their electors by direct popular vote except South Carolina, which did so only after the American Civil War. In choosing electors, most states adopted a general-ticket system in which slates of partisan electors were selected on the basis of a statewide vote. Thus, the winner of a state's popular vote would win its entire electoral vote. Only Maine and Nebraska have chosen to deviate from this method, instead allocating electoral votes to the victor in each House district and a two-electoral-vote bonus to the statewide winner. The winner-take-all system generally

PRIMARY DOCUMENT: THE CONSTITUTION OF THE UNITED STATES: TWELFTH AMENDMENT

The electors shall meet in their respective states and vote by ballot for President and Vice President, one of whom, at least, shall not be an inhabitant of the same state with themselves; they shall name in their ballots the person voted for as President, and in distinct ballots the person voted for as Vice President, and they shall make distinct lists of all persons voted for as President, and of all persons voted for as Vice President, and of the number of votes for each, which lists they shall sign and certify, and transmit sealed to the seat of the government of the United States, directed to the President of the Senate;—The President of the Senate shall, in the presence of the Senate and House of Representatives, open all the certificates and the votes shall then be counted;—The person having the greatest number of votes for President, shall be the President, if such number be a majority of the whole number of Electors appointed; and if no person have such majority, then from the persons having the highest numbers not exceeding three on the list of those voted for as President, the House of Representatives shall choose immediately, by ballot, the President. But in choosing the President, the votes shall be taken by states, the representation from each state having one vote; a quorum for this purpose shall consist of a member or members from two-thirds of the states, and a majority of all the states shall be necessary to a choice. The person having the greatest number of votes as Vice President, shall be the Vice President, if such number be a majority of the whole number of Electors appointed, and if no person have a majority, then from the two highest numbers on the list, the Senate shall choose the Vice President; a quorum for the purpose shall consist of two-thirds of the whole number of Senators, and a majority of the whole number shall be necessary to a choice. But no person constitutionally ineligible to the office of President shall be eligible to that of Vice President of the United States.

favoured major parties over minor parties, large states over small states, and cohesive voting groups concentrated in large states over those that were more diffusely dispersed across the country.

The Evolution of the Nomination Process

"King Caucus"

The word *caucus* originated in Boston in the early part of the 18th century, when it was used as the name of a political club, the Caucus, or Caucus Club. The club hosted public discussions and the election of candidates for public office. In its subsequent usage in the United States, the term came to denote a meeting of the managers or other officials of a political party.

Because the selection of presidential candidates after 1796 was controlled by political parties, the general public had no direct input in the process. The subsequent demise in the 1810s of the Federalist Party, which failed even to nominate a presidential candidate in 1820, made nomination by the Democratic-Republican Party caucus tantamount to election as president. This early nomination system—dubbed "King Caucus" by its critics—evoked widespread resentment, even from some members of the Democratic-Republican caucus itself. By 1824 it had fallen into such disrepute that only one-fourth of the Democratic-Republican congressional delegation took part in the caucus that nominated Secretary of the Treasury William Crawford, instead of more popular figures such as John Quincy Adams and Andrew Jackson. Jackson, Adams, and Henry Clay eventually joined Crawford in contesting the subsequent presidential election, in which Jackson received the most popular and electoral votes but was denied the presidency by the House of Representatives (which selected Adams) after he failed to win the required majority in the electoral college. Jackson, who was particularly enraged following Adams's appointment of Clay as secretary of state, called unsuccessfully for the abolition of the electoral college, but he would get his revenge by defeating Adams in the presidential election of 1828.

The Convention System

In a saloon in Baltimore, Md., in 1832, Jackson's Democratic Party held one of the country's first national conventions (the first such convention had been held the previous year—in the same saloon—by the Anti-Masonic Party). The Democrats nominated Jackson as their presidential candidate and Martin Van Buren as his running mate and drafted a party platform. It was assumed that open and public conventions would be more democratic, but they soon came under the control of small groups of state and local party leaders, who handpicked many of the delegates. The conventions were often tense affairs, and sometimes multiple ballots were needed to overcome party divisions—particularly at conventions of the Democratic Party, which required its presidential and vice presidential nominees to secure the support of two-thirds of the delegates (a rule that was abolished in 1936).

The convention system was unaltered until the beginning of the 20th century, when general disaffection with elitism led to the growth of the Progressive movement and the introduction in some states of binding presidential primary elections to select delegates to the conventions; the primary system gave rank-and-file party members more control over the delegate-selection process.

By 1916 some 20 states were using primaries, though in subsequent decades several states abolished them. From 1932 to 1968 the number of states holding presidential primaries was fairly constant (between 12 and 19), and presidential nominations remained the province of convention delegates and party bosses rather than of voters. Indeed, in 1952 Democratic convention delegates selected Adlai Stevenson as the party's nominee though Estes

Dwight D. Eisenhower (left) *and Richard M. Nixon after being renominated at the 1956 Republican National Convention in San Francisco.* Courtesy of the Dwight D. Eisenhower Library/U.S. Army

Kefauver had won more than three-fifths of the votes in that year's presidential primaries. In 1968, at a raucous convention in Chicago that was marred by violence on the city's streets and chaos in the convention hall, Vice Pres. Hubert Humphrey captured the Democratic Party's presidential nomination despite his not having contested a single primary.

To unify the Democratic Party, Humphrey appointed a committee that proposed reforms that later fundamentally altered the nomination process for both major national parties. The reforms introduced a largely primary-based system that reduced the importance of the national party conventions. Although the presidential and vice presidential candidates of both the Democratic Party and the Republican Party are still formally selected by national conventions, most of the delegates are selected through

primaries—or, in a minority of states, through caucuses—
and the delegates gather merely to ratify the choice of
the voters.

THE MODERN NOMINATION PROCESS

Deciding to Run

Although there are few constitutional requirements for
the office of the presidency—presidents must be natural-
born citizens, at least 35 years of age, and residents of the
United States for at least 14 years—there are considerable informal barriers. No woman has yet been elected
president, and all presidents but one have been Protestants
(John F. Kennedy was the only Roman Catholic to occupy
the office). Until Barack Obama's election as president in
2008, no ethnic minority had been a major party nominee
for either the presidency or vice presidency. Successful
presidential candidates generally have followed one of
two paths to the White House: from prior elected office
(some four-fifths of presidents have been members of the
U.S. Congress or state governors) or from distinguished
service in the military (e.g., Washington, Jackson, and
Eisenhower).

The decision to become a candidate for president is
often a difficult one, in part because candidates and their
families must endure intensive scrutiny of their entire
public and private lives by the news media. Before officially entering the race, prospective candidates usually
organize an exploratory committee to assess their political viability. They also travel the country extensively to
raise money and to generate grassroots support and favourable media exposure. Those who ultimately opt to run
have been described by scholars as risk takers who have a
great deal of confidence in their ability to inspire the public and handle the rigours of the office they seek.

The Money Game

Political campaigns in the United States are expensive—none more so than those for the presidency. Presidential candidates generally need to raise tens of millions of dollars to compete for their party's nomination. Even candidates facing no internal party opposition, such as incumbent presidents Bill Clinton in 1996 and George W. Bush in 2004, raise enormous sums to dissuade prospective candidates from entering the race and to campaign against their likely opponent in the general election before either party has officially nominated a candidate. Long before the first vote is cast, candidates spend much of their time fund-raising, a fact that has prompted many political analysts to claim that in reality the so-called "money primary" is the first contest in the presidential nomination process. Indeed, much of the early media coverage of a presidential campaign focuses on fund-raising, particularly at the end of each quarter, when the candidates are required to file financial reports with the Federal Election Commission (FEC). Candidates who are unable to raise sufficient funds often drop out before the balloting has begun.

In the 1970s legislation regulating campaign contributions and expenditures was enacted to address increasing concerns that the largely private funding of presidential elections enabled large contributors to gain unfair influence over a president's policies and legislative agenda. Presidential candidates who agree to limit their expenditures in the primaries and caucuses to a fixed overall amount are eligible for federal matching funds, which are collected through a taxpayer "check-off" system that allows individuals to contribute a portion of their federal income tax to the Presidential Election Campaign Fund. To become eligible for such funds, candidates are required to raise a minimum of $5,000 in at least 20 states (only the first $250 of each contribution counts toward the $5,000); they then receive from the FEC a sum equivalent to the first $250 of each individual contribution (or a fraction thereof if there is a shortfall in the fund). Candidates opting to forgo federal matching funds for the primaries and caucuses, such as George W. Bush in 2000 and 2004, John Kerry in 2004, and self-financed candidate Steve Forbes in 1996, are not subject to spending limits. From 1976 through 2000, candidates could collect from individuals a maximum contribution of $1,000, a sum subsequently raised to $2,000 and indexed for inflation by the Bipartisan Campaign Reform Act of 2002. (The figure was $2,300 for the 2008 presidential election.)

Despite these reforms, money continues to exert a considerable influence in the nomination process and in presidential elections. Although prolific fund-raising by itself is not sufficient for winning the Democratic or Republican nominations or for being elected president, it is certainly necessary.

The Primary and Caucus Season

Most delegates to the national conventions of the Democratic and Republican parties are selected through primaries or caucuses and are pledged to support a particular candidate. Each state party determines the date of its primary or caucus. Historically, Iowa held its caucus in mid-February, followed a week later by a primary in New Hampshire; the campaign season then ran through early June, when primaries were held in states such as New Jersey and California. Winning in either Iowa or New Hampshire—or at least doing better than expected there—often boosted a campaign, while faring poorly sometimes led candidates to withdraw. Accordingly, candidates often spent years organizing grassroots support in these states.

Primary elections may be closed (partisan), allowing only declared party members to vote, or open (nonpartisan), enabling all voters to choose which party's primary they wish to vote in without declaring any party affiliation. Primaries may also be direct or indirect. A direct primary, which is now used in some form in all U.S. states, functions as a preliminary election whereby voters decide their party's candidates. In an indirect primary, voters elect delegates who choose the party's candidates at a nominating convention.

Because of criticism that Iowa and New Hampshire were unrepresentative of the country and exerted too much influence in the nomination process, several other states began to schedule their primaries earlier. In 1988, for example, 16 largely Southern states moved their primaries to a day in early March that became known as "Super Tuesday." Such "front-loading" of primaries and caucuses continued during the 1990s, prompting Iowa and New Hampshire to schedule their contests even earlier, in January, and causing the Democratic Party to adopt rules to protect the privileged status of the two states. By 2008 some 40 states had scheduled their primaries or caucuses for January or February; few primaries or caucuses are now held in May or June. For the 2008 campaign, several states attempted to blunt the influence of Iowa and New Hampshire by moving their primaries and caucuses to January, forcing Iowa to hold its caucus on January 3 and New Hampshire its primary on January 8. Some states, however, scheduled primaries earlier than the calendar sanctioned by the Democratic and Republican National Committees, and, as a result, both parties either reduced or, in the case of the Democrats, stripped states of their delegates to the national convention for violating party rules. For example, Michigan and Florida held their primaries on Jan. 15 and Jan. 29, 2008, respectively; both states were stripped of half their Republican and all their Democratic delegates to the national convention. Front-loading has severely truncated the campaign season, requiring candidates to raise more money sooner and making it more difficult for lesser-known candidates to gain momentum by doing well in early primaries and caucuses.

Presidential Nominating Conventions

One important consequence of the front-loading of primaries is that the nominees of both major parties are now usually determined by March or April. To secure a party's nomination, a candidate must win the votes of a majority of the delegates attending the convention. (More than 4,000 delegates attend the Democratic convention, while the Republican convention usually has some 2,500 delegates.) In most Republican primaries the candidate who wins the statewide popular vote is awarded all the state's delegates. By contrast, the Democratic Party requires that delegates be allocated proportionally to each candidate who wins at least 15 percent of the popular vote. It thus takes Democratic candidates longer than Republican candidates to amass the required majority. In 1984 the Democratic Party created a category of "superdelegates," who are unpledged to any candidate. Consisting of federal officeholders, governors, and other high-ranking party officials, they usually constitute 15 to 20 percent of the total number of delegates. Other Democratic delegates are required on the first ballot to vote for the candidate whom they are pledged to support, unless that candidate has withdrawn from consideration. If no candidate receives a first-ballot majority, the convention becomes open to bargaining, and all delegates are free to support any candidate. The last convention to require a second ballot was held in 1952, before the advent of the primary system.

The Democratic and Republican nominating conventions are held during the summer prior to the November general election and are publicly funded through the taxpayer check-off system. (The party that holds the presidency usually holds its convention second.) Shortly before the convention, the presidential candidate selects a vice presidential running mate, often to balance the ticket ideologically or geographically or to shore up one or more of the candidate's perceived weaknesses.

In the early days of television, the conventions were media spectacles, covered by the major commercial networks gavel to gavel. As the importance of the conventions declined, however, so too did the media coverage of them. Nevertheless, the conventions are still considered vital. It is at the conventions that the parties draft their platforms, which set out the policies of each party and its presidential candidate. The convention also serves to unify each party after what may have been a bitter primary season. Finally, as the nominees do not receive federal money until they have been formally chosen by the convention delegates, the conventions mark the formal start of the general election campaign, providing the candidates with a large national audience and an opportunity to explain their agendas to the American public.

The national conventions in the United States have been criticized throughout their history as undemocratic spectacles. Critics have proposed replacing them with some form of national presidential primary. By contrast, defenders argue that besides promoting party unity and enthusiasm, conventions allow compromise and tend to produce nominees and platforms that represent the political centre rather than the extremes. Because elected officials must appeal to both party leaders and the public to function effectively, supporters of conventions claim that they are a good test of how well a candidate will perform in office.

THE GENERAL ELECTION CAMPAIGN

Although the traditional starting date of the general election campaign is Labor Day (the first Monday in September), in practice the campaign begins much earlier, because the nominees are known long before the national conventions. Like primary campaigns and the national conventions, the general election campaign is publicly funded through the taxpayer check-off system. Since public financing was introduced in the 1970s, all Democratic and Republican candidates have opted to receive federal matching funds for the general election; in exchange for such funds, they agree to limit their spending to an amount equal to the federal matching funds they receive, plus a maximum personal contribution of $50,000. By 2004 each major party nominee received some $75 million. In 2008 Democratic nominee Barack Obama became the first presidential candidate ever to opt out of public financing for both the primary and the general election campaign; he raised more than $745 million.

Minor party presidential candidates face formidable barriers. Whereas Democratic and Republican presidential candidates automatically are listed first and second on general election ballots, minor party candidates must navigate the complex and varied state laws to gain ballot access. In addition, a new party is eligible for federal financing in an election only if it received at least 5 percent of the vote in the previous election. All parties that receive at least 25 percent of the vote in the prior presidential election are entitled to equivalent public funding.

A candidate's general election strategy is largely dictated by the electoral college system. All states except Maine and Nebraska follow the unit rule, by which all of a state's electoral votes are awarded to the candidate who receives the most popular votes in that state. Candidates therefore focus their resources and time on large states and states that are considered toss-ups, and they tend to ignore states that are considered safe for one party or the other and states with few electoral votes.

Modern presidential campaigns are media driven, as candidates spend millions of dollars on television advertising and on staged public events (photo ops) designed to generate favourable media coverage. The most widely viewed campaign spectacles are the debates between the Democratic and Republican presidential and vice presidential candidates (minor parties are often excluded from such debates, a fact cited by critics who contend that the current electoral process is undemocratic and inimical to viewpoints other than those of the two major parties). First televised in 1960, such debates have been a staple of the presidential campaign since 1976. They are closely analyzed in the media and sometimes result in a shift of public opinion in favour of the candidate who is perceived to be the winner or who is seen as more attractive or personable by most viewers. Some analysts have argued, for example, that John F. Kennedy's relaxed and self-confident manner, as well as his good looks, aided him in his televised debate with Richard Nixon, contributing to his narrow victory in the presidential election of 1960. (Most who listened rather than watched, though, thought Nixon to be the winner.) Because of the potential impact and the enormous audience of the debates—some 80 million people watched the single debate between Jimmy Carter and Ronald Reagan in 1980—the campaigns usually undertake intensive negotiations over the number of debates as well as their rules and format.

The presidential election is held on the Tuesday following the first Monday in November. Voters do not actually vote for presidential and vice presidential candidates, but rather vote for electors pledged to a particular candidate. Only on rare occasions, such as the disputed presidential election in 2000 between Al Gore and George W. Bush, is it not clear on election day (or the following morning) who has won the presidency. Although it is possible for the candidate who has received the most popular votes to lose the electoral vote (as also occurred in 2000), such inversions are infrequent. The electors gather in their respective state capitals to cast their votes on the Monday following the second Wednesday in December, and the results are formally ratified by Congress in early January.

Upon winning the election, a nonincumbent president-elect appoints a transition team to effect a smooth transfer of power between the incoming and outgoing administrations. The formal swearing-in ceremony and inauguration of the new president occurs on January 20 in Washington, D.C. The chief justice of the United States administers the formal oath of office to the president-elect: "I do solemnly swear (or affirm) that I will faithfully execute the office of President of the United States, and will to the best of my ability, preserve, protect and defend the Constitution of the United States." The new president's first speech, called the inaugural address, is then delivered to the nation.

THE VICE PRESIDENCY OF THE UNITED STATES

THE OFFICE

The officer next in rank to the president is the vice president, who ascends to the presidency on the event of the president's death, disability, resignation, or removal. The vice president also serves as the presiding officer of the Senate, a role that is mostly ceremonial but that gives the vice president the tie-breaking vote when the Senate is deadlocked.

Though famously if somewhat coarsely decried by vice president John Nance Garner as being a worthless office, 14 vice presidents have gone on to become president. Since Garner's term as Franklin D. Roosevelt's vice president, the office has been strengthened and expanded, notably under Dick Cheney, the two-term vice president under George W. Bush. Though Cheney never set his sights on becoming president, it is widely acknowledged that he turned the vice presidency into a more muscular and influential office. During his tenure, Cheney used his influence to help shape the administration's energy policy and foreign policy in the Middle East. He played a central, controversial role in conveying intelligence reports that Ṣaddām Ḥussein of Iraq had developed weapons of mass destruction in violation of resolutions passed by the United Nations—reports used by the Bush administration to initiate the Iraq War. Following the collapse of Saddam's regime, Cheney's former company, Halliburton, secured lucrative reconstruction contracts from the U.S. government, raising the spectre of favouritism and possible wrongdoing—allegations that damaged Cheney's public reputation. Critics, who had long charged Cheney with being a secretive public servant, included members of Congress who brought suit against him for not disclosing records used to form the national energy policy.

VICE PRESIDENT JOE BIDEN
(b. Nov. 20, 1942, Scranton, Pa.)

In 2009 Joe Biden became the United States's 47th vice president, serving in the Democratic administration of Pres. Barack Obama. Biden was born Joseph Robinette Biden on Nov. 20, 1942 in Scranton, Pa. Raised in Scranton and in New Castle county, Del., Biden received a bachelor's degree from the University of Delaware in 1965 and a law degree from Syracuse University in New York in 1968. After graduating from law school, he returned to Delaware to work as an attorney before quickly turning to politics, serving on the New Castle county council from 1970 to 1972. Biden was elected to the U.S. Senate in 1972 at the age of 29, becoming the fifth youngest senator in history. He went on to win reelection six times and became Delaware's longest-serving senator. In addition to his role as U.S. senator, Biden also served as an adjunct professor at the Wilmington, Del., branch of the Widener University School of Law in 1991.

As a senator, Biden focused on foreign relations, criminal justice, and drug policy. He served on the Senate's Foreign Relations Committee, twice as its chair (2001–03; 2007–09), and on the Committee on the Judiciary, serving as its chair from 1987 to 1995. He was particularly outspoken on issues related to the Kosovo conflict of the late '90s, urging U.S. action against Serbian forces to protect Kosovars against an offensive by Serbian Pres. Slobodan Milošević. On the Iraq War, Biden proposed a partition plan as a way to maintain a united, peaceful Iraq. Biden also was a member of the International Narcotics Control Caucus and was the lead senator in writing the law that established the office of "drug czar," a position that oversees the national drug-control policy.

Biden pursued the 1988 Democratic presidential nomination but withdrew after it was revealed that parts of his campaign stump speech had been plagiarized from British Labour Party leader Neil Kinnock without appropriate attribution. His 2008 presidential campaign never gained momentum, and he withdrew from the race after placing fifth in the Iowa Democratic caucus in January of that year. After Barack Obama amassed enough delegates to secure the Democratic presidential nomination, Biden emerged as a front-runner to be Obama's vice presidential

Michelle and Barack Obama (couple at left) *and Jill and Joe Biden at Invesco Field on the final night of the Democratic National Convention in Denver, Aug. 28, 2008.* Carol M. Highsmith/Library of Congress, Washington, D.C.

running mate. On August 23 Obama officially announced his selection of Biden as the Democratic Party's vice presidential nominee, and on August 27 Obama and Biden secured the Democratic Party's nomination. On November 4 the Obama-Biden ticket defeated John McCain and his running mate, Sarah Palin, Biden also easily winning reelection to his U.S. Senate seat. He resigned from the Senate post shortly before taking the oath of office as vice president on Jan. 20, 2009.

As vice president, Biden acted as an influential adviser to the president on both domestic and foreign policy. During his first months in office he headed a White House task force to improve economic conditions for middle-class and working-class families, oversaw the distribution of $787 billion in federal funds designed to stimulate the economy, and helped to formulate the administration's policies on Afghanistan and Pakistan.

THE FIRST LADY OF THE UNITED STATES

The wife of the president of the United States is known as the first lady. Although the president's wife played a public role from the founding of the republic, the title *first lady* did not come into general use until much later, near the end of the 19th century.

Although the first lady's role has never been codified or officially defined, she figures prominently in the political and social life of the nation. Representative of her husband on official and ceremonial occasions both at home and abroad, the first lady is closely watched for some hint of her husband's thinking and a clue to his future actions. Although unpaid and unelected, her prominence provides her a platform from which to influence behaviour and opinion. Popular first ladies have served as models for how American

First Lady Barbara Bush (centre) *with her predecessors at the opening of the Ronald Reagan Presidential Library, November 1991.* (From left) *Lady Bird Johnson, Pat Nixon, Nancy Reagan* (back row), *Bush, Rosalynn Carter, and Betty Ford.* Marcy Nighswander—Associated Press/U.S. Department of Defense

women should dress, speak, decorate their homes, and cut their hair. Some first ladies have used their influence to affect legislation on important matters such as temperance reform, housing improvement, and women's rights. By the end of the 20th century, the title had been absorbed into other languages and was often used, without translation, for the wife of the nation's leader—even in countries where the leader's consort received far less attention and exerted much less influence than in the United States.

THE EARLY YEARS

Because the framers of the Constitution left the chief executive considerable latitude in choosing advisers, he was able to seek counsel from a wide variety of friends and family, including his wife. The first president made decisions that highlighted the consort's role. When Martha Washington (first lady from 1789 to 1797) joined Pres. George Washington in New York City a month after his April 1789 inauguration, she arrived on a conspicuous barge and was greeted as a public hero. The president had already arranged to combine his office and residence in one building, thus providing her with ample opportunity to receive his callers and participate in official functions. Although she refrained from taking a stand on important issues, she was carefully watched and widely hailed as "Lady Washington."

Abigail Adams (1797–1801), the wife of John Adams, enlarged what had been primarily a social role. She took an active part in the debate over the development of political parties, and she sometimes pointed out to her husband people she considered his enemies. Although she did not disdain the household management role that her predecessor had played (she oversaw the initial move to the new White House in Washington, D.C., in November 1800), critics focused on the political counsel she gave her husband, and some referred to her sarcastically as "Mrs. President."

Because Thomas Jefferson (1801–09) was a widower during his presidency, he often turned to the wife of Secretary of State James Madison to serve as hostess. Thus Dolley Madison had ample time (two Jefferson administrations and her husband's two terms, 1809–17) to leave a strong mark. With the assistance of architect Benjamin Latrobe, she decorated the president's residence elegantly and entertained frequently. Her egalitarian mix of guests increased her popularity. During the British assault on the White House in August 1814, near the end of the War of 1812, she provided for the rescue of some of the residence's first acquisitions, which endeared her to many Americans and solidified the role of the president's wife as overseer of the nation's most famous home.

Elizabeth Monroe (1817–25), the wife of James Monroe, appealed to elitists who insisted that the presidential family should illustrate "the very best" of American society, but she had few supporters among those who were more egalitarian. Although she helped her husband select furnishings for the presidential mansion, newly rebuilt after the British assault in 1814 (this furniture became prized possessions of later tenants), she entertained much less than Dolley Madison had, and Washingtonians reacted by boycotting some of her parties. Louisa Adams (1825–29), the wife of John Quincy Adams, struggled with the same problem her predecessor had faced: how to deal with the tension already evident in American culture concerning whether the president's family should mix freely and live simply or reside in luxury and be revered from afar.

1829 TO 1901

The presidential candidacy of Andrew Jackson illustrated how important the role of the president's wife could be.

Rachel Jackson did not live to see her husband inaugurated, but earlier she had been attacked by the press, with one newspaper questioning whether she was qualified to serve "at the head of the female society of the United States."

By 1829 the outline for the job of president's wife was clear: hostess and social leader, keeper of the presidential residence, and role model for American women. When the president respected his wife's opinion (as John Adams did), she could also function as political counsel and strategist.

Between 1829 and 1900 many presidents' wives—such as Margaret Taylor (1849–50), who was chronically ill, and Jane Pierce (1853–57), whose son had been killed in a train accident—sought to avoid public attention by withdrawing behind invalidism and personal grief. Their husbands, as well as other presidents who were widowers or bachelors, often turned over hostess duties to young female relatives (daughters, daughters-in-law, or nieces), whose youth gained them admirers and excused their lapses in etiquette or lack of sophistication. Among the handful of 19th-century presidential wives who did seek a public role, Sarah Polk (1845–49), the wife of James Polk, was well versed in the political issues of the day and was considered a major influence on her husband. Mary Todd Lincoln (1861–65), the wife of Abraham Lincoln, though insecure in a visible role, prevailed on her husband to grant favours to friends and hangers-on. Julia Grant (1869–77), the wife of Ulysses S. Grant, was an extravagant and popular hostess during the Gilded Age and was the first of the presidents' wives to write an autobiography, though it was not published until 1975.

Before the Civil War the president's wife had remained a local figure, little known outside the capital, but in the last third of the 19th century she began to receive national attention. Magazines carried articles about her and the

presidential family. With the completion of the transcontinental railroad in 1869, travel across the country
became easier, and Lucy Hayes (1877–81), the wife of
Rutherford B. Hayes, became the first president's wife
to travel from coast to coast. This exposure, plus her
association with the popular temperance movement and
her own simplicity in matters of dress and decoration,
contributed to her immense popularity. After journalists hailed her as "first lady of the land," the title entered
common usage. Following the production of a popular
play, *First Lady*, in 1911, the title became still more
popular, and in 1934 it entered Merriam-Webster's *New
International Dictionary*.

1901 TO 1953

In the 20th century—as the United States began to play a
greater role in world affairs, as the president assumed
increasing importance both at home and abroad, and as
women's educational and job opportunities improved—
the role of first lady grew considerably. Edith Roosevelt
(1901–09), the wife of Theodore Roosevelt, extended the
role in two ways: first, by hiring a secretary who publicized
her activities and, second, by overseeing major architectural renovations to the Executive Mansion, which was
officially renamed the White House by her husband.

Helen Taft (1909–13), the wife of William Howard Taft,
was intensely political and ambitious for her husband, but
she suffered a paralyzing stroke in May 1909 and for a year
could not undertake public duties. Her major contribution as first lady was the planting of ornamental cherry
trees in the capital. In 1914 her autobiography, *Recollections
of Full Years*, became the first such book published by a
president's wife during her lifetime.

Ellen Wilson (1913–14), the first wife of Woodrow
Wilson, lived in the White House only 17 months before

dying of kidney disease, but she advanced the cause of housing reform by bringing together specialists and legislators at the White House and by conducting tours of slum areas. When Congress passed a housing bill at the time of her death, she became the first president's wife to have her name so prominently attached to legislation. Edith Wilson (1915–21), Woodrow Wilson's second wife, was an attentive companion to her hardworking husband, but was decidedly less devoted to reform. At the end of World War I in 1918, she accompanied him to the peace talks at Versailles, France, becoming the first president's wife to travel internationally amid such publicity. After the president suffered a stroke in October 1919, she served as a vigilant gatekeeper, monitoring all his visitors and messages. Critics complained of "petticoat government," though she later characterized her actions as simply watching over her husband's convalescence while making no major decisions herself. Historians remain divided over the exact nature of her role during this period.

Florence Harding (1921–23), the wife of Warren G. Harding, illustrated the extent to which Americans had come to accept that women—including first ladies—played an important role in public life. She had assisted in running her husband's newspaper in Marion, Ohio, and assumed a prominent social role when he went to Washington, D.C., as a U.S. senator in 1915. As first lady, she paid close attention to press coverage and kept the White House open to a wide variety of visitors.

Although some of her predecessors had gone to college, Grace Coolidge (1923–29), the wife of Calvin Coolidge, was the first president's wife to earn a university degree. Her enormous personal popularity offset her husband's reputation for laconic dourness. Often photographed in glamorous gowns or with some of her menagerie of animals, she also made news by attempting (unsuccessfully) to refurbish the family quarters of the White House with furniture from the colonial period.

Lou Hoover (1929–33), the wife of Herbert Hoover, held the same Stanford University degree as her husband, and the two had collaborated on the translation of an important mining textbook, but she distanced herself from the substantive decisions he made as president. Although she confined herself to domestic management and to leading widely approved causes such as the Girl Scouts and physical education for women, she set one precedent when she became the first president's wife to give speeches on national radio. Her effort to catalog White House holdings and to furnish one of the upstairs rooms as the Monroe Drawing Room foreshadowed later restoration efforts of her successors.

Eleanor Roosevelt (1933–45), the wife of Franklin D. Roosevelt, entered the White House with grave reservations about undertaking the job of first lady, but, before she left, had set new standards for how her successors would be judged. First lady for longer than any other woman, she extended the limits on what unelected, unappointed public figures could do. Her husband's paralysis as a result of poliomyelitis suffered in 1921 led her to travel for him, and she often said that she acted as his "eyes and ears." She was also motivated by her early exposure to reform movements and her feeling of responsibility toward others, gained from a family that had long been involved in liberal causes and that prominently featured its women as well as its men. In the 1920s her association with a network of politically powerful women helped to augment her zeal. Inspired by all these factors, she was an extremely active first lady, writing articles, giving speeches, and taking stands on controversial issues. Moreover, she was widely viewed as appealing to constituencies different from her husband's, including women, African Americans, youth, the poor, and others who had formerly felt shut out of the political process. Although she regularly disclaimed any influence, she was credited with gaining appointments to important posts for many individuals from these groups. Throughout her tenure she held regular press conferences, limiting attendance to women until the start of World War II, thus ensuring that news agencies would hire more women correspondents. Her continued participation in public affairs after her husband's death further underlined the prestige she held in her own right. As a U.S. representative to the United Nations, she helped to shape the Universal Declaration of Human Rights and secure its unanimous passage. She continued to be active in the Democratic Party in the 1950s, and in 1961 Pres. John F. Kennedy named her chair of his Commission on the Status of Women, a post she held until her death in 1962.

The fact that Bess Truman (1945–53), the wife of Harry S. Truman, could achieve enormous popularity as first lady and yet act so differently from Eleanor Roosevelt showed how malleable the role of first lady had become. Intensely private, she refused to hold press conferences and revealed little when she answered written questions from reporters. As a result, the extent of her influence on her husband is difficult to assess. After leaving office, Pres. Truman said that he had talked over his most important decisions with his wife because "her judgment was always good," but their daughter, Margaret, suggested that Bess Truman was not so closely involved.

1953 TO 1977

Mamie Eisenhower (1953–61), the wife of Dwight D. Eisenhower, did not significantly change the role of first lady. Popular with many Americans for her down-to-earth style, she saw her first name attached to a hairstyle ("Mamie bangs") and a chocolate fudge recipe. Her press conferences were limited to social matters, and, when she published an article before the 1952 election, she refused to take sides, telling readers to vote for her husband or for Adlai Stevenson but to "please vote."

Jacqueline Kennedy Onassis (1961–63) was, as the wife of John F. Kennedy, the youngest first lady in 75 years. She gained enormous popularity at home and abroad because of her youth, her glamour and style, and her two photogenic young children. The first president's wife to name her own press secretary, she struggled to guard her privacy. Her White House renovation, which was aimed at restoring the mansion to its original elegance, gained wide approval. In 1961 she established the White House Historical Association, which later facilitated the mansion's official designation as a museum (1988).

Lady Bird Johnson (1963–69) had been a member of Washington society for nearly three decades while her husband, Lyndon B. Johnson, served in the House of Representatives and the Senate. An efficient household administrator, she had also taken an active part in her husband's political campaigns, and during World War II had briefly run his Washington office. By the presidential election of 1960, she was such a seasoned campaigner that Robert Kennedy credited her with carrying Texas for the Democrats. In 1964, when her husband's popularity in some parts of the country was low because of his support for civil rights, she undertook a whistle-stop campaign through the South. After he won the presidential election that year, she spearheaded a program encouraging Americans to do more to improve the appearance of their neighbourhoods and that resulted in the Highway Beautification Act of 1965.

Pat Nixon (1969–74), the wife of Richard M. Nixon, also had a long Washington apprenticeship, but received little credit for her accomplishments in the White House.

A dutiful consort, she traveled thousands of miles, giving speeches and greeting potential voters. She opened the White House to groups that had not been invited before—including the blind, who were permitted to touch the furnishings—and staged special holiday functions for senior citizens. Her program to encourage volunteerism never really caught on, however, and her reluctance to discuss her role or highlight her achievements diminished her place in history. Nevertheless, she continued to be named one of the most-admired American women long after she had returned to private life.

Betty Ford (1974–77), the wife of Gerald R. Ford, often said that because she entered the White House in the wake of the Watergate affair, which forced Nixon's resignation, she felt an enormous responsibility to be candid. During a press conference within a month of becoming first lady, she openly expressed opinions that differed from her husband's on several important issues, including abortion. A few weeks later, after undergoing a mastectomy for breast cancer, she insisted on telling the truth instead of concealing the matter, as some of her predecessors had done during their own serious illnesses. Following her example, many women went for medical examinations, a fact that, as she later wrote, made her realize the power of the first lady. Some of the interviews she gave, including one in which she discussed her teenage daughter's sex life, led to criticism, but, on balance, Americans approved of her openness. After she left the White House, her confessions of alcoholism and drug dependence won additional approval.

1977 TO PRESENT

Rosalynn Carter (1977–81), the wife of Jimmy Carter, broke new ground for first ladies in several ways. Eighteen months before the 1976 election, she began campaigning for her husband on her own. In 1977, soon after becoming first lady, she traveled to seven Latin American countries, where she met with political leaders and discussed substantive matters such as trade and defense. This marked a departure from the kind of "fact-finding" trips that Eleanor Roosevelt had undertaken, and, after encountering criticism, she confined future trips to ceremonial or goodwill missions. Nevertheless, she attended cabinet meetings when the subject of discussion interested her—the first president's wife to do so. She also made headlines by testifying in support of the Mental Health Systems Act before a committee of the U.S. Senate. After leaving the White House, she wrote *First Lady from Plains*, an insightful look at her husband's administration.

Nancy Reagan (1981–89), the wife of Ronald Reagan, insisted that she had little influence on her husband's decisions, but, before she left the White House, the *New York Times* wrote that she had "expanded the job of First Lady into a sort of Associate Presidency." She was often credited with influencing personnel decisions (both in hiring and firing), setting her husband's travel schedule, and shaping his agenda. She was criticized for what many considered "elitist" social behaviour and excessive spending, though private donors footed the bills. Her early association with a foster-grandparents program brought little favourable attention. However, her self-deprecating performance at a private dinner for journalists in 1982 and her leadership in an antidrug campaign, "Just Say No," increased her popularity.

Barbara Bush (1989–93), the wife of George Bush, followed tradition in refusing to specify how her own opinions differed from her husband's. White-haired and full-figured, she was enormously popular for her personal style, laughingly reporting that there were "a lot of fat, white-haired wrinkled ladies . . . tickled pink" to see someone like themselves in the White House. Her association with a campaign to increase literacy also won her admirers, and all the revenue earned from her best-selling book about her dog Millie was donated to the Barbara Bush Foundation for Family Literacy.

Hillary Rodham Clinton (1993–2001), the wife of Bill Clinton, entered the White House with a law degree, a successful career of her own, and connections to a large network of successful professionals, including other lawyers and activists. When she took an office in the West Wing of the White House (the first president's wife to do so) and was named by the president to head a task force on health care reform, many expected that she would carve out a substantive policy role for herself. Although the deliberations of the task force did not result in important legislation, they did highlight the first lady's power. After a group of physicians complained that she was not a "government official" and thus had no right to keep the task force meetings closed, a federal appeals court ruled in her favour, citing a long tradition of presidents' wives acting "as advisers and personal representatives of their husbands." Her appearance before five congressional committees to discuss the recommendations of the task force focused attention on the leading role she had taken in health care reform. Her public pronouncements on foreign policy and her changing stance on several other issues were frequently criticized, and they sometimes even conflicted with positions taken by her husband's administration. But her social activism, her frequent trips abroad without the president, the interviews she gave before, during, and after her husband's impeachment, and her successful candidacy for a U.S. Senate seat from New York State in 2000 all highlighted the independent power that a first lady could attain. And though her bid for the presidency in 2008 was unsuccessful, Clinton became the first first lady to attempt to win the highest office in the land. In December of that year, former adversary and then President-elect Barack Obama selected Clinton to serve as secretary of State—another first lady first.

Laura Welch Bush (2001–09), the wife of George W. Bush, was less of an activist than her predecessor but more of a public figure than her traditional mother-in-law. She publicly disagreed with her husband's position on *Roe* v. *Wade* (1973), the U.S. Supreme Court decision that guaranteed the legality of abortion (she supported the ruling, he opposed it). She also invited writers to the White House who had openly criticized her husband, and she agreed to testify before a Senate committee on education. A schoolteacher and librarian, she organized a national book fair to promote literacy and to encourage Americans to use libraries, organized a foundation for American libraries, and in a more traditional, maternal vein, devoted considerable time to comforting Americans after the September 11 attacks of 2001.

Michelle Obama (2009–), the wife of Barack Obama, was the first African American first lady. A successful lawyer and a mother of two young children, she put her own unique stamp on the role. As first lady she promoted volunteerism and community service, drew attention to the problems of military and working-class families, and worked to educate children on the importance of healthy eating.

FIRST LADY MICHELLE OBAMA

(b. Jan. 17, 1964, Chicago, Ill.)

Born Michelle LaVaughn Robinson, America's first lady Michelle Obama is the first African American first lady. She grew up on Chicago's South Side, the daughter of Marian, a homemaker, and Frasier Robinson, a worker in the city's water-purification plant. Robinson studied sociology and

African American studies at Princeton University (B.A., 1985) in New Jersey before attending Harvard Law School (J.D., 1988). Returning to Chicago, she took a job as a junior associate at Sidley Austin LLP, where she specialized in intellectual property law. In 1989, while at the firm, she met Barack Obama, who had been hired as a summer associate. Seeking a more public-service-oriented career path, in 1991 she became an assistant to Chicago Mayor Richard M. Daley. The following year she and Barack, then a community organizer, were married. From 1992 to 1993 Michelle was the assistant commissioner for the Chicago Department of Planning and Development, and in 1993 she founded the Chicago branch of Public Allies, a leadership-training program for young adults; she served as the branch's executive director until 1996.

Barack was elected to the Illinois Senate in 1996, and that year Michelle became the associate dean of student services at the University of Chicago, where she helped organize the school's community outreach programs. In 2002 she became the executive director of community and external affairs for the University of Chicago. Two years later Barack was elected to the U.S. Senate and came to national prominence with a speech he gave on the final night of the 2004 Democratic National Convention. In 2005 she became vice president of community and external affairs for the University of Chicago Medical Center.

When her husband announced his candidacy for the 2008 Democratic presidential nomination, Michelle took a prominent role in his campaign, taking leave from her position at the University of Chicago to devote herself more fully to campaigning while still maintaining time to care for her and Barack's two young daughters. An adept speaker, she stumped extensively for her husband during the long Democratic primary race, and in June 2008 Barack became the party's presumptive

nominee. Michelle's openness on the campaign trail and
in interviews—she often humanized her husband by dis-
cussing his faults and implored observers not to "deify
him"—endeared her to many. However, critics of her husband's campaign took issue with some of her
comments—such as when she remarked, while campaigning in Wisconsin in February 2008, that "for the first time
in my adult lifetime, I am really proud of my country."
Michelle later clarified her statement—saying that she
meant to say that she was proud that Americans were
eagerly engaging in the political process during the 2008
election—and she continued to have an active role in her
husband's campaign. Indeed, campaign aides referred to
her as "the closer," for her persuasiveness on the stump
among uncommitted voters who attended rallies. On
Nov. 4, 2008, Barack was elected 44th president of the
United States, defeating Arizona Sen. John McCain.

Michelle was an active first lady. During her first six
months in the role she visited military families to help
publicize the difficult problems they faced, encouraged
volunteerism and community service, and started an
organic vegetable garden at the White House grounds to
promote healthy eating.

THE WHITE HOUSE

The White House is the official office and residence of the
president of the United States at 1600 Pennsylvania Avenue
N.W. in Washington, D.C. The White House and its land-
scaped grounds occupy 18 acres (7.2 hectares). Since the
administration of George Washington (1789–97), who
occupied presidential residences in New York and
Philadelphia, every American president has resided at the
White House. Originally called the "President's Palace" on
early maps, the building was officially named the Executive

The White House at night, Washington, D.C. Hisham F. Ibrahim/ Getty Images

Mansion in 1810 in order to avoid connotations of royalty. Although the name "White House" was commonly used from about the same time (because the mansion's white-gray sandstone contrasted strikingly with the red brick of nearby buildings), it did not become the official name of the building until 1902, when it was adopted by Pres. Theodore Roosevelt (1901–09). The White House is the oldest federal building in the nation's capital.

The building's history begins in 1792, when a public competition was held to choose a design for a presidential residence in the new capital city of Washington. Thomas Jefferson, later the country's third president (1801–09), using the pseudonymous initials "A.Z.," was among those who submitted drawings, but Irish American architect James Hoban won the commission (and a $500 prize) with his plan for a Georgian mansion in the Palladian style. The structure was to have three floors and more than 100 rooms and would be built in sandstone imported from quarries along Aquia Creek in Virginia. The cornerstone was laid on Oct. 13, 1792. Labourers, including local slaves, were housed in temporary huts built on the north side of the premises. They were joined by skilled stonemasons from Edinburgh, Scotland, in 1793.

In 1800 the entire federal government was relocated from Philadelphia to Washington. John Adams, the country's second president (1797–1801), moved into the still unfinished presidential mansion on November 1 and the next night wrote in a letter to his wife, Abigail Adams:

> *I Pray Heaven Bestow the Best of Blessings on This House and All that shall hereafter inhabit it. May none but Honest and Wise Men ever rule under this Roof.*

At the insistence of Pres. Franklin Roosevelt (1933–45), the quotation was inscribed on the fireplace of the State Dining Room immediately below the portrait of Abraham Lincoln, by George Healy. When Abigail Adams finally arrived in Washington several days later, she was disappointed with the inadequate state of the residence. The first lady wrote,

> *There is not a single apartment finished. We have not the least fence, yard, or other convenience outside. I use the great unfinished audience room [East Room] as a drying room for hanging up the clothes.*

THE WHITE HOUSE IN THE 19TH CENTURY

The mansion quickly became a focal point of the new federal city and was symbolically linked to the United States Capitol by way of Pennsylvania Avenue. Following his inauguration in March 1801 Jefferson became the second president to reside in the executive mansion. In keeping with his ardent republicanism, he opened the house to public visitation each morning, a tradition that was continued (during peacetime) by all his successors. He personally drew up landscaping plans and had two earthen mounds installed on the south lawn to remind him of his beloved Virginia piedmont. Meanwhile, construction continued on the building's interior, which still lacked ample staircases and suffered from a persistently leaky roof. During Jefferson's tenure, the White House was elegantly furnished in Louis XVI style (known in America as Federal style).

During the War of 1812 the building was burned by the British, and Pres. James Madison (1809–17) and his family were forced to flee the city. The Madisons eventually moved into the nearby Octagon House, the Washington mansion of John Tayloe, a Virginia plantation owner. Reconstruction and expansion began under Hoban's direction, but the building was not ready for occupancy until 1817, during the administration of Pres. James Monroe (1817–25). Hoban's reconstruction included the addition of east and west terraces on the main building's flanks; a semicircular south portico and a colonnaded north portico were added in the 1820s.

During the 19th century the White House became a symbol of American democracy. In the minds of most Americans, the building was not a "palace" from which the president ruled, but merely a temporary office and residence from which he served the people he governed. The White House belonged to the people, not the president, and the president occupied it only for as long as the people allowed him to stay. The idea of a president refusing to leave the White House after losing an election or an impeachment trial was unthinkable.

The inauguration of Andrew Jackson (1829–37), the "people's president," attracted thousands of well-wishers to the nation's capital. As Jackson rode on horseback down

Pennsylvania Avenue to the White House, he was surrounded by a frenetic throng of 20,000 people, many of
whom attempted to follow him into the mansion to get a
better look at their hero. A contemporary, Margaret Bayer
Smith, recounts what happened next: "The halls were
filled with a disorderly rabble . . . scrambling for the
refreshments designed for the drawing room." While
friends of the new president joined arms to protect him
from the mob, "china and glass to the amount of several
thousand dollars were broken in the struggle to get at the
ices and cakes, though punch and other drinkables had
been carried out in tubs and buckets to the people." Said
Supreme Court Justice Joseph Story, "I was glad to escape
from the scene as soon as possible." During his administration Jackson spent more than $50,000 refurbishing the
residence, including $10,000 on decorations for the East
Room and more than $4,000 on a sterling silver dinner
and dessert set decorated with an American eagle.

In 1842 the visit to the United States of the English
novelist Charles Dickens brought an official invitation to
the White House. After his calls at the White House
door went unanswered, Dickens let himself in and walked
through the mansion from room to room on the lower
and upper floors. Finally coming upon a room filled with
nearly two dozen people, he was shocked and appalled to
see many of them spitting on the carpet. Dickens later
wrote, "I take it for granted the Presidential housemaids
have high wages." Until the Civil War, however, most
White House servants were slaves. Moreover, the wages
of all White House employees—as well as the expenses
for running the White House, including staging official
functions—were paid for by the president. Not until
1909 did Congress provide appropriations to pay White
House servants.

Dickens was not the only foreign visitor to be disappointed with the White House. On a trip to Washington just before the Civil War, Aleksandr Borisovich Lakier, a Russian nobleman, wrote that "the home of the president . . . is barely visible behind the trees." The White House, he said, was "sufficient for a private family and not at all conforming to the expectations of a European." Subsequent changes to the building in the 19th century were relatively minor. The interior was redecorated during various presidential administrations and modern conveniences were regularly added, including a refrigerator in 1845, gas lighting in 1849, and electric lighting in 1891.

The White House was the scene of mourning after the assassination of Pres. Abraham Lincoln (1861–65). While Mary Todd Lincoln lay in her room for five weeks grieving for her husband, many White House holdings were looted. Responding to charges that she had stolen government property when she left the White House, she angrily inventoried all the items she had taken with her, including gifts of quilts and waxworks from well-wishers.

THE WHITE HOUSE SINCE 1900

During the presidency of Theodore Roosevelt, the mansion's second-floor rooms were converted from presidential offices to family living quarters, not least because of the president's six children. For them, one observer said, "nothing [in the White House] was too sacred for amusement and no place too good for a playroom." Additional space was needed for the children's exotic pets, which included raccoons, snakes, a badger, and a bear. To accommodate a growing presidential staff and to provide more office space for the president, the West Wing was constructed in 1902. More office space was made available with the building of the East Wing in 1942. (The East and

West wings are connected to the main building by the east and west terraces.)

In 1948, during the presidency of Harry Truman (1945–53), the main building was discovered to be structurally unsound; during the next four years the entire interior was carefully rebuilt, though the original exterior walls were left standing. A second-floor balcony was likewise added on the south portico. The last major alterations to the White House were made in the 1960s by Jacqueline Kennedy, wife of Pres. John F. Kennedy (1961–63). Renowned for her beauty and refined taste, she collected and displayed items of historic and artistic value throughout its rooms. She made the White House a centre of national culture and awakened public interest in its beauties by conducting a televised tour of the mansion in 1962.

The White House building complex has a total of more than 130 rooms. The main building still contains the presidential family's living quarters and various reception rooms, all decorated in styles of the 18th and 19th centuries. Parts of the main building are open to the public. The west terrace contains the press briefing room, and the east terrace houses a movie theatre. The presidential office, known as the Oval Office, is located in the West Wing, as are the cabinet and press rooms; the East Wing contains other offices.

Over the years the White House has become a major American historic site, attracting more than 1.5 million visitors annually. In 1995 the section of Pennsylvania Avenue in front of the White House was closed to automobile traffic because of concerns about terrorism, and the area has since became popular with pedestrians and skaters. The allure of the building has never waned, and few who enter its environs—visitors and occupants alike—leave unaffected by its ambience and rich history. Jefferson thought that the

White House was too large, "big enough for two emperors, one Pope, and the grand lama," and Caroline Harrison, wife of Pres. Benjamin Harrison (1889–93), complained that there was "no feeling of privacy" on the property. But Franklin Roosevelt found it warm and comfortable. "My husband liked to be in the White House on New Year's Eve," remembered Eleanor Roosevelt:

> *We always gathered a few friends, and at midnight in the oval study the radio was turned on and we waited with the traditional eggnog in hand for midnight to be announced. Franklin always sat in his chair and, as the President, would raise his glass and say: "To the United States of America." All of us stood and repeated the toast after him. Somehow, the words were especially meaningful and impressive in that house.*

The White House is a unit of the National Capital Parks system and was accredited as a museum in 1988.

EXECUTIVE DEPARTMENTS AND AGENCIES

If the White House is the nerve centre of the presidency, the departments and agencies of the executive branch are the neurons. The members of the cabinet—the attorney general and the secretaries of State, Treasury, Defense, Homeland Security, Interior, Agriculture, Commerce, Labor, Health and Human Services, Housing and Urban Development, Transportation, Education, Energy, and Veterans Affairs—are appointed by the president and approved by the Senate. Although they are described in the Twenty-fifth Amendment as "the principal officers of the executive departments," significant power has flowed to non-cabinet-level presidential aides, such as those serving in the Office of Management and Budget (OMB), the Council of Economic Advisers, the National Security Council (NSC), and the office of the White House Chief of Staff; cabinet-level rank may be conferred to the heads of such institutions at the discretion of the president. Members of the cabinet and presidential aides serve at the pleasure of the president and may be dismissed by him at any time.

The executive branch also includes independent regulatory agencies such as the Federal Reserve System and the Securities and Exchange Commission. Governed by commissions appointed by the president and confirmed by the Senate (commissioners may not be removed by the president), these agencies protect the public interest by enforcing rules and resolving disputes over federal regulations. Also part of the executive branch are government corporations (e.g., the Tennessee Valley Authority, the National Railroad Passenger Corporation [Amtrak], and the U.S. Postal Service), which supply services to consumers that could be provided by private corporations, and independent executive agencies (e.g., the Central Intelligence Agency, the National Science Foundation, and the National Aeronautics and Space Administration), which comprise the remainder of the federal government.

THE CABINET

THE INSTITUTION OF THE CABINET

The cabinet serves as a collective body of advisers to a chief of state, and individual members of the cabinet serve as the heads of government departments. The cabinet has become an important element of government wherever legislative powers have been vested in a parliament, but its form differs markedly in various countries, the two most striking examples being the United Kingdom and the United States.

The cabinet system of government developed in Britain from the Privy Council in the 17th and early 18th centuries, when that body grew too large to debate affairs of state effectively. The English monarchs Charles II (reigned 1660–85) and Anne (1702–14) began regularly consulting leading members of the Privy Council in order to reach decisions before meeting with the more unwieldy full council. By the reign of Anne, the weekly, and some-times daily, meetings of this select committee of leading ministers had become the accepted machinery of execu-tive government, and the Privy Council's power was in inexorable decline. After George I (1714–27), who spoke little English (he was German), ceased to attend meetings with the committee in 1717, the decision-making process within that body, or cabinet, as it was now known, gradu-ally became centred on a chief, or prime, minister. This office began to emerge during the long chief ministry (1721–42) of Sir Robert Walpole and was definitively estab-lished by Sir William Pitt later in the century.

The passage of the Reform Bill in 1832 clarified two basic principles of cabinet government: that a cabinet should be composed of members drawn from the party or political faction that holds a majority in the House of Commons and that a cabinet's members are collectively responsible to the Commons for their conduct of the gov-ernment. Henceforth, no cabinet could maintain itself in power unless it had the support of a majority in the Commons. Unity in a political party proved the best way to organize support for a cabinet within the House of Commons, and the party system thus developed along with cabinet government in England.

In the United Kingdom today, the cabinet consists of about 15 to 25 members, or ministers, appointed by the prime minister, who in turn has been appointed by the monarch on the basis of his ability to command a majority of votes in the Commons. Although formerly empowered to select the cabinet, the sovereign is now restricted to the mere formal act of inviting the head of Parliament's majority party to form a government. The prime minister must put together a cabinet that represents and balances the various factions within his own party (or within a coalition of parties). Cabinet members must all be members of Parliament, as must the prime minister himself. The members of a cabinet head the principal government departments, or ministries, such as Home Affairs, Foreign Affairs, and the Exchequer (treasury). Other ministers may serve without portfolio or hold sinecure offices and are included in the cabinet on account of the value of their counsel or debating skills. The cabinet usually meets in the prime minister's official residence at 10 Downing Street in London.

Cabinet ministers are responsible for their departments, but the cabinet as a whole is accountable to Parliament for its actions, and its individual members must be willing and able to publicly defend the cabinet's policies. Cabinet members can freely disagree with each other within the secrecy of cabinet meetings, but once a decision has been reached, all are obligated to support the cabinet's policies, both in the Commons and before the general public. The loss of a vote of confidence or the defeat of a major legislative bill in the Commons can mean a cabinet's fall from power and the collective resignation of its members.

The U.S. president's cabinet is entirely different from the British-style cabinet. As noted above, it is composed of the heads of executive departments chosen by the president with the consent of the Senate, but the members do not (and cannot) hold seats in Congress, and their tenure, like that of the president himself, does not depend on favourable congressional votes on administration measures. Cabinet meetings are not required under the U.S. Constitution, which in fact makes no mention of such a body. The existence of the cabinet and its operations are matters of custom rather than of law, and the cabinet as a collective body has no legal existence or power. The first American president, George Washington, began the custom of consulting regularly with his department heads as a group. The term *cabinet* was first used for the heads of the State, Treasury, and War departments by James Madison in 1793. Gradually, as administrative duties increased and different problems arose, new executive departments were created by Congress; by the early 21st century, the U.S. cabinet consisted of 15 department heads, or secretaries.

Washington's habit of calling regular and frequent cabinet meetings began a tradition that has been followed by every succeeding president. But it is important to remember that the cabinet exists solely to help the president carry out his functions as the nation's chief executive. He is virtually free to use it or not to use it as he pleases. Presidents have thus varied greatly in their use of the cabinet. Ordinarily, all members of a cabinet are of the same political party, though in recent times—as in the presidencies of Bill Clinton, George W. Bush, and Barack Obama—the administration has attempted to include at least one cabinet member of the opposition party. Attendance at U.S. cabinet meetings is not restricted exclusively to those department heads that are of cabinet rank. Cabinet appointments are for the duration of the administration, but the president may dismiss any member at his own pleasure, without approval of the Senate.

CABINET DEPARTMENTS

As discussed previously, the U.S. cabinet is composed of the heads of 15 executive departments: Agriculture, Commerce, Defense, Education, Energy, Health and Human Services, Homeland Security, Housing and Urban Development, Interior, Justice, Labor, State, Transportation, Treasury, and Veterans Affairs.

The Department of Agriculture, also known as the USDA, is in charge of programs and policies relating to the farming industry and the use of national forests and grasslands. Formed in 1862, the USDA works to stabilize or improve domestic farm income, develop foreign markets for American agricultural products, curb poverty and hunger, protect soil and water resources, make credit available for rural development, and ensure the quality of food supplies.

The Deparment of Commerce is responsible for programs and policies relating to international trade, national economic growth, and technological advancement. Established in 1913, it administers the Bureau of the Census, the National Oceanic and Atmospheric Administration (NOAA), the Patent and Trademark Office, and the U.S. Travel and Tourism Administration (USTTA).

The Department of Defense is responsible for ensuring national security and supervising U.S. military forces. Based in the Pentagon building in Washington, D.C., it includes the Joint Chiefs of Staff, the departments of the U.S. Army, U.S. Navy, and U.S. Air Force, and numerous defense agencies and allied services. It was formed in 1947 by an act of Congress (amended 1949) that combined the former departments of War and the Navy.

The Department of Education is responsible for carrying out government education programs. Established in 1980 by Pres. Jimmy Carter, it seeks to ensure access to education and to improve the quality of education nation-wide. It administers programs in elementary and secondary education, higher education, vocational and adult education, special education, bilingual education, civil rights, and educational research. (The Carter family received much media attention for sending their daughter, Amy, to public school in Washington, D.C.)

The Department of Energy is responsible for administering national energy policy. Established in 1977, it promotes energy efficiency and the use of renewable energy. Its national security programs serve to develop and oversee nuclear-energy resources. Its Office of Environmental Management oversees waste management and cleanup activities at inactive facilities. The Fossil Energy Office develops policies and regulations concerning the use of natural gas, coal, and electric energy. Its regional power administrations transmit electric power produced at federal hydroelectric projects.

The Department of Health and Human Services (HHS) is responsible for carrying out government programs and policies relating to human health, welfare, and income security. Established in 1980, when responsibility for education was removed from the former Department of Health, Education, and Welfare, it consists of several agencies, including the Administration for Children and Families, the Administration on Aging, the Centers for Disease Control and Prevention, the Health Resources and Services Administration, the Indian Health Service, the National Institutes of Health, and the Substance Abuse and Mental Health Services Administration.

The Department of Homeland Security is responsible for safeguarding the United States against terrorist attacks and ensuring preparedness for natural disasters and other emergencies. In the wake of the September 11 attacks in 2001, Pres. George W. Bush created the Office of Homeland

Security to coordinate counterterrorism efforts by federal, state, and local agencies; and the Homeland Security Council to advise the president on homeland security matters. Both offices were superseded in January 2003 with the creation of the Department of Homeland Security, which assumed control of several agencies responsible for domestic security and emergency preparedness, including the Customs Service and Border Patrol (now U.S. Customs and Border Protection), the Federal Emergency Management Agency (FEMA), the Transportation Security Administration (TSA), the Secret Service, and the Coast Guard.

The Department of Housing and Urban Development (HUD) is responsible for carrying out government housing and community-development programs. Established in 1965 under Pres. Lyndon B. Johnson, it ensures equal access to housing and community-based employment opportunities; finances new housing, public housing, and housing rehabilitation projects; insures mortgages; and carries out programs that serve the housing needs of low-income and minority families and the elderly, the disabled, and the mentally ill. It also protects consumers against fraudulent practices by land developers, ensures the safety of manufactured homes, and defends homebuyers against abusive mortgage-loan practices.

The Department of the Interior is responsible for managing most federally owned lands and natural resources in the United States and for administering reservation communities for American Indians and Alaska Natives. Created in 1849, it encompasses the Bureau of Indian Affairs, the Bureau of Land Management, the Bureau of Reclamation, the Minerals Management Service, the Office of Surface Mining, the National Park Service, the U.S. Fish and Wildlife Service, and the U.S. Geological Survey.

The Department of Justice is responsible for the enforcement of federal laws. Headed by the U.S. attorney general, it investigates and prosecutes cases under federal antitrust, civil rights, criminal, tax, and environmental laws. It controls the Federal Bureau of Investigation (FBI), the Federal Bureau of Prisons, the Drug Enforcement Administration (DEA), the Office of Justice Programs, the U.S. Marshals Service, and the U.S. National Central Bureau of Interpol, among many other agencies.

The Department of Labor is responsible for enforcing labour statutes and promoting the general welfare of U.S. wage earners. Established in 1913, it controls the Employment Standards Administration, the Occupational Safety and Health Administration (OSHA), the Pension Benefit Guaranty Corporation, and numerous other agencies that administer programs concerned with employment and training, trade adjustment assistance, unemployment insurance, veterans and senior citizens, and mine safety.

The Department of State, also called the State Department, is responsible for carrying out U.S. foreign policy. Established in 1789, it is the oldest of the federal departments and the president's principal means of conducting treaty negotiations and forging agreements with foreign countries. Under its administration are the U.S. Mission to the United Nations, the Foreign Service Institute, and various offices of diplomatic security, foreign intelligence, policy analysis, international narcotics control, protocol, and passport services.

The Department of Transportation is responsible for programs and policies relating to transportation. Established in 1966, it controls the Federal Aviation Administration (FAA), the Federal Highway Administration, the Federal Motor Carrier Safety Administration, the Federal Railroad Administration, the Federal Transit Administration, the

Maritime Administration, the National Highway Traffic Safety Administration, the Pipeline and Hazardous Materials Safety Administration, and the Research and Innovative Technology Administration.

The Department of Veterans Affairs (VA) is responsible for programs and policies relating to veterans and their families. Established in 1989, it succeeded the Veterans Administration (formed in 1930). The VA administers benefits for medical care, educational assistance and vocational rehabilitation, pensions and life insurance, and payments for disability or death related to military service.

EXECUTIVE AGENCIES AND OFFICES

The principal executive agencies in the United States are the Central Intelligence Agency (CIA), the Environmental Protection Agency (EPA), the Federal Reserve System, the National Aeronautics and Space Administration (NASA), the National Security Council (NSC), the Office of Management and Budget (OMB), the Securities and Exchange Commission (SEC), and the U.S. Postal Service (USPS).

CENTRAL INTELLIGENCE AGENCY

Formally created in 1947, the Central Intelligence Agency (CIA) is the country's principal foreign intelligence and counterintelligence agency. It grew out of the World War II Office of Strategic Services (OSS). Previous U.S. intelligence and counterintelligence efforts had been conducted by the military and the Federal Bureau of Investigation (FBI), and suffered from duplication, competition, and lack of coordination.

In 1947 Congress passed the National Security Act, which created the National Security Council (NSC) and, under its direction, the CIA. Given extensive power to conduct foreign intelligence operations, the CIA was charged with advising the NSC on intelligence matters, correlating and evaluating the intelligence activities of other government agencies, and carrying out other intelligence activities as the NSC might require. Although it did not end rivalries with the military services and the FBI, the law established the CIA as the country's preeminent intelligence service.

The CIA is headed by a director and deputy director, only one of whom may be a military officer. The director of central intelligence (DCI) is responsible for managing all U.S. intelligence-gathering activities. DCIs have been drawn from various fields, including not only intelligence but also the military, politics, and business. The DCI serves as the chief intelligence adviser to the president and is often his close confidant.

The CIA is organized into four major directorates. The Intelligence Directorate analyzes intelligence gathered by overt means from sources such as the news media and by covert means from agents in the field, satellite photography, and the interception of telephone and other forms of communication. These analyses attempt to incorporate intelligence from all possible sources. During the Cold War in the second half of the 20th century, most of this work was focused on the military and the military-industrial complex of the Soviet Union.

The Directorate of Operations is responsible for the clandestine collection of intelligence (i.e., espionage) and special covert operations. Clandestine activities are carried out under various covers, including the diplomatic cloak used by virtually every intelligence service, as well as corporations and other "front" companies that the CIA creates or acquires. Despite the elaborate nature of some covert operations, these activities represent only a small fraction of the CIA's overall budget.

The Directorate of Science and Technology is responsible for keeping the agency abreast of scientific and technological advances, for carrying out technical operations (e.g., coordinating intelligence from reconnaissance satellites), and for supervising the monitoring of foreign media.

The Directorate of Administration is responsible for the CIA's finances and personnel matters. It also contains the Office of Security, which is responsible for the security of personnel, facilities, and information as well as for uncovering spies within the CIA.

ENVIRONMENTAL PROTECTION AGENCY

The Environmental Protection Agency (EPA) sets and enforces national pollution-control standards. In 1970, in response to the welter of confusing, often ineffective environmental protection laws enacted by states and communities, Pres. Richard Nixon created the EPA to fix national guidelines and to monitor and enforce them. The EPA was initially charged with the administration of the Clean Air Act (1970), enacted to abate air pollution primarily from industries and motor vehicles; the Federal Environmental Pesticide Control Act (1972); and the Clean Water Act (1972), regulating municipal and industrial wastewater discharges and offering grants for building sewage-treatment facilities. By the mid-1990s the EPA was enforcing 12 major statutes, including laws designed to control uranium mill tailings; ocean dumping; toxins in drinking water; insecticides, fungicides, and rodenticides; and asbestos hazards in schools.

One of the EPA's early successes was an agreement with automobile manufacturers to install catalytic converters in cars, thereby reducing emissions of unburned hydrocarbons by 85 percent. The EPA's enforcement was in large part responsible for a decline of one-third to one-half in

most air-pollution emissions in the United States from
1970 to 1990; significant improvements in water quality
and waste disposal also occurred. The Comprehensive
Environmental Response, Compensation, and Liability
Act (also called the Superfund), providing billions of dollars for cleaning up abandoned waste dumps, was first
established in 1980, but the number of those waste sites
and the difficulties of the cleanups remained formidable
for years thereafter.

FEDERAL RESERVE SYSTEM

The Federal Reserve System is the central banking
authority of the United States. It acts as a fiscal agent for
the U.S. government, is custodian of the reserve accounts
of commercial banks, makes loans to commercial banks,
and oversees the supply of currency, including coin, in
coordination with the U.S. Mint. The system was created
by the Federal Reserve Act, which Pres. Woodrow Wilson
signed into law on Dec. 23, 1913. It consists of the Board
of Governors of the Federal Reserve System, the 12
Federal Reserve banks, the Federal Open Market
Committee, the Federal Advisory Council, and, since
1976, a Consumer Advisory Council; there are several
thousand member banks.

The seven-member Board of Governors of the Federal
Reserve System determines the reserve requirements of
the member banks within statutory limits, reviews and
determines the discount rates established by the 12 Federal
Reserve banks, and reviews the budgets of the reserve
banks. The chairman of the Board of Governors is
appointed to a four-year term by the president of the
United States.

A Federal Reserve bank is a privately owned corporation established pursuant to the Federal Reserve Act to
serve the public interest.

The 12 Federal Reserve banks are located in Boston; New York City; Philadelphia; Chicago; San Francisco; Cleveland, Ohio; Richmond, Virginia; Atlanta, Georgia; St. Louis, Missouri; Minneapolis, Minnesota; Kansas City, Missouri; and Dallas, Texas.

The 12-member Federal Open Market Committee, consisting of the seven members of the Board of Governors, the president of the Federal Reserve Bank of New York, and four members elected by the Federal Reserve banks, is responsible for the determination of Federal Reserve bank policy. The Federal Advisory Council, whose role is purely advisory, consists of one representative from each of the 12 Federal Reserve districts.

The Federal Reserve System exercises its regulatory powers in several ways, the most important of which may be classified as instruments of direct or indirect control. One form of direct control can be exercised by adjusting the legal reserve ratio—i.e., the proportion of its deposits that a member bank must hold in its reserve account— thus increasing or reducing the amount of new loans that the commercial banks can make. Because loans give rise to new deposits, the potential money supply is, in this way, expanded or reduced.

The money supply may also be influenced through manipulation of the discount rate, which is the rate of interest charged by Federal Reserve banks on short-term secured loans to member banks. Since these loans are typically sought by banks to maintain reserves at their required level, an increase in the cost of such loans has an effect similar to that of increasing the reserve requirement.

The classic method of indirect control is through open-market operations, first widely used in the 1920s and now employed daily to make small adjustments in the market. Federal Reserve bank sales or purchases of securities on the open market tend to reduce or increase the size of commercial-bank reserves; for example, when the Federal Reserve sells securities, the purchasers pay for them with checks drawn on their deposits, thereby reducing the reserves of the banks on which the checks are drawn.

NATIONAL AERONAUTICS AND SPACE ADMINISTRATION

The National Aeronautics and Space Administration (NASA) was established in 1958 to conduct research and development of vehicles and activities for the exploration of space within and outside of Earth's atmosphere.

NASA is composed of five program offices: Aeronautics and Space Technology, for the development of equipment; Space Science and Applications, dealing with programs for understanding the origin, structure, and evolution of the universe, the solar system, and the Earth; Space Flight, concerning manned and unmanned space transportation; Space Tracking and Data, involving tracking and data acquisition; and Space Station, which has a long-term goal of establishing a manned space station. A number of additional research centres are affiliated, including the Goddard Space Flight Center in Greenbelt, Md.; the Jet Propulsion Laboratory in Pasadena, Calif.; the Lyndon B. Johnson Space Center in Houston, Texas; and the Langley Research Center in Hampton, Va. The headquarters of NASA are in Washington, D.C.

NASA was created largely in response to the Soviet launching of Sputnik in 1957. NASA's organization was well under way by the early years of Pres. John F. Kennedy's administration, when Kennedy proposed that the United States put a man on the Moon by the end of the 1960s. To that end the Apollo program was designed, and in 1969 U.S. astronaut Neil Armstrong became the first human being to set foot on the Moon. Later unmanned programs—such as Viking, Mariner, Voyager, and Galileo—explored other bodies of the solar system.

NASA was also responsible for the development and launching of a number of satellites, including Earth-science satellites, communications satellites, and weather satellites. It also planned and developed the space shuttle, a reusable vehicle capable of carrying out missions that cannot be conducted with conventional spacecraft.

NATIONAL SECURITY COUNCIL

The National Security Council (NSC) was established by the National Security Act in 1947 to advise the president on domestic, foreign, and military policies related to national security. The president of the United States is chairman of the NSC; other members include the vice president and the secretaries of state and defense. Advisers to the NSC are the chairman of the Joint Chiefs of Staff, the director of the CIA, and other officials whom the president may appoint with Senate approval. The NSC staff is headed by a special assistant for national security affairs, who generally acts as a close adviser of the president.

OFFICE OF MANAGEMENT AND BUDGET

The Office of Management and Budget is an agency of the executive branch of the federal government that assists the president in preparing the federal budget and in supervising the budget's administration in executive agencies. It is involved in the development and resolution of all budget, policy, legislative, regulatory, procurement, and management issues on behalf of the president. The agency also evaluates the effectiveness of, and sets funding priorities for, the programs, policies, and procedures of other agencies.

SECURITIES AND EXCHANGE COMMISSION

The Securities and Exchange Commission was established by Congress in 1934 after the Senate Committee on

Banking and Currency investigated the New York Stock Exchange's operations. The commission's purpose was to restore investor confidence by ending misleading sales practices and stock manipulations that led to the collapse of the stock market in 1929. It prohibited the buying of stock without adequate funds to pay for it, provided for the registration and supervision of securities markets and stockbrokers, established rules for solicitation of proxies, and prevented unfair use of nonpublic information in stock trading. It also stipulated that a company offering securities make full public disclosure of all relevant information. The commission acts as adviser to the court in corporate bankruptcy cases.

UNITED STATES POSTAL SERVICE

The United States Postal Service (USPS) is a government-owned corporation responsible for delivering mail within the United States and between the United States and other countries. Established in 1970, it replaced the Post Office Department, which itself had evolved from the postal system created in 1775 by the first postmaster general of the United States, Benjamin Franklin.

The postal service expanded rapidly after U.S. independence. Although annual revenue also increased dramatically, the heavy cost of establishing a postal structure to keep pace with the remarkable economic progress of the country and the accelerating extension of its settled area caused expenditures to rise even faster.

By the end of the 19th century, however, this expenditure had produced remarkable results. The accessibility, quality, and range of services provided had improved immeasurably.

The first supplementary postal service, registered mail, was introduced in 1855. Other milestones in this progress were postal money order service (1864); international money orders (1867); special delivery (1885); parcel post, with its accessory collect on delivery (COD) and insurances services (1913); and certified mail (1955), which provided proof of posting for items without intrinsic value. Mail was formally divided into three classes in 1863, and a fourth was added in 1879. First-class, or letter, mail is the class of mail most commonly used by the public. The other classes were established according to mail content: second-class for newspapers and magazines, third-class for other printed matter and merchandise weighing less than one pound, and fourth-class for merchandise or printed matter weighing one pound or more.

The post office has played a vital role as a pioneer and major user of all systems of transport as each was developed: the stagecoach, steamboat, canals, and railroads; the short-lived Pony Express; and airlines and motor vehicles. It also helped subsidize their development.

To deal with the problem of increasing deficits and to improve the overall management and efficiency of the post office, the U.S. Congress approved the Postal Reorganization Act of 1970, signed into law Aug. 12, 1970, which transformed the Post Office Department into a government-owned corporation, called the United States Postal Service.

Presidents of the United States: George Washington to William McKinley

Chapter 2

GEORGE WASHINGTON

(b. Feb. 22, 1732, Westmoreland county, Va.—d. Dec. 14, 1799, Mount Vernon, Va.)

George Washington was an American general and commander in chief of the colonial armies in the American Revolution (1775–83) and subsequently the first president of the United States (1789–97).

CHILDHOOD AND YOUTH

Little is known of George Washington's early childhood, spent largely on the Ferry Farm on the Rappahannock River, opposite Fredericksburg, Va. Mason L. Weems's stories of the hatchet and cherry tree and of young Washington's repugnance to fighting are apocryphal efforts to fill a manifest gap. He attended school irregularly from his 7th to his 15th year, first with the local church sexton and later with a schoolmaster named Williams. His best training, however, was given him by practical men and outdoor occupations, not by books. He mastered tobacco growing and stock raising, and early in his teens he was sufficiently familiar with surveying to plot the fields about him. At his father's death, the 11-year-old boy became the ward of his eldest half brother, Lawrence.

Washington turned first to surveying as a profession. In 1749 he received an appointment as official surveyor of Culpeper county in Virginia, and for more than two years he was kept almost constantly busy. Surveying taught him resourcefulness and endurance and toughened him in both body and mind; it also gave him an interest in western development that endured throughout his life.

Upon the death of Lawrence and his daughter Sarah in 1751, Washington gained control of the family's Virginia estate, Mount Vernon. For the next 20 years the main background of Washington's life was the work and society of Mount Vernon. He gave assiduous attention to the rotation of crops, fertilization of the soil, and the management of livestock. He had to manage the 18 slaves that came with the estate and others he bought later; by 1760 he had paid taxes on 49 slaves—though he strongly disapproved of the institution and hoped for some mode of abolishing it. At the time of his death, more than 300 slaves were housed in the quarters on his property. In his will, he bequeathed the slaves in his possession to his wife and ordered that upon her death they be set free.

PREREVOLUTIONARY
MILITARY AND POLITICAL CAREER

EARLY MILITARY CAREER

Traditions of his ancestor John Washington's feats as Indian fighter and Lawrence Washington's talk of service days helped imbue George with military ambition. Just after Lawrence's death, Lieutenant Governor Robert Dinwiddie appointed George adjutant for the southern district of Virginia; in 1753 he became adjutant of the Northern Neck and Eastern Shore.

In 1754 the enterprising governor planned an expedition to hold the Ohio Valley lands claimed by the crown against encroachments by the French. He made Joshua Fry colonel of a provincial regiment, appointed Washington lieutenant colonel, and set them to recruiting troops. Two agents of the Ohio Company, which Lawrence Washington and others had formed to develop lands on the upper Potomac and Ohio rivers, had begun building a fort at what later became Pittsburgh, Pa. Dinwiddie, ready to launch into his own war, sent Washington with two companies to reinforce this post. In April 1754 the lieutenant colonel set out from Alexandria with about 160 men at his back. He marched to Cumberland only to learn that the French had anticipated the British blow; they had taken possession of the fort of the Ohio Company and had renamed it Fort Duquesne. Happily, the Indians of the area offered support. Washington therefore struggled cautiously forward to within about 40 miles (60 km) of the French position and erected his own post at Great Meadows, near what is now Confluence, Pa. From this base, he made a surprise attack (May 28, 1754) on an advance detachment of 30 French, killing the commander, Coulon de Jumonville, and nine others and taking the rest prisoners. The French and Indian War had begun.

Washington at once received promotion to a full colonelcy and was reinforced, commanding a considerable body of Virginia and North Carolina troops, with Indian auxiliaries. But his attack soon brought the whole French force down upon him. They drove his 350 men into the Great Meadows fort (Fort Necessity) on July 3, besieged it with 700 men, and, after an all-day fight, compelled him to surrender. The French agreed to let the disarmed colonials march back to Virginia with the honours of war, but they compelled Washington to promise that Virginia would not build another fort on the Ohio for a year. He returned to Virginia, chagrined but proud, to receive the thanks of the House of Burgesses and to find that his name had been mentioned in the London gazettes.

The arrival of Gen. Edward Braddock and his army in Virginia in February 1755, as part of the triple plan of campaign that called for his advance on Fort Duquesne and in New York Governor William Shirley's capture of Fort Niagara and Sir William Johnson's capture of Crown Point, brought Washington new opportunities and responsibilities. He had resigned his commission in October 1754 in resentment of an untactful order of the British war office that provincial officers of whatever rank would be subordinate to any officer holding the king's commission. But he ardently desired a part in the war; when Braddock showed appreciation of his merits and invited him to join the expedition as personal aide-de-camp with the courtesy title of colonel, he accepted.

At the table he had frequent disputes with Braddock, who, when contractors failed to deliver their supplies, attacked the colonials as supine and dishonest while Washington defended them warmly. His freedom of utterance is proof of Braddock's esteem. Braddock accepted Washington's unwise advice that he divide his army, leaving half of it to come up with the slow wagons and cattle train and taking the other half forward against Fort Duquesne at a rapid pace. Washington was by Braddock's side when on July 9 the army was ambushed and bloodily defeated. Braddock was fatally wounded on his fifth horse. Washington was at Braddock's deathbed, helped bring the troops back, and was repaid by being appointed, in August 1755, while still only 23 years old, commander of all Virginia troops.

But no part of his later service was conspicuous. In 1757 his health failed and in the closing weeks of that year he was so ill of a "bloody flux" (dysentery) that his physician ordered him home to Mount Vernon. In the spring of 1758 he had recovered sufficiently to return to duty as colonel in command of all Virginia troops. As part of the grand sweep of several armies organized by British statesman William Pitt, the Elder, Gen. John Forbes led a new advance upon Fort Duquesne. Late in the autumn the French evacuated and burned the fort. Washington, who had just been elected to the House of Burgesses, was able to resign with the honorary rank of brigadier general.

MARRIAGE AND PLANTATION LIFE

Immediately on resigning his commission, Washington was married (Jan. 6, 1759) to Martha Dandridge, the widow of Daniel Parke Custis. She was a few months older than he, the mother of two children living and two dead, and possessed one of the considerable fortunes of Virginia. Washington had met her the previous March, asking for her hand before his campaign with Forbes. Though it does not seem to have been a romantic love match, the marriage united two harmonious temperaments and proved happy. Some estimates of the property brought to him by this marriage have been exaggerated, but it did include a number of slaves and about 15,000 acres (6,000 hectares), much of it valuable for its proximity to Williamsburg.

From the time of his marriage Washington added to the care of Mount Vernon the supervision of the Custis estate at the White House on the York River. As his holdings expanded, they were divided into farms, each under its own overseer; but he minutely inspected operations every day and according to one visitor often pulled off his coat and performed ordinary labour.

Though the practice of slavery of any form is, to modern sensibilities, intolerable, it is however true that Washington's care of his slaves was exemplary. He carefully clothed and fed them, engaged a doctor for them by the year, generally refused to sell them—"I am principled against this kind of traffic in the human species"—and administered correction mildly. They showed so much attachment that few ran away.

PREREVOLUTIONARY POLITICS

Washington's contented life was interrupted by the rising storm in imperial affairs. The British ministry, facing a heavy postwar debt, high home taxes, and continued military costs in America, decided in 1764 to obtain revenue from the colonies. Up to that time, Washington had shown no signs of personal greatness and few signs of interest in state affairs. He nevertheless played a silent part in the House of Burgesses and was a thoroughly loyal subject. But he was also present when Patrick Henry introduced his resolutions against the Stamp Act in May 1765 and shortly thereafter gave token of his adherence to the cause of the colonial Whigs against the Tory ministries of England.

He was not a member of the Virginia committee of correspondence formed in 1773 to communicate with other colonies, but when the Virginia legislators, meeting irregularly again at the Raleigh tavern in May 1774, called for a Continental Congress, he was present and signed the resolutions. Moreover, he was a leading member of the first provincial convention or revolutionary legislature late that summer.

The Virginia provincial convention promptly elected Washington one of the seven delegates to the first Continental Congress. He was by this time known as a radical rather than a moderate, and in several letters of the time he opposed a continuance of petitions to the British crown, declaring that they would inevitably meet with a humiliating rejection.

Returning to Virginia in November, he took command of the volunteer companies drilling there and served as chairman of the Committee of Safety in Fairfax county. Although the province contained many experienced officers and Colonel William Byrd of Westover had succeeded Washington as commander in chief, the unanimity with which the Virginia troops turned to Washington was a tribute to his reputation and personality; it was understood that Virginia expected him to be its general. He was elected to the second Continental Congress at the March 1775 session of the legislature and again set out for Philadelphia.

REVOLUTIONARY LEADERSHIP

HEAD OF THE COLONIAL FORCES

The choice of Washington as commander in chief of the military forces of all the colonies followed immediately upon the first fighting.

The first phase of Washington's command covered the period from July 1775 to the British evacuation of Boston in March 1776. In those eight months he imparted discipline to the army, which at maximum strength slightly exceeded 20,000; he dealt with subordinates who, as John Adams said, quarrelled "like cats and dogs"; and he kept the siege of Boston vigorously alive.

The British general, Sir William Howe, abandoned the city on March 17, leaving 200 cannons and invaluable stores of small arms and munitions.

Washington had won the first round, but there remained five years of the war, during which the American cause was repeatedly near complete disaster. It is unquestionable that Washington's strength of character, his ability to hold the confidence of army and people and to diffuse his own courage among them, his unremitting activity, and his strong common sense constituted the chief factors in achieving American victory. He was not a great tactician: as Jefferson said later, he often "failed in the field"; he was sometimes guilty of grave military blunders. One of his chief faults was his tendency to subordinate his own judgment to that of the generals surrounding him.

One element of Washington's strength was his sternness as a disciplinarian. The army was continually dwindling and refilling, politics largely governed the selection of officers by Congress and the states, and the ill-fed, ill-clothed, ill-paid forces were often half-prostrated by sickness and ripe for mutiny. Troops from each of the three sections, New England, the middle states, and the South, showed a deplorable jealousy of the others. Washington was rigorous in breaking cowardly, inefficient, and dishonest men, boasting in front of Boston that he had "made a pretty good sort of slam among such kind of officers."

The darkest chapter in Washington's military leadership was opened when, reaching New York in April 1776, he placed half his army, about 9,000 men, under Israel Putnam, on the perilous position of Brooklyn Heights, Long Island, where a British fleet in the East River might cut off their retreat. Howe thrust a crushing force along feebly protected roads against the American flank. The patriots were outmaneuvered, defeated, and suffered a total loss of 5,000 men, of whom 2,000 were captured. Their whole position might have been carried by storm, but, fortunately for Washington, General Howe delayed. While the enemy lingered, Washington succeeded under cover of a dense fog in ferrying the remaining force across the East River to Manhattan, where he took up a fortified position.

THE TRENTON-PRINCETON CAMPAIGN

It was at this darkest hour of the Revolution that a 44-year-old Washington struck his brilliant blows at Trenton and

Princeton, N.J., reviving the hopes and energies of the nation. Howe, believing that the American army soon would dissolve totally, retired to New York, leaving strong forces in Trenton and Burlington. Washington, at his camp west of the Delaware River, planned a simultaneous attack on both posts, using his whole command of 6,000 men. But his subordinates in charge of both wings failed him, and he was left on the night of Dec. 25, 1776, to march on Trenton with about 2,400 men. With the help of Colonel John Glover's regiment, which was composed of fishermen and sailors from Marblehead, Mass., Washington and his troops were ferried across the Delaware River. In the dead of night and amid a blinding snowstorm, they then marched 10 miles (16 km) downstream and in the early hours of the morning caught the enemy at Trenton unaware. In less than two hours and without the loss of a single man in battle, Washington's troops defeated the Hessians, killed their commander (Johann Rall), and captured nearly 1,000 prisoners and arms and ammunition. This historic Christmas crossing proved to be a turning point in the war and was immortalized for posterity by Emanuel Gottlieb Leutze in his famous 1851 painting of the event. (The painting is, however, historically inaccurate: the depicted flag is anachronistic, the boats are the wrong size and shape, and it is questionable whether Washington could have crossed the icy Delaware while standing in the manner depicted.)

The year 1777 was marked by the British capture of Philadelphia and the surrender of British General John Burgoyne's invading army to Gen. Horatio Gates at Saratoga, N.Y., followed by intrigues to displace Washington from his command. Congress fled to the interior of Pennsylvania, and Washington, after an unsuccessful effort to repeat his stroke at Trenton against the British troops posted at Germantown, had to take up winter quarters at Valley Forge. His army, ill housed and ill fed, with thousands of men "barefoot and otherwise naked," was at the point of exhaustion; it could not keep the field, for inside of a month it would have disappeared. Under these circumstances, there is nothing that better proves the true fibre of Washington's character and the courage of his soul than the unyielding persistence with which he held his strong position at Valley Forge through a winter of semistarvation, of justified grumbling by his men, of harsh public criticism, and of captious meddling by a Congress that was too weak to help him.

With the conclusion of the French alliance in the spring of 1778, the aspect of the war was radically altered. The British army in Philadelphia, fearing that a French fleet would blockade the Delaware while the militia of New Jersey and Pennsylvania invested the city, hastily retreated upon New York City. The arrival of the French fleet under Admiral Charles-Hector Estaing on July 1778 completed the isolation of the British, who were thenceforth held to New York City and the surrounding area.

The final decisive stroke of the war, the capture of Cornwallis at Yorktown, is to be credited chiefly to Washington's vision. He hurried his troops through New Jersey, embarked them on transports in Delaware Bay, and landed them at Williamsburg, Va., where he had arrived on September 14. Cornwallis had retreated to Yorktown and entrenched his army of 7,000 British regulars. Their works were completely invested before the end of the month; the siege was pressed with vigour by the allied armies under Washington, consisting of 5,500 Continentals, 3,500 Virginia militia, and 5,000 French regulars; and on October 19 Cornwallis surrendered. By this campaign, probably the finest single display of Washington's generalship, the war was brought to a virtual close.

Washington remained during the winter of 1781–82 with the Continental Congress in Philadelphia, exhorting it to maintain its exertions for liberty and to settle the army's claims for pay. He was present at the entrance of the American army into New York on the day of the British evacuation, Nov. 25, 1783, and on December 4 took leave of his closest officers in an affecting scene at Fraunces Tavern. Traveling south, on December 23, in a solemn ceremony, he resigned his commission to the Continental Congress in the state senate chamber of Maryland in Annapolis and received the thanks of the nation. Washington left Annapolis at sunrise on December 24 and before nightfall was at home in Mount Vernon. In the next four years he found sufficient occupation in his estates, wishing to close his days as a gentleman farmer and to give to agriculture as much energy and thought as he had to the army.

PRESIDENCY

POSTREVOLUTIONARY POLITICS

Viewing the chaotic political condition of the United States after 1783, Washington at first he believed that the Articles of Confederation might be amended. Later he took the view that a more radical reform was necessary. Washington approved in advance the call for a gathering of all the states to meet in Philadelphia in May 1787 to "render the Constitution of the Federal Government adequate to the exigencies of the Union." Although he hoped to the last to be excused, he was chosen one of Virginia's five delegates.

Washington arrived in Philadelphia on May 13, the day before the opening of the Constitutional Convention, and as soon as a quorum was obtained he was unanimously

George Washington, engraving by C. Burt, c. 1790. Hulton Archive/Getty Images

chosen its president. For four months he presided over the convention, breaking his silence only once upon a minor question of congressional apportionment. Although he said little in debate, no one did more outside the hall to insist on stern measures. When ratification of the new constitution was obtained, he wrote to leaders in the various states urging that men staunchly favourable to it be elected to Congress. For a time he sincerely believed that when the new framework was completed, he would be allowed to retire again to privacy. But all eyes immediately turned to him for the first president; in no state was any other name considered. The electors chosen in the first days of 1789 cast a unanimous vote for him, and reluctantly he accepted. He was inaugurated in New York City on April 30.

Washington and his wife, to considerable public criticism, traveled about in a coach-and-four like monarchs. Moreover, during his presidency, Washington did not shake hands, and he met his guests on state occasions while standing on a raised platform and displaying a sword on his hip. Slowly, feeling his way, Washington was defining the style of the first president of a country in the history of the world. The people, too, were adjusting to a government without a king. Even the question of how to address a president had to be discussed. It was decided that in a republic the simple salutation "Mr. President" would do.

THE WASHINGTON ADMINISTRATION

Washington's administration of the government in the next eight years was marked by the caution, the methodical precision, and the sober judgment that had always characterized him. A painstaking inquiry into all the problems confronting the new nation laid the basis for a series of judicious recommendations to Congress in his first message. The four members of his first cabinet were Thomas Jefferson as secretary of state, Alexander Hamilton as secretary of treasury, Henry Knox as secretary of war, and Edmund Randolph as attorney general. When war was declared between France and England in 1793, he took Hamilton's view that the United States should completely disregard the treaty of alliance with France and pursue a course of strict neutrality. He had a firm belief that the United States must insist on its national identity, strength, and dignity.

Although the general voice of the people compelled him to acquiesce reluctantly to a second term in 1792 and his election that year was again unanimous, during his last four years in office he suffered from a fierce personal and partisan animosity. This culminated when the publication of the terms of the Jay Treaty, which Washington signed in August 1795, provoked a bitter discussion, and the House of Representatives called upon the president for the instructions and correspondence relating to the treaty. Washington, who had already clashed with the Senate on foreign affairs, refused to deliver these items, and, in the face of an acrimonious debate, he firmly maintained his position.

RETIREMENT

Earnestly desiring leisure, feeling a decline of his physical powers, and wincing under abuses of the opposition,

Washington refused to yield to the general pressure for a third term. This refusal was blended with a testament of sagacious advice to his country in the farewell address of Sept. 19, 1796, written largely by Hamilton but remolded by Washington and expressing his ideas. Retiring in March 1797 to Mount Vernon, he devoted himself for the last two and a half years of his life to his family, farm operations, and care of his slaves. In 1798 his seclusion was briefly interrupted when the prospect of war with France caused his appointment as commander in chief of the provisional army, and he was much worried by the political quarrels over high commissions; but the war cloud passed away.

On Dec. 12, 1799, after riding on horseback for several hours in cold and snow, he returned home exhausted and was attacked late the next day with quinsy or acute laryngitis. His strength sank rapidly, and he died at 10:00 PM on December 14.

JOHN ADAMS

(b. Oct. 30, 1735, Braintree [now in Quincy], Mass.—d. July 4, 1826, Quincy, Mass.)

John Adams was the second president of the United States (1797–1801), the first vice president (1789–97), and a major figure in the Continental Congress (1774–77).

EARLY LIFE

Adams was the eldest of the three sons of Deacon John Adams and Susanna Boylston of Braintree, Mass. His father, a farmer and shoemaker, could trace the family lineage back to the first generation of Puritan settlers in New England. Adams graduated from Harvard College in 1755 and in 1758 began practicing law in nearby Boston.

In 1764 Adams married Abigail Smith, a minister's daughter from neighbouring Weymouth. Intelligent, well-read, vivacious, and just as fiercely independent as her new husband, Abigail Adams became a confidante and political partner who helped to stabilize and sustain the ever-irascible and highly volatile Adams throughout his long career. The letters between them afford an extended glimpse into their deepest thoughts and emotions and provide modern readers with the most revealing record of personal intimacy between husband and wife in the revolutionary era. Their first child, Abigail Amelia, was born in 1765. Their first son, John Quincy, who would become the sixth president of the United States, arrived two years later. Two other sons, Thomas Boylston and Charles, followed shortly thereafter. (Another child, Susanna, did not survive infancy.)

By then Adams's legal career was on the rise, and he had become a visible member of the resistance movement that questioned Parliament's right to tax the American colonies. Despite his hostility toward the British government, in 1770 Adams agreed to defend the British soldiers who had fired on a Boston crowd in what became known as the Boston Massacre. His insistence on upholding the legal rights of the soldiers, who in fact had been provoked, made him temporarily unpopular but also marked him as one of the most principled radicals in the burgeoning movement for American independence.

CONTINENTAL CONGRESS

In the summer of 1774, Adams was elected to the Massachusetts delegation that joined the representatives from 12 of 13 colonies in Philadelphia at the First Continental Congress. He and his cousin, Samuel Adams, quickly became the leaders of the radical faction, which rejected the prospects for reconciliation with Britain.

John Adams lithograph, based on a painting by Gilbert Stuart.
Library of Congress Prints and Photographs Division

By the time the Second Continental Congress convened in 1775, Adams had gained the reputation as "the Atlas of independence." Over the course of the following year, he made several major contributions to the patriot cause destined to ensure his place in American history. First, he nominated George Washington to serve as commander of the fledging Continental Army. Second, he selected Jefferson to draft the Declaration of Independence. (Both decisions were designed to ensure Virginia's support for the revolution.) Third, he dominated the debate in the Congress on July 2–4, 1776, defending Jefferson's draft of the declaration and demanding unanimous support for a decisive break with Great Britain.

Adams remained the central figure of the Continental Congress for the following two years. As the prospects for a crucial wartime alliance with France improved late in 1777, he was chosen to join Benjamin Franklin in Paris to conduct the negotiations. In February 1778 he sailed for Europe, accompanied by 10-year-old John Quincy.

FOREIGN SERVICE

By the time Adams arrived in Paris, the treaty creating an alliance with France had already been concluded. He quickly returned home in the summer of 1779, just in time to join the Massachusetts Constitutional Convention.

The other delegates, acknowledging his constitutional expertise, simply handed him the job of drafting what became the Massachusetts constitution (1780), which immediately became the model for the other state constitutions and—in its insistence on a bicameral legislature and the separation of powers—a major influence on the Constitution of the United States.

The Congress then ordered Adams to rejoin Franklin in Paris to lead the American delegation responsible for negotiating an end to the war with Britain. The favourable terms achieved in the Peace of Paris (1783) can be attributed to the effective blend of Franklin's discretion and Adams's bulldog temperament.

In 1784 Jefferson arrived in Paris to replace Franklin as the American minister at the French court. Over the next few months, Jefferson became an unofficial member of the Adams family, and the bond of friendship between Adams and Jefferson was sealed, a lifelong partnership and rivalry that made the combative New Englander and the elegant Virginian the odd couple of the American Revolution.

POLITICAL PHILOSOPHY

Because he was the official embodiment of American independence from the British Empire, Adams was largely ignored and relegated to the periphery of the court during his nearly three years in London. Still brimming with energy, he spent his time studying the history of European politics for patterns and lessons that might assist the fledgling American government in its efforts to achieve what no major European nation had managed to produce—namely, a stable republican form of government.

Adams wished to warn his fellow Americans against all revolutionary manifestos that envisioned a fundamental break with the past and a fundamental transformation in human nature or society that supposedly produced a new age. All such utopian expectations were illusions, he believed, driven by what he called "ideology," the belief that imagined ideals, so real and seductive in theory, were capable of being implemented in the world. The same kind of conflict between different classes that had bedeviled medieval Europe would, albeit in muted forms, also afflict the United States, because the seeds of such competition were planted in human nature itself. Adams blended the psychological insights of New England Puritanism, with its emphasis on the emotional forces throbbing inside all creatures, and the Enlightenment belief that government must contain and control those forces, to construct a political system capable of balancing the ambitions of individuals and competing social classes.

VICE PRESIDENCY AND PRESIDENCY

Soon after his return to the United States, Adams found himself on the ballot in the presidential election of 1789. He finished second to Washington (69 votes to 34 votes), which signaled three political realities: first, his standing as a leading member of the revolutionary generation was superseded only by that of Washington himself; second, his combative style and his political writings had hurt his reputation enough to preclude the kind of overwhelming support Washington enjoyed; third, according to the electoral rules established in the recent ratified Constitution, he was America's first vice president.

Adams himself described the vice presidency as "the most insignificant office that ever the Invention of man contrived or his Imagination conceived." His main duty was to serve as president of the Senate, casting a vote only to break a tie. He steadfastly supported all the major initiatives of the Washington administration, and when Washington announced his decision not to seek a third term in 1796, Adams was the logical choice to succeed him.

In the first contested presidential election in American history, Adams won a narrow electoral majority (71–68) over Jefferson, who thereby became vice president. This burdened the Adams presidency with a vice president who was the acknowledged head of the rival political party, the Republicans (subsequently the Democratic-Republicans).

Despite Washington's plea for a bipartisan foreign policy in his farewell address (1796), the "quasi-war" produced a bitter political argument between Federalists, who preferred war with France to alienating Britain, and Democratic-Republicans, who viewed France as America's only European ally and the French Revolution as a continuation of the American Revolution on European soil. In 1797 he sent a peace delegation to Paris to negotiate an end to hostilities, but when the French directory demanded bribes before any negotiations could begin, Adams ordered the delegates home. Rather than ask Congress for a declaration of war he acted with characteristic independence by sending yet another, and this time successful, peace delegation to France against the advice of his cabinet and his Federalist supporters. The move ruined him politically but avoided a costly war that the infant American republic was ill-prepared to fight.

If ending the "quasi-war" with France was Adams's major foreign policy triumph, his chief domestic failure was passage of the Alien and Sedition Acts (1798), which permitted the government to deport foreign-born residents and indict newspaper editors or writers who published "false, scandalous, and malicious writing or writings against the government of the United States." A total of 14 indictments were brought against the Republican press under the sedition act, but the crudely partisan prosecutions quickly became infamous persecutions that backfired on the Federalists.

The election of 1800 again pitted Adams against Jefferson. Adams ran ahead of the Federalist candidates for Congress, who were swept from office in a Republican landslide. However, thanks to the deft maneuvering of Aaron Burr, all 12 of New York's electoral votes went to Jefferson, giving the tandem of Jefferson and Burr the electoral victory (73–65). Jefferson was eventually elected president by the House of Representatives, which chose him over Burr on the 36th ballot. In his last weeks in office, Adams made several Federalist appointments to the judiciary, including John Marshall as chief justice of the United States. These "midnight judges" offended Jefferson, who resented the encroachment on his own presidential prerogatives. Adams, the first president to reside in the presidential mansion in Washington, D.C., was also the first—and one of the very few—presidents not to attend the inauguration of his successor. On March 4, 1801, he was already on the road back to Quincy.

RETIREMENT

In 1812, thanks in part to prodding from Benjamin Rush, the Philadelphia physician and political leader, he overcame his bitterness toward Jefferson and initiated a correspondence with his former friend and rival that totaled 158 letters. Generally regarded as the most intellectually impressive correspondence between American statesmen in all of American history, the dialogue between Adams and Jefferson touched on a host of timely and timeless subjects: the role of religion in history, the aging process, the emergence of an American language, the French Revolution, and the party battles of the 1790s. Adams put it most poignantly to Jefferson: "You and I ought not to die, before

We have explained ourselves to each other." As if according to a script written by providence, the "Sage of Quincy" and the "Sage of Monticello" died within hours of each other on July 4, 1826, the 50th anniversary to the day of the Declaration of Independence.

THOMAS JEFFERSON

(b. April 13, 1743, Shadwell, Va. — d. July 4, 1826, Monticello, Va.)

Thomas Jefferson was the third president of the United States (1801–09), the second vice president (1797–1801), and the chief draftsman of the Declaration of Independence (1776). He also was the founder and architect of the University of Virginia and the most eloquent American proponent of individual freedom as the core meaning of the American Revolution.

EARLY YEARS

Albermarle county, where he was born, lay in the foothills of the Blue Ridge Mountains in what was then regarded as a western province of the Old Dominion. His father, Peter Jefferson, was a self-educated surveyor who amassed a tidy estate that included 60 slaves. His mother, Jane Randolph Jefferson, was descended from one of the most prominent families in Virginia. He boarded with the local schoolmaster to learn his Latin and Greek until 1760, when he entered the College of William and Mary in Williamsburg.

Thomas Jefferson, c. 1805. MPI/ Hulton Archive/Getty Images

By all accounts he was an obsessive student, often spending 15 hours of the day with his books, 3 hours practicing his violin, and the remaining 6 hours eating and sleeping. He read law with George Wythe, the leading legal scholar in Virginia, from 1762 to 1767, then left Williamsburg to practice, though he handled no landmark cases.

In 1768 he made two important decisions: first, to build his own home atop an 867-foot- (264-metre-) high mountain near Shadwell that he eventually named Monticello and, second, to stand as a candidate for the House of Burgesses. His political timing was also impeccable, for he entered the Virginia legislature just as opposition to the taxation policies of the British Parliament was congealing.

In 1772 he married Martha Wayles Skelton, an attractive and delicate young widow whose dowry more than doubled his holdings in land and slaves. In 1774 he wrote *A Summary View of the Rights of British America*, which was quickly published, though without his permission, and catapulted him into visibility beyond Virginia as an early advocate of American independence. His reputation thus enhanced, the Virginia legislature appointed him a delegate to the Second Continental Congress in the spring of 1775.

DECLARING INDEPENDENCE

Jefferson's inveterate shyness prevented him from playing a significant role in the debates within the Congress. John Adams, a leader in those debates, remembered that Jefferson was silent even in committee meetings, though consistently staunch in his support for independence. His chief role was as a draftsman of resolutions. In that capacity, on June 11, 1776, he was appointed to a five-person committee, which also included Adams and Benjamin Franklin, to draft a formal statement of the reasons why a break with Great Britain was justified. Adams asked him to prepare the first draft, which he did within a few days. It contained the following 55 words, which are generally regarded as the seminal statement of American political culture:

> *We hold these truths to be self-evident; that all men are created equal; that they are endowed by their Creator with certain inalienable rights; that among these are life, liberty and the pursuit of happiness; that to secure these rights, governments are instituted among men, deriving their just powers from the consent of the governed.*

On July 3–4 the Congress debated and edited Jefferson's draft, deleting and revising fully one-fifth of the text. But they made no changes whatsoever in this passage, which over succeeding generations became the lyrical sanction for every liberal movement in American history.

Jefferson's political philosophy was less a comprehensive body of thought than a visionary prescription. He regarded the past as a "dead hand" of encrusted privileges and impediments that must be cast off to permit the natural energies of individual citizens to flow freely. The American Revolution, as he saw it, was the first shot in what would eventually became a global battle for human liberation from despotic institutions and all coercive versions of government.

AMERICAN IN PARIS

Jefferson agreed, albeit reluctantly, to serve as a delegate to the Continental Congress in December 1782. Then, in 1784 he agreed to replace Franklin as American minister to France.

During his five-year sojourn in Paris, Jefferson accomplished very little in any official sense. His only significant achievement, the negotiation of a $400,000 loan from Dutch bankers that allowed the American government to consolidate its European debts, was conducted primarily by John Adams, then serving as American minister to the Court of St. James' in London. There is considerable evidence to suggest, but not to prove conclusively, that Jefferson initiated a sexual liaison with his attractive young slave Sally Hemings during his stay in Paris.

During the latter stages of Jefferson's stay in Paris, Louis XVI, the French king, was forced to convene the Assembly of Notables in Versailles to deal with France's deep financial crisis. Jefferson initially regarded the assembly as a French version of the Constitutional Convention, then meeting in Philadelphia, and he expected the French Revolution to remain a bloodless affair that would culminate in a revised French government, probably a constitutional monarchy along English lines. He was fortunate to depart France late in 1789, just at the onset of mob violence.

PARTY POLITICS

Jefferson returned to the United States in 1789 to serve as the first secretary of state under Pres. George Washington. During his tenure as secretary of state (1790–93), a three-pronged division within the cabinet soon emerged over American policy toward the European powers. While all parties embraced some version of the neutrality doctrine, the specific choices posed by the ongoing competition for supremacy in Europe between England and France produced a bitter conflict. Washington and Adams, who was serving as vice president, insisted on complete neutrality;

Alexander Hamilton pushed for a pro-English version of neutrality—chiefly commercial ties with the most potent mercantile power in the world; and Jefferson favoured a pro-French version of neutrality, arguing that the Franco-American treaty of 1778 obliged the United States to honour past French support during the war for independence, and that the French Revolution embodied the "spirit of '76" on European soil. This remained his unwavering position throughout the decade. Serving as vice president during the Adams presidency (1797–1801), Jefferson worked behind the scenes to undermine Adams's efforts to sustain strict neutrality and blamed the outbreak of the "quasi-war" with France in 1797–98 on what he called "our American Anglophiles" rather than the French Directory. His foreign-policy vision was dominated by a dichotomous view of England as a corrupt and degenerate engine of despotism and France as the enlightened wave of the future.

Jefferson's position on domestic policy during the 1790s was a variation on the same dichotomy. As Hamilton began to construct his extensive financial program—to include funding the national debt, assuming the state debts, and creating a national bank—Jefferson came to regard the consolidation of power at the federal level as a diabolical plot to subvert the true meaning of the American Revolution. As Jefferson saw it, the entire Federalist commitment to an energetic central government with broad powers over the domestic economy replicated the arbitrary policies of Parliament and George III, which the American Revolution had supposedly repudiated as monarchical and aristocratic practices, incompatible with the principles of republicanism.

By the middle years of the decade two distinctive political camps had emerged, calling themselves Federalists and Republicans (later Democratic-Republicans). As an embryonic version of party structure was congealing, and Jefferson, assisted and advised by Madison, established the rudiments of the first opposition party in American politics under the Republican banner.

The highly combustible political culture of the early republic reached a crescendo in the election of 1800, one of the most fiercely contested campaigns in American history. The Federalist press described Jefferson as a pagan and atheist, a treasonable conspirator against the duly elected administrations of Washington and Adams, a utopian dreamer with anarchistic tendencies toward the role of government, and a cunning behind-the-scenes manipulator of Republican propaganda. In the final tally of electoral votes the tandem of Jefferson and Aaron Burr won by a margin of 73 to 65. A quirk in the Constitution, subsequently corrected in the Twelfth Amendment, prevented electors from distinguishing between their choice of president and vice president, so Jefferson and Burr tied for the top spot, even though voter preference for Jefferson was incontestable. The decision was thrown into the House of Representatives where, after several weeks of debate and backroom wheeling and dealing, Jefferson was elected on the 36th ballot.

PRESIDENCY

The major message of Jefferson's inaugural address was conciliatory. Its most famous line ("We are all republicans—we are all federalists") suggested that the party battles of the previous decade must cease. He described his election as a recovery of the original intentions of the American Revolution, this after the hostile takeover of those "ancient and sacred truths" by the Federalists, who had erroneously assumed that a stable American nation required a powerful central government. In Jefferson's truly distinctive and original formulation, the coherence of the American republic did not require the mechanisms of a powerful state to survive or flourish. Indeed, the health of the emerging American nation was inversely proportional to the power of the federal government, for in the end the sovereign source of republican government was voluntary popular opinion, "the people," and the latent energies these liberated individuals released when unburdened by government restrictions.

In 1804 Jefferson was easily reelected over Federalist Charles Cotesworth Pinckney, winning 162 electoral votes to Pinckney's 14. Initially, at least, his policies as president reflected his desire for decentralization, which meant dismantling the embryonic federal government, the army and navy, and all federal taxation programs, as well as placing the national debt, which stood at $112 million, on the road to extinction.

There were very few cabinet discussions during Jefferson's presidency because he preferred to do the bulk of business within the executive branch in writing. Crafting language on the page was his most obvious talent, and he required all cabinet officers to submit drafts of their recommendations, which he then edited and returned for their comments. The same textual approach applied to his dealings with Congress. All of his annual messages were delivered in writing rather than in person. Indeed, apart from his two inaugural addresses, there is no record of Jefferson delivering any public speeches whatsoever.

The major achievement of his first term was the purchase of the vast Louisiana region, which stretched from the Mississippi Valley to the Rocky Mountains, from France for $15 million. Although the price substantially increased the national debt, Jefferson reasoned that the opportunity to double the national domain was too good to miss. In one fell swoop he removed the threat of a major European power from America's borders and extended the life span of the uncluttered agrarian values he so cherished. In private, however, Jefferson agreed with critics who claimed that the purchase was unconstitutional.

If the Louisiana Purchase was the crowning achievement of Jefferson's presidency, it also proved to be the high point from which events moved steadily in the other direction. Despite his eloquent testimonials to the need for a free press, Jefferson was outraged by the persistent attacks on his policies and character from Federalist quarters, and he instructed the attorneys general in the recalcitrant states to seek indictments, in clear violation of his principled commitment to freedom of expression.

But Jefferson's major disappointment had its origins in Europe with the resumption of the Napoleonic Wars, which resulted in naval blockades in the Atlantic and Caribbean that severely curtailed American trade and pressured the U.S. government to take sides in the conflict. Jefferson's response was the Embargo Act (1807), which essentially closed American ports to all foreign imports and American exports. The embargo assumed that the loss of American trade would force England and France to alter their policies, but this fond hope was always an illusion, since the embryonic American economy lacked the size to generate such influence and was itself wrecked by Jefferson's action. Moreover, the enforcement of the Embargo Act required the exercise of precisely those coercive powers by the federal government that Jefferson had previously opposed. By the time he left office in March 1809, Jefferson was a tired and beaten man, anxious to escape the consequences of his futile efforts to preserve American neutrality and eager to embrace the two-term precedent established by Washington.

RETIREMENT

During the last 17 years of his life Jefferson maintained a crowded and active schedule. He rose with the dawn each day, bathed his feet in cold water, then spent the morning on his correspondence (one year he counted writing 1,268 letters) and working in his garden. Each afternoon he took a two-hour ride around his grounds. Dinner, served in the late afternoon, was usually an occasion to gather his daughter Martha and her 12 children, along with the inevitable visitors. Monticello became a veritable hotel during these years, on occasion housing 50 guests. The lack of privacy caused Jefferson to build a separate house on his Bedford estate about 90 miles (140 km) from Monticello, where he periodically fled for seclusion.

A considerable share of Jefferson's attention during the last 17 years was occupied with his architectural projects. Throughout his life Monticello remained a work-in-progress; even during his retirement Jefferson's intensive efforts at completing the renovations never quite produced the masterpiece of neoclassical design he wanted to achieve. A smaller but more architecturally distinctive mansion at Bedford, called Poplar Forest, was completed on schedule. Finally there was the campus of the University of Virginia at Charlottesville, which Jefferson called his "academical village." Jefferson surveyed the site and chose the Pantheon of Rome as the model for the rotunda. He also selected all the books for the library, defined the curriculum, and picked the faculty. Unlike every other American college at the time, "Mr. Jefferson's university" had no religious affiliation and imposed no religious requirement on its students. There were no curricular requirements, no mandatory code of conduct except the self-enforced honour system, no president or administration. Every aspect of life at the University of Virginia reflected Jefferson's belief that the only legitimate form of governance was self-governance.

In 1812 his vast correspondence began to include an exchange with his former friend and more recent rival John Adams. The exchange of 158 letters between 1812 and 1826 permitted the two sages to pose as philosopher-kings and create what is arguably the most intellectually impressive correspondence between statesmen in all of American history.

Jefferson's twilight years were darkened by the shadow of debt. He had been chronically in debt throughout most of his life, mostly because of his own lavish lifestyle. By the end, he was more than $100,000 — in modern terms several million dollars — in debt. Monticello, including land, mansion, furnishings, and the vast bulk of the slave population, was auctioned off the year after his death, and his surviving daughter, Martha, was forced to accept charitable contributions to sustain her family.

Jefferson died in his bed at Monticello at about half past noon on July 4, 1826. His last conscious words were "Is it the Fourth?" Remarkably, up in Quincy on that same day his old rival and friend John Adams also died later in the afternoon. His last words — "Thomas Jefferson still lives" — were wrong at the moment but right for the future, since Jefferson's complex legacy was destined to become the most resonant and controversial touchstone in all of American history.

JAMES MADISON

(b. March 16, 1751, Port Conway, Va. —d. June 28, 1836, Montpelier, Va.)

James Madison was the fourth president of the United States (1809–17) and one of the Founding Fathers of his country. At the Constitutional Convention (1787), he influenced the planning and ratification of the U.S. Constitution and collaborated with Alexander Hamilton and John Jay in the publication of the Federalist papers. As a member of the new House of Representatives, he sponsored the first 10 amendments to the Constitution, commonly called the Bill of Rights. He was secretary of state under Pres. Thomas Jefferson when the Louisiana Territory was purchased from France. The War of 1812 was fought during his presidency.

EARLY LIFE AND POLITICAL ACTIVITIES

Madison was born at the home of his maternal grandmother. The son and namesake of a leading Orange county landowner and squire, he maintained his lifelong home in Virginia at Montpelier, near the Blue Ridge Mountains. In 1769 he rode horseback to the College of New Jersey (Princeton University), where he completed the four-year course in two years. Overwork produced several years of epileptoid hysteria and premonitions of early death but did not prevent home study of public law.

His health improved, and he was elected to Virginia's 1776 Revolutionary convention, where he drafted the state's guarantee of religious freedom. In the convention-turned-legislature he helped Thomas Jefferson disestablish the church but lost reelection by refusing to furnish the electors with free whiskey. After two years on the governor's council, he was sent to the Continental Congress in March 1780.

Five feet four inches tall and weighing about 100 pounds, small boned, boyish in appearance, and weak of voice, he waited six months before taking the floor, but strong actions belied his mild demeanour. He rose quickly to leadership against the devotees of state sovereignty and enemies of Franco-U.S. collaboration in

peace negotiations, contending also for the establishment of the Mississippi as a western territorial boundary
and the right to navigate that river through its Spanish-
held delta.

THE FATHER OF THE CONSTITUTION

Reentering the Virginia legislature in 1784, Madison defeated
Patrick Henry's bill to give financial support to "teachers
of the Christian religion." To avoid the political effect of
his extreme nationalism, he persuaded the states-rights
advocate John Tyler to sponsor the calling of the Annapolis
Convention of 1786, which, aided by Madison's influence,
produced the Constitutional Convention of 1787.

James Madison. National
Archives/Getty Images

There his Virginia, or large-
state, Plan, put forward through
Governor Edmund Randolph,
furnished the basic framework
and guiding principles of the
Constitution, earning him the title
of father of the Constitution.
Madison believed keenly in the
value of a strong government in
which power was well controlled
because it was well balanced
among the branches.

Madison took day-by-day notes
of debates at the Constitutional
Convention, which furnish the
only comprehensive history of
the proceedings. To promote
ratification he collaborated with
Alexander Hamilton and John Jay
in newspaper publication of the

Federalist papers (Madison wrote 29 out of 85), which became the standard commentary on the Constitution.

Elected to the new House of Representatives, Madison sponsored the first 10 amendments to the Constitution—the Bill of Rights—placing emphasis in debate on freedom of religion, speech, and press. His leadership in the House came to an end when he split with Secretary of the Treasury Hamilton over methods of funding the war debts. Hamilton's aim was to strengthen the national government by cementing men of wealth to it; Madison sought to protect the interests of Revolutionary veterans.

Hamilton's victory turned Madison into a strict constructionist of the congressional power to appropriate for the general welfare. He denied the existence of implied power to establish a national bank to aid the Treasury. Later, as president, he asked for and obtained a bank as "almost [a] necessity" for that purpose, but he contended that it was constitutional only because Hamilton's bank had gone without constitutional challenge. The break over funding split Congress into Madisonian and Hamiltonian factions, though Madisonians later turned into Jeffersonians after Thomas Jefferson, having returned from France, became secretary of state.

In 1794 Madison married a widow, Dolley Payne Todd, a Quaker 17 years his junior. She periodically served as official hostess for Pres. Jefferson, who was a widower. As Madison's wife, she may be said to have created the role of First Lady as a political partner of the president, although that label did not come into use until much later.

Madison left Congress in 1797, disgusted by John Jay's treaty with England, which frustrated his program of commercial retaliation against the wartime oppression of U.S. maritime commerce. The Alien and Sedition Acts of 1798 inspired him to draft the Virginia Resolutions of that year, denouncing those statutes as violations of the First Amendment of the Constitution and affirming the right and duty of the states "to interpose for arresting the progress of the evil."

During eight years as Jefferson's secretary of state (1801–09), Madison used the words "The President has decided" so regularly that his own role can be discovered only in foreign archives. Senators John Adair and Nicholas Gilman agreed in 1806 that he "governed the President," an opinion held also by French minister Louis-Marie Turreau.

MADISON'S PRESIDENCY

Although he was accused of weakness in dealing with France and England, Madison won the presidency in 1808 by publishing his vigorous diplomatic dispatches. Faced with a scheming senatorial clique on taking office, he made a senator's lacklustre brother, Robert Smith, secretary of state and wrote all important diplomatic letters for two years before replacing him with James Monroe, who would succeed Madison as the fifth president of the United States in 1817. Although he had fully supported Jefferson's wartime shipping embargo, Madison reversed his predecessor's policy two weeks after assuming the presidency by secretly notifying both Great Britain and France, then at war, that, in his opinion, if the country addressed should stop interfering with U.S. commerce and the other belligerent continued to do so, "Congress will, at the next ensuing session, authorize acts of hostility . . . against the other."

Believing that England was bent on permanent suppression of American commerce, Madison proclaimed nonintercourse with England on Nov. 2, 1810, and notified France on the same day that this would "necessarily lead to war" unless England stopped its impressment of American seamen and seizure of American goods and vessels. He was reelected in 1812, despite strong opposition and the vigorous candidacy of DeWitt Clinton.

With his actions buried in secrecy, Federalists and politicians pictured Madison as a timorous pacifist dragged into the War of 1812 (1812–15) by congressional War Hawks, and they denounced the conflict as "Mr. Madison's War." In fact, the president had sought peace but accepted war as inevitable.

By lowering the average age of generals from 60 to 36 years, Madison managed to turn the tide of the war in favour of the United States, and by 1814 victory over the British was secured. Still the country would never forget the ignominy of the president and his wife having to flee in the face of advancing British troops bent on laying waste Washington, D.C., including setting afire the executive mansion, the Capitol, and other public buildings.

The Federalist Party was killed by its opposition to the war, and the president was lifted to a pinnacle of popularity. On leaving the presidency, Madison was eulogized at a Washington mass meeting for having won national power and glory "without infringing a political, civil, or religious right."

LATER LIFE

Never again leaving Virginia, Madison managed his 5,000-acre (2,000-hectare) farm for 19 years, cultivating the land by methods regarded today as modern innovations. He hated slavery, which held him in its economic chains, and worked to abolish it through the government purchase of slaves and their resettlement in Liberia, financed by the sale of public lands. Madison participated in Jefferson's creation of the University of Virginia (1819) and later served as its rector. His last years were spent in bed; he was barely able to bend his rheumatic fingers, which nevertheless turned out an endless succession of letters and articles combating nullification and secession—the theme of his final "Advice to My Country." Henry Clay called him, after George Washington, "our greatest statesman."

JAMES MONROE

(b. April 28, 1758, Westmoreland county, Va.—d. July 4, 1831, New York, N.Y.)

James Monroe was the fifth president of the United States (1817–25). He issued an important contribution to U.S. foreign policy in the Monroe Doctrine, a warning to European nations against intervening in the Western Hemisphere. The period of his administration has been called the Era of Good Feelings.

EARLY LIFE AND CAREER

Monroe's father, Spence Monroe, was of Scottish descent, and his mother, Elizabeth Jones Monroe, of Welsh descent. The family were owners of a modest 600 acres (240 hectares) in Virginia. At age 16 Monroe entered the College of William and Mary but in 1776 left to fight in the American Revolution.

In 1780, having resigned his commission in the army, he began the study of law under Thomas Jefferson, then governor of Virginia, and between the two men there developed an intimacy and a sympathy that had a powerful influence upon Monroe's later career. Jefferson also fostered a friendship between Monroe and James Madison.

Monroe was elected to the Virginia House of Delegates in 1782 and was chosen a member of the governor's council. From 1783 to 1786 he served in the Congress under the Articles of Confederation, the first constitution of the new nation.

During his term he vigorously insisted on the right of the United States to navigate the Mississippi River, then controlled by the Spanish, and attempted, in 1785, to secure for the weak Congress the power to regulate commerce, thereby removing one of the great defects in the existing central government.

In 1786 Monroe, 27 years old, and Elizabeth Kortright of New York, 17 years old, were married. They had two daughters, Eliza Kortright and Maria Hester, and a son who died in infancy. Eliza often was at her father's side as official hostess when he was president, substituting for her ailing mother.

James Monroe. National Archives/Getty Images

Retiring from Congress in 1786, Monroe began practicing law at Fredericksburg, Va. He was chosen a member of the Virginia House of Delegates in 1787 and in 1788 a member of the state convention at which Virginia ratified the new federal Constitution. In 1790 he was elected to the U.S. Senate, where he vigorously opposed Pres. George Washington's administration; nevertheless, in 1794 Washington nominated him as minister to France.

MINISTER TO FRANCE

It was the hope of the administration that Monroe's well-known French sympathies would secure for him a favourable reception and that his appointment would also conciliate France's friends in the United States. His warm welcome in France and his enthusiasm for the French Revolution, which he regarded as a natural successor to the American Revolution, displeased the Federalists (the party of Alexander Hamilton, which encouraged close ties not to France but to England) at home. Monroe did nothing, moreover, to reconcile the French to the Jay Treaty, which regulated commerce and navigation between the United States and Great Britain during the French Revolutionary wars.

Monroe led the French government to believe that the Jay Treaty would never be ratified by the United States and that better things might be expected after the election in 1796 of a new president, perhaps Thomas Jefferson. Washington, though he did not know of this intrigue, sensed that Monroe was unable to represent his government properly and, late in 1796, recalled him.

In 1799 Monroe was chosen governor of Virginia and was twice reelected, serving until 1802.

THE LOUISIANA PURCHASE

There was much uneasiness in the United States when Spain restored Louisiana to France in October 1800. In January 1803 Pres. Jefferson appointed Monroe envoy extraordinary and minister plenipotentiary to France to aid Robert R. Livingston, the resident minister, in purchasing the territory at the mouth of the Mississippi, including the island of New Orleans. On April 18 Monroe was further commissioned as the regular minister to Great Britain.

Monroe joined Livingston in Paris on April 12, after the latter's negotiations were well under way, and the two ministers, on finding Napoleon willing to dispose of the entire province of Louisiana, decided to exceed their instructions and effect its purchase. Accordingly, on

May 2, 1803, they signed a treaty and two conventions (antedated to April 30) whereby France sold Louisiana to the United States.

Monroe returned to the United States in December 1807. He was elected to the Virginia House of Delegates in the spring of 1810. In the following winter he was again chosen governor, serving from January to November 1811, when he resigned to become secretary of state under James Madison, a position he held until March 1817. The direction of foreign affairs in the troubled period immediately preceding and during the War of 1812, with Great Britain, thus fell upon him. On Sept. 27, 1814, after the capture of Washington, D.C., by the British, he was appointed secretary of war and discharged the duties of this office, in addition to those of the Department of State, until March 1815.

PRESIDENCY

In 1816 Monroe was elected president of the United States as the Republican candidate, defeating Rufus King, the Federalist candidate. By 1820, when he was reelected, the Federalists had ceased to function as a party. The chief events of his calm and prosperous administration, which has been called the Era of Good Feelings, were the First Seminole War (1817–18); the acquisition of the Floridas from Spain (1819–21); the Missouri Compromise (1820), by which the first conflict over slavery under the Constitution was peacefully settled; recognition of the new Latin American states, former Spanish colonies, in Central and South America (1822); and—most intimately connected with Monroe's name—the enunciation, in the presidential message of Dec. 2, 1823, of the Monroe Doctrine, which has profoundly influenced the foreign policy of the United States.

The "principles of President Monroe," as the message was referred to in Congress, consisted of three openly proclaimed dicta: no further European colonization in the New World, abstention of the United States from the political affairs of Europe, and nonintervention of Europe in the governments of the American hemisphere.

On the expiration of his second term Monroe retired to his home at Oak Hill, Va. In 1826 he became a regent of the University of Virginia and in 1829 was a member of the convention called to amend the state constitution. Monroe died in 1831—like Jefferson and Adams before him on the Fourth of July—in New York City at the home of his daughter, Maria, with whom he was living after the death of his wife the year before. After Liberia was created in 1821 as a haven for freed slaves, its capital city was named Monrovia in honour of the American president, who had supported the repatriation of blacks to Africa.

JOHN QUINCY ADAMS

(b. July 11, 1767, Braintree [now Quincy], Mass.—d. Feb. 23, 1848, Washington, D.C.)

John Quincy Adams, the eldest son of Pres. John Adams, was the sixth president of the United States (1825–29). In his prepresidential years he was one of America's greatest diplomats; in his postpresidential years (as U.S. congressman, 1831–48) he conducted a consistent and often dramatic fight against the expansion of slavery.

EARLY LIFE AND CAREER

John Quincy Adams grew up as a child of the American Revolution. His patriot father, John Adams, at that time a delegate to the Continental Congress, and his patriot mother, Abigail Smith Adams, had a strong moulding influence on his education. In 1778 and again in 1780 the boy accompanied his father to Europe. He studied at a private school in Paris in 1778–79 and at the University of Leiden, Neth., in 1780.

When his father was appointed United States minister to the Court of St. James', he chose to return to Massachusetts, where he attended Harvard College, graduating in 1787. He then read law at Newburyport and in 1790 was admitted to the bar in Boston. While struggling to establish a practice, he wrote a series of articles for the newspapers in which he ably supported the neutrality policy of George Washington's administration as it faced the war

John Quincy Adams. National Archives/Getty Images

that broke out between France and England in 1793. These articles were brought to Pres. Washington's attention and resulted in Adams's appointment as U.S. minister to the Netherlands in May 1794.

John Quincy Adams was married in London in 1797 to Louisa Catherine Johnson, daughter of the United States consul Joshua Johnson, a Marylander by birth, and his wife, Katherine Nuth, an Englishwoman. Accompanying her husband on his various missions in Europe, she came to be regarded as one of the most-traveled women of her time.

While in Berlin as minister to Prussia, Adams negotiated (1799) a treaty of amity and commerce. Recalled from Berlin by Pres. Adams after the election of Thomas Jefferson to the presidency in 1800, the younger Adams reached Boston in 1801 and the next year was elected to the Massachusetts Senate. In 1803 the Massachusetts legislature elected him a member of the Senate of the United States.

BREAK WITH THE FEDERALISTS

Up to this time John Quincy Adams was regarded as belonging to the Federalist Party, though he found its general policy displeasing. Adams arrived in Washington too late to vote for ratification of the treaty for the purchase of Louisiana. In December 1807 he supported Pres. Jefferson's suggestion of an embargo to essentially stop all commerce with other nations (an attempt to gain British recognition of American rights) and vigorously urged instant action. Support of this measure, hated by the Federalists and unpopular in New England because it stifled the region's economy, cost Adams his seat in the Senate. His successor was chosen on June 3, 1808, several months before the usual time of electing a senator for the next term, and five days later Adams resigned. In the same year he attended the Republican congressional caucus, which nominated James Madison for the presidency, and thus he allied himself with that party. From 1806 to 1809 Adams was Boylston professor of rhetoric and oratory at Harvard College.

In 1809 Pres. Madison sent Adams to Russia to represent the United States at the court of Tsar Alexander I. On the outbreak of the war between the United States and England in 1812, he was still in St. Petersburg. In December 1814 Adams went to London, where he helped to negotiate (1815) a "Convention to Regulate Commerce and Navigation." Soon afterward he became U.S. minister to Great Britain, as his father had been before him, and as his son, Charles Francis Adams, was to be after him. After accomplishing little in London, he returned to the United States in the summer of 1817 to become secretary of state in the cabinet of Pres. James Monroe.

SECRETARY OF STATE

As secretary of state, Adams played the leading part in the acquisition of Florida. Ever since the acquisition of Louisiana, successive administrations had sought to include at least a part of Florida in that purchase. In 1819, after long negotiations, Adams succeeded in getting the Spanish minister to agree to a treaty in which Spain would abandon all claims to territory east of the Mississippi River, the United States would relinquish all claims to what is now Texas, and a boundary of the United States would be drawn (for the first time) from the Atlantic to the Pacific Ocean. This Transcontinental Treaty was perhaps the greatest victory ever won by a single man in the diplomatic history of the United States. As secretary of state, Adams was also responsible for conclusion of the treaty of 1818 with Great Britain, laying down the northern boundary of the United States from the Lake of the Woods to the Rocky Mountains along the line of latitude 49° N.

PRESIDENCY AND FEUD WITH JACKSON

As Pres. Monroe's second term drew to a close in 1824, three of his advisors—Secretary of State John Quincy Adams, Secretary of War John C. Calhoun, and Secretary of the Treasury William H. Crawford—aspired to succeed him. Henry Clay, speaker of the House, and Gen. Andrew Jackson were also candidates. Calhoun was nominated for the vice presidency. Clay, who had for years assumed a censorious attitude toward Jackson, cast his influence for

Adams, whose victory in the electoral was thereby secured on the first ballot.

Up to this point Adams's career had been almost uniformly successful, but his presidency (1825–29), during which the country prospered, was in most respects a political failure because of the virulent opposition of the Jacksonians.

In 1828 Jackson was elected president over Adams, with 178 electoral votes to Adams's 83. It was during Jackson's administration that irreconcilable differences developed between his followers and those of Adams. Adams's intense dislike of Jackson and what he represented remained unabated. When Harvard College in 1833 awarded Jackson an honorary degree, Adams refused to attend the ceremony at his alma mater. He avowed that he would not "be present to witness [Harvard's] disgrace in conferring its highest honors upon a barbarian who could not write a sentence of grammar and could hardly spell his own name."

Adams had retired to private life in 1829 in the Massachusetts town of Quincy, but only for a brief period; in 1830, supported largely by members of the Anti-Masonic movement (a political force formed initially in opposition to Freemasonry), he was elected a member of the national House of Representatives. He served in the House of Representatives from 1831 until his death.

SECOND CAREER IN CONGRESS

Adams's long second career in Congress was at least as important as his earlier career as a diplomat. Throughout, he was conspicuous as an opponent of the expansion of slavery and was at heart an abolitionist, though he never became one in the political sense of the word. Adams championed the cause of Africans arrested aboard the slave ship *Amistad*—slaves who had mutinied and escaped from their Spanish owners off the coast of Cuba and had wound up bringing the ship into United States waters near Long Island, N.Y. Adams defended them as freemen before the Supreme Court in 1841 against efforts of the administration of Pres. Martin Van Buren to return them to their masters and inevitable death. Adams won their freedom.

Perhaps the most dramatic event in Adams's life was its end. On Feb. 21, 1848, in the act of protesting an honorary grant of swords by Congress to the generals who had won what Adams considered a "most unrighteous war" with Mexico, he suffered a cerebral stroke, fell unconscious to the floor of the House, and died two days later in the Capitol building.

ANDREW JACKSON

(b. March 15, 1767, Waxhaws region, S.C. —d. June 8, 1845, the Hermitage, near Nashville, Tenn.)

Andrew Jackson was a military hero and the seventh president of the United States (1829–37). He was the first U.S. president to come from the area west of the Appalachians and the first to gain office by a direct appeal to the mass of voters. His political movement has since been known as Jacksonian Democracy.

EARLY LIFE

Jackson was born on the western frontier of the Carolinas, an area that was in dispute between North Carolina and South Carolina. The area offered little opportunity for formal education, and what schooling he received was interrupted by the British invasion of the western Carolinas in 1780–81. His mother and two brothers died during the closing years of the war, direct or indirect casualties of

Andrew Jackson. Library of Congress Prints and Photographs Division

the invasion of the Carolinas. This sequence of tragic experiences fixed in Jackson's mind a lifelong hostility toward Great Britain. After the end of the American Revolution, he studied law in an office in Salisbury, N.C., and was admitted to the bar of that state in 1787. In 1788 he went to the Cumberland region as prosecuting attorney of the western district of North Carolina—the region west of the Appalachians, soon to become the state of Tennessee.

When Jackson arrived in Nashville, the community was still a frontier settlement. As prosecuting attorney, Jackson was principally occupied with suits for the collection of debts. Jackson boarded in the home of Colonel John Donelson, where he met and married the colonel's daughter, Rachel Robards.

TENNESSEE POLITICS

Jackson's interest in public affairs and in politics had always been keen. He had gone to Nashville as a political appointee, and in 1796 he became a member of the convention that drafted a constitution for the new state of Tennessee. In the same year he was elected as the first representative from Tennessee to the U.S. House of Representatives. An undistinguished legislator, he refused to seek reelection and served only until March 4, 1797. Before the end of the year, however, he was elected to the U.S. Senate. He resigned his seat in 1798 after an uneventful year. Soon after his return to Nashville he was elected major general of the Tennessee militia, a position he still held when the War of 1812 opened the door to a command in the field and a hero's role.

MILITARY FEATS

In March 1812, when it appeared that war with Great Britain was imminent, Jackson issued a call for 50,000 volunteers to be ready for an invasion of Canada. After the declaration of war, in June 1812, Jackson offered his services and those of his militia to the United States. The government was slow to accept this offer, and, when Jackson finally was given a command in the field, it was to fight against the Creek Indians, who were allied with the British and who were threatening the southern frontier. In a campaign of about five months, in 1813–14, Jackson defeated them so decisively that they never again menaced the frontier, and Jackson was established as the hero of the West.

In August 1814, Jackson moved his army south to Mobile, where he learned that an army of British regulars had landed at the Spanish post of Pensacola. In the first week in November, he led his army into Florida and, on November 7, occupied that city just as the British evacuated it to go by sea to Louisiana. Jackson then marched his army overland to New Orleans, where his forces inflicted a decisive defeat upon the British army in the Battle of New Orleans on Jan. 8, 1815. This victory and the signing of the Treaty of Ghent (Belgium) between the United States and Great Britain on Dec. 24, 1814, made Jackson the hero not only of the West but of a substantial part of the country as well.

PRESIDENTIAL PROSPECTS

Jackson's military triumphs led to suggestions that he become a candidate for president, but he disavowed any interest, and political leaders in Washington assumed that the flurry of support for him would prove transitory. The campaign to make him president, however, was kept alive by his continued popularity, and was carefully nurtured by a small group of his friends in Nashville, who combined devotion to the general with a high degree of political astuteness.

In the election of 1824 four candidates, including Jackson, received electoral votes. Jackson received the highest number (99), but because no one had a majority, the House of Representatives was required to elect a president from the three with the highest number of votes. Henry Clay, who as speaker of the House was in a strategic and perhaps decisive position to determine the outcome, threw his support to Adams, who was elected on the first ballot. When Adams appointed Clay secretary of state, it seemed to admirers of Jackson to confirm rumours of a "corrupt bargain" between Adams and Clay. Jackson's friends persuaded him that the popular will had been thwarted by intrigues, and he thereupon determined to vindicate himself and his supporters by becoming a candidate again in 1828.

In 1828 Jackson defeated Adams by an electoral vote of 178 to 83 after a campaign in which personalities and slander played a larger part than in any previous U.S. national election. Jackson's hour of triumph was soon overshadowed by personal tragedy—his wife died at the Hermitage on Dec. 22, 1828. Rachel Jackson's niece, Emily Donelson, the wife of Andrew Jackson Donelson, served as the president's hostess until 1836. At times, Sarah Yorke Jackson, the wife of Andrew Jackson's adopted son, also served as his hostess.

JACKSONIAN DEMOCRACY

The election of 1828 is commonly regarded as a turning point in the political history of the United States. Jackson was the first president from the area west of the Appalachians, but it was equally significant that the initiative in launching his candidacy and much of the leadership in the organization of his campaign also came from the West. The victory of Jackson indicated a westward movement of the centre of political power. He was also the first man to be elected president through a direct appeal to the mass of the voters rather than through the support of a recognized political organization.

Jackson was the first president born in poverty. In time he became one of the largest landholders in Tennessee, yet he had retained the frontiersmen's prejudice against people of wealth. Although the Jacksonian organization successfully portrayed its candidate as the embodiment of democracy, in fact Jackson had been aligned with the conservative faction in Tennessee politics for 30 years, and in the financial crisis that swept the West after 1819 he had vigorously opposed legislation for the relief of debtors.

THE FIRST TERM

When Jackson was inaugurated on March 4, 1829, it was the first time in more than a quarter of a century that the election of a new president reflected the repudiation of his predecessor. Hundreds who had worked for the election of Jackson hoped this would mean that incumbent officeholders would be replaced by friends of the new

president, and within a few weeks the process of removing opponents of Jackson to make way for supporters
had begun.

In 1832 South Carolina adopted a resolution declaring the protective tariffs of 1828 and 1832 null and void
and prohibiting the enforcement of either within its
boundaries after Feb. 1, 1833. Jackson accepted the challenge, denounced the theory of nullification, and asked
Congress for authority to send troops into South
Carolina to enforce the law. When Congress passed the
Force Bill, which empowered the president to use the
armed forces to enforce federal laws, South Carolina
repealed its nullification ordinance. Jackson thus pre-
served the integrity of the Union against the most serious
threat it had yet faced.

In 1829 Georgia extended its jurisdiction to about
9,000,000 acres (4,000,000 hectares) of land that lay
within its boundaries but was still occupied by the
Cherokee Indians. The Cherokees appealed to the federal
courts, as their title to the land—on which gold had been
discovered—had been guaranteed by a treaty with the
United States. In two separate cases, the Supreme Court
ruled against Georgia, but the state ignored those decisions and continued to enforce its jurisdiction within the
territory claimed by the Cherokees. In contrast to his
strong reaction against South Carolina's defiance of federal authority, Jackson made no effort to restrain Georgia;
his failure to support the Supreme Court remains an
indelible stain on his record. The Cherokee, left without
a choice, signed another treaty in 1835, giving up their land
in exchange for land in the Indian Territory west of
Arkansas. Three years later, some 15,000 Cherokees were
forced to wend their way westward, mostly on foot, on a
journey that became known as the Trail of Tears. Along

the way, during the cold and wet of winter, nearly a quarter of them died of starvation, illness, and exposure.

REELECTION IN 1832

In the meantime, Jackson acquiesced to the pressure of friends and sought a second term. As the election of 1832 approached, Jackson's opponents hoped to embarrass him by posing a new dilemma. The charter of the Bank of the United States was due to expire in 1836. The president had not clearly defined his position on the bank, but he was increasingly uneasy about how it was then organized. More significant in an election year was the fact that large blocs of voters who favoured Jackson were openly hostile to the bank. In the summer of 1832, Jackson's opponents rushed through Congress a bill to recharter the bank, thus forcing Jackson either to sign the measure and alienate many of his supporters or to veto it and appear to be a foe of sound banking. Jackson's cabinet was divided between friends and critics of the bank, but the obviously political motives of the recharter bill reconciled all of them to the necessity of a veto. The question before Jackson actually was whether the veto message should leave the door open to future compromise.

Few presidential vetoes have caused as much controversy in their own time or later as the one Jackson sent to Congress on July 10, 1832. The veto of the bill to recharter the bank was the prelude to a conflict over financial policy that continued through Jackson's second term, which he nevertheless won easily.

Jackson retired to his home, the Hermitage, in 1837. For decades in poor health, he was virtually an invalid during the remaining eight years of his life, but he continued to have a lively interest in public affairs.

MARTIN VAN BUREN

(b. Dec. 5, 1782, Kinderhook, N.Y.—d. July 24, 1862, Kinderhook)

Martin Van Buren was the eighth president of the United States (1837–41) and one of the founders of the Democratic Party. He was known as the "Little Magician" to his friends (and the "Sly Fox" to his enemies) in recognition of his reputed cunning and skill as a politician.

Van Buren was the son of Abraham Van Buren, a farmer and tavern keeper, and Maria Hoes Van Alen, both of Dutch descent. Apprenticed to the lawyer Francis Silvester in 1796, Van Buren began his own practice in Kinderhook in 1803. In 1807 he married his cousin Hannah Hoes, with whom he had four children. Van Buren served two terms in the New York Senate (1812–20) and during his tenure he was appointed state attorney general. After his election to the U.S. Senate in 1821, he created the Albany Regency, an informal political organization in New York State that was a prototype of the modern political machine.

Martin Van Buren, portrait by Henry Inman. Library of Congress Prints and Photographs Division

Van Buren regarded himself as a disciple of Thomas Jefferson. As a member of the Jeffersonian faction of the Republican Party, he supported the doctrine of states' rights, opposed a strong federal government, and disapproved of federally sponsored internal improvements. After John Quincy Adams was elected president in 1824, Van Buren brought together a diverse coalition of Jeffersonian Republicans, including followers of Andrew Jackson, William H. Crawford, and John C. Calhoun, to found a new political party, which was soon named the Democratic Party.

In 1828 Van Buren resigned his Senate seat and successfully ran for governor of New York. However, he gave up the governorship within 12 weeks to become Pres. Andrew Jackson's secretary of state. In this role he was criticized for expanding the system of political patronage, though some later historians considered the criticism unfair. Resigning as secretary of state in 1831 to permit reorganization of the cabinet, he served briefly as minister to Great Britain.

Nominated for the vice presidency in 1832 by the first national convention of the Democratic Party, Van Buren was elected with Jackson on a ticket opposing the continued operation of the Bank of the United States. With Jackson's endorsement, Van Buren was unanimously nominated for president in May 1835. In the election the following year, Van Buren defeated three candidates fielded by the splintered Whig Party. He took office in 1837, at the onset of a national financial panic brought about in part by the transfer of federal funds from the Bank of the United States to state banks during Jackson's second term. Van Buren's popularity was eroded by the long and costly war with the Seminole Indians in Florida (the second of the Seminole Wars) and by his failure to support the proposed annexation of the newly independent state of Texas. In an effort to win the proslavery vote in the election of 1840, Van Buren sided against African slaves on trial in the United States for their part in the Amistad mutiny in 1839. One of Van Buren's last acts in office was to order that no person should work more than 10 hours a day on federal public works.

Unanimously renominated by the Democrats in 1840, Van Buren was overwhelmingly defeated by the Whig candidate William Henry Harrison. Four years later the Democrats were bitterly divided over the question of the annexation of Texas, and Van Buren, who opposed annexation, was passed over in favour of James K. Polk, who won the election on a platform calling for the annexation of both Texas and Oregon. In 1848 Van Buren ran as a candidate of the Free Soil Party, which included members of the antislavery factions of the Democratic Party (the "Barnburners") and the Whig Party, but he received only 10 percent of the vote. He spent several years in Europe and then retired to his estate, Lindenwald, in Kinderhook.

WILLIAM HENRY HARRISON

(b. Feb. 9, 1773, Charles City county, Va. —d. April 4, 1841, Washington, D.C.)

William Henry Harrison was the ninth president of the United States (1841). His Indian campaigns, while he was a territorial governor and army officer, thrust him into the national limelight and led to his election in 1840. At age 67, he was the oldest man ever elected president up to that time, the last president born under British rule, and the first to die in office—after only one month's service. His grandson Benjamin Harrison was the 23rd president of the United States (1889–93).

Born at Berkeley, a Virginia plantation, Harrison was descended from two wealthy and well-connected Virginia families. His father, Benjamin Harrison, was a signer of the Declaration of Independence and a member of the Continental Congress. William Henry Harrison attended Hampden-Sydney College in 1787, then studied medicine in Richmond, Va., and in Philadelphia.

At age 18 Harrison enlisted as an army officer, serving as an aide-de-camp to Gen. Anthony Wayne, who was engaged in a struggle against the Northwest Indian Confederation over the westward encroachment of white settlers. He was named secretary of the Northwest Territory, a vast tract of land encompassing most of the future states of Ohio, Indiana, Michigan, Illinois, and Wisconsin, in 1798, and was sent to Congress as a territorial delegate the following year. In May 1800 Harrison was appointed governor of the newly created Indiana Territory, where, succumbing to the demands of land-hungry whites, he negotiated between 1802 and 1809 a

A c. 1838 engraving of William Henry Harrison. Hulton Archive/Getty Images

number of treaties that stripped the Indians of that region of millions of acres. Resisting this expansionism, the Shawnee intertribal leader Tecumseh organized an Indian uprising. Harrison, leading a force of seasoned regulars and militia, defeated the Indians at the Battle of Tippecanoe (Nov. 7, 1811), near present-day Lafayette, Ind., a victory that largely established his military reputation in the public mind. A few months after the War of 1812 broke out with Great Britain, Harrison was made a brigadier general and placed in command of all federal forces in the Northwest Territory. On Oct. 5, 1813, troops under his command decisively defeated the British and their Indian allies at the Battle of the Thames, in Ontario, Canada. Tecumseh was killed in the battle, and the British-Indian alliance was permanently destroyed; thus ended resistance in the Northwest.

After the war, Harrison settled in Ohio, where he quickly became active in politics. He served in the U.S. House of Representatives (1816–19), the Ohio Senate (1819–21), the U.S. Senate (1825–28), and as minister to Colombia (1828–29). In 1836 he was one of three presidential candidates of the splintered Whig Party, but he lost the election to Democrat Martin Van Buren. Nonetheless, his popular vote totals were large enough to encourage him to make another attempt. In 1840 Harrison won the Whig nomination over Sen. Henry Clay of Kentucky, largely because of his military record and his noncommittal political views. To pull in Southern Democrats, the Whigs nominated John Tyler of Virginia for vice president. Capitalizing on voters' distress over the severe economic depression caused by the panic of 1837, the campaign deliberately avoided discussion of national issues and substituted political songs, partisan slogans, and appropriate insignia: miniature log cabins and jugs of hard cider were widely distributed to emphasize Harrison's frontier identification, and the cry of "Tippecanoe and Tyler too" rang throughout the land, calling up Harrison's dramatic triumph on the field of battle 29 years earlier. These appeals worked, with Harrison winning 234 electoral votes to incumbent Martin Van Buren's 60.

Harrison was the first president-elect to travel by railroad to Washington, D.C., for his inauguration. Wearing no gloves and no overcoat despite the freezing weather, he rode up Pennsylvania Avenue on a white horse to take the oath of office on March 4, 1841. In the cold drizzle he delivered an inaugural address in which he highlighted a common Whig concern—"executive usurpation"—and reconfirmed his belief in a limited role for the U.S.

president. He said he would serve but one term, limit his use of the veto, and leave revenue schemes to Congress.

Harrison tried to do everything expected of him, even trudging around Washington to purchase supplies for the White House. But a cold he had contracted on inauguration day developed into pneumonia, and he died just a month later, on April 4, bringing "His Accidency," John Tyler, to the presidency. The first president to lie in state in the Capitol, Harrison was buried in Washington. In June his remains were reinterred in what is now the William Henry Harrison Memorial State Park in North Bend, Ohio.

JOHN TYLER

(b. March 29, 1790, Charles City county, Va.—d. Jan. 18, 1862, Richmond)

John Tyler was the 10th president of the United States (1841–45). He took office upon the death of Pres. William Henry Harrison. A maverick Democrat who refused allegiance to the program of party leader Andrew Jackson, Tyler was rejected in office by both the Democratic Party and the Whig Party and functioned as a political independent.

Tyler was the son of John Tyler, a member of the Virginia House of Delegates during the American Revolution and later governor of Virginia, and Mary Armistead. After graduating from the College of William and Mary in 1807, young Tyler studied law with his father, gaining admission to the bar in 1809. He married his first wife, Letitia Christian, on his 23rd birthday in 1813. His political career began in the Virginia legislature, where he served from 1811 to 1816, 1823 to 1825, and in 1839. He served as United States representative (1817–21), as state governor (1825–27), and as

John Tyler is shown in this engraving, c. 1835. Hulton Archive/Getty Images

United States senator (1827–36). His service in Washington was marked by his consistent support of states' rights and his strict constructionist interpretation of the Constitution.

In an unusual show of independence, Tyler resigned from the Senate in 1836 rather than yield to his state legislature's instructions to reverse his vote on Senate resolutions censuring Pres. Jackson for removal of deposits from the Bank of the United States. This anti-Jackson stand endeared Tyler to the opposition Whig Party, which in 1840 nominated him for the vice presidency in an effort to attract Southern support. Harrison and Tyler defeated the Democratic incumbents Martin Van Buren and Richard M. Johnson after a campaign that sedulously avoided the issues.

Pres. Harrison's sudden death one month after his inauguration created a constitutional crisis. Because the Constitution was silent on the matter, it was unclear whether, upon the death of a president, the vice president would become president or merely "vice president acting as president," as John Quincy Adams maintained at the time. Defying his opponents, who dubbed him "His Accidency," Tyler decided that he was president and moved into the White House, thereby establishing a precedent that was never successfully challenged.

After Tyler vetoed two bills aimed at reestablishing a national bank, all but one member of the cabinet Tyler inherited from Harrison, Daniel Webster, resigned, and two days later he was formally ostracized by congressional Whigs. Tyler was now a president without a party. Nevertheless, his administration managed to accomplish a great deal. It reorganized the navy, established the United States Weather Bureau, brought an end to the Second Seminole War (1835–42) in Florida, and put down the rebellion (1842) led by Thomas Dorr against the state government of Rhode Island. Tyler's wife Letitia Christian Tyler died in 1842, the first president's wife to die in the White House. Tyler married Julia Gardiner in 1844, thus becoming the first president to marry while in office.

Tyler entered the presidential election of 1844 as the candidate of his own party, which he created from a core of loyal appointees. His candidacy attracted little support, however, and in August 1844 he withdrew in favour of the Democratic nominee, James K. Polk.

On the eve of the Civil War Tyler stood firmly against secession and worked to preserve the Union. Early in 1861 he presided over the Washington Peace Conference, an abortive effort to resolve sectional differences. When the Senate rejected the proposals of the conference, he relinquished all hope of saving the Union and returned to Virginia, where he served as a delegate to the Virginia Secession Convention. Shortly before his death Tyler was elected to the Confederate House of Representatives.

JAMES K. POLK

(b. Nov. 2, 1795, Mecklenburg county, N.C. – d. June 15, 1849, Nashville, Tenn.)

James Knox Polk was the 11th president of the United States (1845–49). Under his leadership the country fought the Mexican War (1846–48) and acquired vast territories along the Pacific coast and in the Southwest.

James K. Polk, daguerreotype by Mathew Brady, 1849. Library of Congress, Washington, D.C.

EARLY LIFE AND CAREER

Polk was the eldest child of Samuel and Jane Knox Polk. At age 11 he moved with his family to Tennessee, where his father operated a prosperous farm in Maury County. Although ill health during his childhood made formal schooling impossible, Polk successfully passed, at age 20, the entrance requirements for the second-year class at the University of North Carolina. As a graduating senior in 1818 he was the Latin salutatorian of his class—a preeminent scholar in both the classics and mathematics.

After graduation he returned to Tennessee and began to practice law in Nashville. In 1820 he was admitted to the bar. Because he was a confirmed Democrat and an unfailing supporter of Andrew Jackson and because his style of political oratory became so popular that he was characterized as the "Napoleon of the stump," his political career was assured.

His rapid rise to political power was furthered by his wife, Sarah Childress Polk (1803–91), whom he married Jan. 1, 1824, while serving in the state House of Representatives (1823–25). She proved to be the most politically dominant president's wife since Abigail Adams. The social prominence of Sarah Polk's family and her personal charm were distinct assets for a politically ambitious lawyer. Year after year she was her husband's closest companion and his eyes and ears in state and national politics.

Polk was not an easy man to know or to like. Even close companions did not relish his austerity, and associates tolerated but did not approve of his inflexible living standards. Among his few close friends was Andrew Jackson, who encouraged and advanced Polk and whose influence carried him from the Tennessee House of Representatives to the United States House of Representatives, where he served from 1825 to 1839.

As speaker of the House during that time, Polk acquired a reputation as an undeviating supporter of Jacksonian principles. In 1839 he left the House to become governor of Tennessee. Two defeats for a second term (1841, 1843) by small majorities convinced him that to strengthen his party he should return to Washington.

At the Democratic convention in Baltimore, Md., in 1844, Polk hoped only for the vice presidential nomination, for the party had more prominent presidential contenders in Martin Van Buren, Lewis Cass, and James Buchanan. But the Democrats could not reconcile their differences, and a compromise candidate had to be found. Because the campaign was to be run on issues and not on personalities, it was decided that Polk would do. Although well known in political circles, to the public Polk was the first "dark horse" nominee in the history of the presidency. His election was close, but it was decisive—a popular plurality of about 38,000 votes and 170 electoral votes against 105 for Clay.

During his campaign Polk surprised the country by taking a positive stand on two burning issues of the day. Whereas other candidates hedged on the question of whether to annex Texas, which had been independent of Mexico since 1836, he demanded annexation. Whereas other candidates evaded the problem of joint occupancy of Oregon with England, he openly laid claim to the whole territory that extended as far north as latitude 54°40′ with the campaign slogan "Fifty-four forty or fight."

PRESIDENCY

Not yet 50 years of age, Polk was the youngest successful presidential candidate up to that time. He entered the presidency full of eagerness and with an expressed zeal to put his aims into effect. He left it four years later exhausted and enfeebled by his efforts. In office he demonstrated remarkable skill in the selection and control of his official advisers, and, in his formal relations with Congress, his legislative experience served him well.

The Polk administration was marked by large territorial gains. The annexation of Texas as a state was concluded and resulted in a two-year war with Mexico, as a consequence of which the Southwest and far West (California) became part of the United States' domain. During this period the northwestern boundary became fixed by treaty, and the continental United States emerged a recognized reality.

The expansion of the country westward led to the creation of a new agency, the Department of the Interior. The Polk administration was also responsible for the establishment of the United States Naval Academy at Annapolis, Md., and the authorization of the Smithsonian Institution, a national foundation for all areas of science.

ZACHARY TAYLOR

(b. Nov. 24, 1784, Montebello, Va.—d. July 9, 1850, Washington, D.C.)

Zachary Taylor was the 12th president of the United States (1849–50). Elected on the ticket of the Whig Party as a hero of the Mexican-American War (1846–48), he died only 16 months after taking office.

Taylor's parents, Richard Taylor and Mary Strother, migrated to Kentucky from Virginia shortly after Zachary, the third of their nine children, was born. After spending his boyhood on the Kentucky frontier, Taylor enlisted in the army in 1806 and was commissioned first lieutenant in the infantry in 1808. In 1810 he married Margaret Mackall Smith, with whom he had six children. His daughter Sarah Knox Taylor married Jefferson Davis, the future president of the Confederate States of America, in 1835, and his son, Richard Taylor, fought in the Civil War as a lieutenant general in the Confederate Army.

Taylor served in the army for almost 40 years, finally advancing to the rank of major general (1846). He commanded troops in the field in the War of 1812, the Black Hawk War (1832), and the second of the Seminole Wars in Florida (1835–42), in which he won promotion to the rank of brigadier general for his leadership in the Battle of Lake Okeechobee (1837). In 1840 he was assigned to a post in Louisiana and established his home in Baton Rouge.

Soon after the annexation of Texas (1845), Pres. James K. Polk ordered Taylor and an army of 4,000 men to the Rio Grande, opposite the Mexican city of Matamoros. A detachment of Mexican troops crossed the Rio Grande and engaged Taylor's forces in a skirmish (April 25, 1846), marking the beginning of the Mexican-American War. Two weeks later Mexican troops again crossed the river to challenge Taylor, whose forces decisively defeated the invaders on two successive days in the battles of Palo Alto and Resaca de la Palma (May 8 and 9). On May 13 the United

Zachary Taylor, daguerreotype by Mathew B. Brady. Library of Congress, Washington, D.C. (neg. no. LC-USZ62-13012)

States formally declared war on Mexico. Taylor then led his troops across the Rio Grande and advanced toward Monterrey, capturing the city on September 22–23 and granting the Mexican army an eight-week armistice, an action that displeased Polk. Taylor further alienated Polk by writing a letter, which found its way into the press, criticizing Polk and his secretary of war, William L. Marcy. Polk then ordered Taylor to confine his actions to those necessary for defensive purposes and transferred Taylor's best troops to the army of Gen. Winfield Scott. The following February, however, Taylor disobeyed these orders and with his diminished force marched south and, in the Battle of Buena Vista, won a brilliant victory over a Mexican army that outnumbered his troops by about four to one.

Having thus won the north of Mexico, Taylor emerged as a hero and began to be seen by Whig politicians as a possible presidential candidate. At the Whig Party convention in 1848 Taylor gained the nomination on the fourth ballot. He defeated the Democratic candidate, Lewis Cass, in the general election, winning the electoral college vote 163 to 127.

Taylor's brief administration was beset with problems, the most perplexing of which was the controversy over the extension of slavery into the newly acquired Mexican territories. By 1848 Taylor had come to oppose the creation of new slave states, and in December 1849 he called for immediate statehood for California, whose new constitution explicitly prohibited slavery. Southerners in Congress, who feared a permanent majority of free states in the Senate, fought bitterly against the proposal, and the controversy was not finally resolved until September of the following year (two months after Taylor's death), with the adoption of the Compromise of 1850. A further problem was the revelation in mid-1850 of financial improprieties on the part of three members of Taylor's cabinet. Deeply humiliated, Taylor, who prided himself on honesty, decided to reorganize his cabinet, but before he could do so he died suddenly of an attack of cholera.

MILLARD FILLMORE

(b. Jan. 7, 1800, Locke Township, N.Y.—d. March 8, 1874, Buffalo)

Millard Fillmore was the 13th president of the United States (1850–53). His insistence on federal enforcement of the Fugitive Slave Act of 1850 alienated the North and led to the destruction of the Whig Party. Elected vice president in 1848, he became chief executive on the death of Pres. Zachary Taylor (July 1850).

Fillmore was born in a log cabin to a poor family and was apprenticed to a wool carder at age 15. He received little formal education until he was 18, when he managed to obtain six consecutive months of schooling. Shortly afterward he secured his release from apprenticeship and started work in a law office, and in 1823 he was admitted to the bar. He married his first wife, Abigail Powers, in 1826.

Fillmore entered politics in 1828 as a member of the democratic and libertarian Anti-Masonic Movement and Anti-Masonic Party. In 1834 he followed his political mentor, New York politician and journalist Thurlow Weed, to the Whigs and was soon recognized as an outstanding leader of the party's Northern wing. Following

Millard Fillmore. Library of Congress, Washington, D.C.

three terms in the New York State Assembly (1829–32), he was elected to Congress (1833–35, 1837–43), where he became a devoted follower of Sen. Henry Clay. Losing the New York gubernatorial election in 1844, he was easily elected the first state comptroller three years later. At the national Whig convention in 1848, Zachary Taylor, hero of the Mexican War (1846–48), was nominated for president and Fillmore for vice president, largely through Clay's sponsorship.

Fillmore, though personally opposed to slavery, supported Henry Clay's Compromise of 1850, which sought to appease both sides on the slavery issue, as necessary to preserving the Union. When the legislation was finally passed two months after Taylor's death, the new president felt obligated to respect the provision that required the federal government to aid in the capture and return of runaway slaves to their former owners (the Fugitive Slave Act of 1850), and he publicly announced that, if necessary, he would call upon the military to aid in the enforcement of this statute. Although this section of the compromise assuaged the South and had the effect of postponing the Civil War for 10 years, it also meant political death for Fillmore because of its extreme unpopularity in the North.

Fillmore was an early champion of American commercial expansion in the Pacific, and in 1853 sent a fleet of warships, under the command of Commodore Matthew C. Perry, to Japan to force its shogunate government to alter its traditional isolationism and enter into trade and diplomatic relations with the United States. The resulting Treaty of Kanagawa (1854) led to similar agreements between Japan and other Western powers and marked the beginning of Japan's transformation into a modern state.

In 1852 Fillmore was one of three presidential candidates of a divided Whig Party in its last national election, which it lost. He ran again in 1856 as the candidate of the Know-Nothing party (also known as the American Party), finishing third behind Democrat James Buchanan and Republican John C. Frémont. Fillmore then retired to Buffalo, where he became a leader in the city's civic and cultural life. In 1858, some five years after the death of his wife Abigail, he married Caroline Carmichael McIntosh.

FRANKLIN PIERCE

(b. Nov. 23, 1804, Hillsboro, N.H.—d. Oct. 8, 1869, Concord)

Franklin Pierce was the 14th president of the United States (1853–57). As president he failed to deal effectively with the corroding sectional controversy over slavery in the decade preceding the American Civil War (1861–65).

The son of a governor of New Hampshire, Benjamin Pierce, and the former Anna Kendrick, Franklin Pierce attended Bowdoin College in Maine, studied law in Northampton, Mass., and was admitted to the bar in 1827. He married Jane Means Appleton, whose father was president of Bowdoin, in 1834.

Pierce entered political life in New Hampshire as a Democrat, serving in the state legislature (1829–33), the U.S. House of Representatives (1833–37), and the Senate (1837–42). Handsome, affable, charming, and possessed of a certain superficial brilliance, Pierce made many friends in Congress, but his career there was otherwise undistinguished. He was a devoted supporter of Pres. Andrew Jackson but was continually overshadowed by older and more prominent men on the national scene. Resigning from the Senate for personal reasons, he returned to Concord, where he resumed his law practice and also served as federal district attorney.

Except for a brief stint as an officer in the Mexican War (1846–48), Pierce remained out of the public eye until

Franklin Pierce. Library of Congress, Washington, D.C.

the nominating convention of the Democratic Party in 1852. After a deadlock developed among supporters of the leading presidential contenders, a coalition of New England and Southern delegates proposed "Young Hickory" (a reference to Andrew Jackson, who had been known as "Old Hickory"), and Pierce was nominated on the 49th ballot. The ensuing presidential campaign was dominated by the controversy over slavery and the finality of the Compromise of 1850. Although both the Democrats and the Whigs declared themselves in favour of the compromise, the Democrats were more thoroughly united in their support. As a result, Pierce, who was almost unknown nationally, unexpectedly won the November election, defeating the Whig candidate Winfield Scott by 254 votes to 42 in the electoral college. Pierce's triumph was quickly marred by tragedy, however, when, a few weeks before his inauguration, he and his wife witnessed the death of their only surviving child, 11-year-old Bennie, in a railroad accident. Jane Pierce, who had always opposed her husband's candidacy, never fully recovered from the shock.

At the time of his election, Pierce, age 47, was the youngest man to have been elected to the presidency. Representing the Eastern element of the Democratic Party, which was inclined for the sake of harmony and business prosperity to oppose antislavery agitation and generally to placate Southern opinion, Pierce tried to promote sectional unity by filling his cabinet with extremists from both sides of the slavery debate. In 1855 an American adventurer, William Walker, conducted a notorious expedition into Central America with the hope of establishing a proslavery government under the control of the United States. In Nicaragua he established himself as military dictator and then as president, and his dubious regime was recognized by the Pierce administration.

Among Pierce's domestic policies were preparations for a transcontinental railroad and the opening of the Northwest for settlement. In 1853, in order to create a southerly route to California, the U.S. minister to Mexico, James Gadsden, negotiated the purchase of almost 30,000 square miles of Mexican territory (the Gadsden Purchase), for $10 million. Mainly to stimulate migration to the Northwest and to facilitate the construction of a central route to the Pacific, Pierce signed the Kansas-Nebraska Act in 1854. This measure, which opened two new territories for settlement, included repeal of the Missouri Compromise of 1820 (by which slavery in the territories was prohibited north of latitude 36° 30') and provided that the status of the territories as "free" or "slave" would be decided by popular sovereignty. The indignation aroused by the act and the resulting period of violent conflict in the Kansas Territory were the main causes of the rise of the Republican Party in the mid-1850s. Owing to his ineptness in handling the situation in Kansas, Pierce was denied renomination by the Democrats, and he remains the only president to be so repudiated by his party. After an extended tour of Europe he retired to Concord. Always a heavy drinker, Pierce descended further into apparent alcoholism, and he died in obscurity.

JAMES BUCHANAN

(b. April 23, 1791, near Mercersburg, Pa.—d. June 1, 1868,
near Lancaster)

James Buchanan was the 15th president of the United States (1857–61). He was a moderate Democrat whose efforts to find a compromise in the conflict between the North and the South failed to avert the Civil War (1861–65).

Buchanan was the son of James Buchanan and Elizabeth Speer, both Scottish Presbyterians from the north of Ireland. His father had immigrated to the United States in 1783 and worked as a storekeeper. Buchanan was educated at Dickinson College in Carlisle, Pa., graduating in 1809, and studied law in Lancaster. He was admitted to the bar in 1812 and soon established a successful law practice. His gift for oratory led him to politics.

James Buchanan, photograph by Mathew Brady. Library of Congress, Washington, D.C.

Buchanan never married and remains the only bachelor president. In 1819, when he was 28 years old, he became engaged to Anne C. Coleman, the daughter of a wealthy Pennsylvania family. He broke off the engagement for an undisclosed reason, and shortly afterward Coleman died, possibly a suicide. When Buchanan became president, he made his 27-year-old niece, Harriet Lane, his hostess.

A Federalist, Buchanan served in the Pennsylvania legislature (1814–16) and in the U.S. House of Representatives (1821–31). When his party disintegrated in the 1820s, Buchanan associated himself with the emerging Democratic Party.

He served as U.S. minister to St. Petersburg (1831–33) for the Andrew Jackson administration, U.S. senator (1834–45), and secretary of state (1845–49) in the cabinet of Pres. James K. Polk. The annexation of Texas and subsequent Mexican War took place during Buchanan's tenure as secretary of state. Buchanan's role in the war was limited, but he played a more active part in the border dispute with Britain over Oregon, which was settled peaceably by treaty. Buchanan had sought the nomination for president in 1844 but had ultimately thrown his support to Polk. Failing to receive the presidential nomination in 1848, Buchanan retired from public service until 1853, when he was appointed minister to Britain by Pres. Franklin Pierce.

In Congress, Buchanan tended to side with the South, and although he felt that slavery was morally wrong, he thought that freeing the slaves would lead to "the massacre of the high-minded, and the chivalrous race of men in the South." Thus in 1846 he opposed the Wilmot Proviso, which would have prohibited the extension of slavery into the U.S. territories, and he supported the Compromise of 1850.

Having thus consolidated his position in the South, Buchanan was nominated for president in 1856 and was elected, winning 174 electoral votes to 114 for the Republican John C. Frémont and 8 for Millard Fillmore, the American (Know-Nothing) Party candidate. Although well-endowed with legal knowledge and experienced in government, Buchanan lacked the soundness of judgment and conciliatory personality to undo the misperceptions the North and South had of one another and thereby to deal effectively with the slavery crisis. His strategy for the preservation of the Union consisted in the prevention of Northern antislavery agitation and the enforcement of the Fugitive Slave Act (1850). Buchanan's position was further weakened by scandals over financial improprieties within his administration. At the 1860 Democratic National

Convention, a split within the Democratic Party resulted in the advancement of two candidates for president, Sen. Stephen A. Douglas of Illinois and Vice Pres. John C. Breckinridge, which opened the way for the election of the Republican Abraham Lincoln as president in 1860.

On Dec. 20, 1860, South Carolina voted to secede from the Union. By February 1861 seven Southern states had seceded. Buchanan denounced secession but admitted that he could find no means to stop it, maintaining that he had "no authority to decide what shall be the relation between the federal government and South Carolina." War was inevitable. The president ordered reinforcements sent to Fort Sumter at Charleston, S.C. However, when the federal supply ship was fired upon by shore batteries, it turned back. The call for a second relief mission came too late for Buchanan to act. As the crisis deepened, he seemed impatient for his time in the White House to run out.

Upon leaving office (March 4), Buchanan retired to Wheatland, his home near Lancaster. He died confident in the belief that posterity would vindicate his presidency.

ABRAHAM LINCOLN

(b. Feb. 12, 1809, near Hodgenville, Ky.—d. April 15, 1865, Washington, D.C.)

Abraham Lincoln was the 16th president of the United States (1861–65). He is remembered for preserving the Union during the American Civil War and for bringing about the emancipation of the slaves.

Among American heroes, Lincoln continues to have a unique appeal for his fellow countrymen as well as people of other lands. His relevance endures and grows especially because of his eloquence as a spokesman for democracy. In his view, the Union was worth saving not only for its own sake but because it embodied the ideal of self-government. The Lincoln Memorial in Washington, D.C., was dedicated to him on May 30, 1922.

LIFE

Born in a backwoods cabin 3 miles (5 km) south of Hodgenville, Ky., Lincoln was two years old when he was taken to a farm in the neighbouring valley of Knob Creek. His father, Thomas Lincoln, was the descendant of a weaver's apprentice who had migrated from England to Massachusetts in 1637. On June 12, 1806, he married Nancy Hanks, with whom he had three children: Sarah, Abraham, and Thomas, who died in infancy.

CHILDHOOD AND YOUTH

In December 1816, faced with a lawsuit challenging the title to his Kentucky farm, Thomas Lincoln moved with his family to southwestern Indiana. Abraham helped to clear the fields and to take care of the crops but early acquired a dislike for hunting and fishing. The unhappiest period of his boyhood followed the death of his mother in the autumn of 1818; as a ragged nine-year-old, he saw her buried in the forest, then faced a winter without the warmth of a mother's love. Fortunately, before the onset of a second winter, Thomas Lincoln brought home from Kentucky a new wife for himself and a new mother for the children, Sarah Bush Johnston Lincoln, a widow with two girls and a boy of her own.

Both of Lincoln's parents were almost completely illiterate, and he himself received little formal education; his entire schooling amounted to no more than one year's attendance. His neighbours later recalled how he used to trudge for miles to borrow a book. According to his own statement, however, his early surroundings provided "absolutely nothing to excite ambition for education. Of course, when I came of age I did not know much. Still, somehow, I could read, write, and cipher to the rule of three; but that was all."

In March 1830 the Lincoln family undertook a second migration, this time to Illinois. Having just reached the age of 21, he was six feet four inches tall, rawboned and lanky but muscular and physically powerful. He was especially noted for the skill and strength with which he could wield an axe.

Having no desire to be a farmer, Lincoln tried his hand at a variety of occupations, including rail-splitting (from which he acquired the byname "The Rail-Splitter"). With the coming of the Black Hawk War (1832), he enlisted as a volunteer and was elected captain of his company. Meanwhile, aspiring to be a legislator, he was defeated in his first try and then repeatedly reelected to the state assembly. He considered blacksmithing as a trade but finally decided in favour of the law. He began to study law books, and in 1836, having passed the bar examination, he began to practice law.

PRAIRIE LAWYER

The next year he moved to Springfield, Ill., the new state capital. Within a few years he was earning $1,200 to $1,500 annually, at a time when the governor of the state received a salary of $1,200 and circuit judges only $750. He found it necessary not only to practice in the capital but also to follow the court as it made the rounds of its circuit, setting out by horseback or buggy to travel hundreds of miles each spring and fall.

The coming of the railroads, especially after 1850, made travel easier and practice more remunerative. Lincoln handled cases for railroads, banks, insurance companies, and mercantile and manufacturing firms. His business also included a number of patent suits and criminal trials. By the time he began to be prominent in national politics, about 20 years after launching his legal career, Lincoln had made himself one of the most distinguished and successful lawyers in Illinois.

He was noted not only for his shrewdness and practical common sense, which enabled him always to see to the heart of any legal case, but also for his invariable fairness and utter honesty, for which he came to be known as "Honest Abe."

PRIVATE LIFE

So far as can be known, the first and only real love of Lincoln's life was Mary Todd. High-spirited, quick-witted, and well-educated, Todd came from a rather distinguished Kentucky family, and her Springfield relatives belonged to the social aristocracy of the town. Although Lincoln sometimes doubted whether he could ever make her happy, they became engaged. Then, on a day in 1841 that Lincoln recalled as the "fatal first of January," the engagement was broken, apparently on his initiative. For some time afterward, Lincoln was overwhelmed by terrible depression and despondency. Finally the two were reconciled, and on Nov. 4, 1842, they married.

Four children, all boys, were born to the Lincolns. Robert Todd, the eldest, was the only one of the children to survive to adulthood, though Lincoln's favourite, Thomas ("Tad"), who had a cleft palate and a lisp, outlived his father.

Mary Lincoln suffered from recurring headaches, fits of temper, and a sense of insecurity and loneliness that was intensified by her husband's long absences on the lawyer circuit. After his election to the presidency, she was afflicted by the death of her son Willie and the unfair public criticisms of her as mistress of the White House. She developed an obsessive need to spend money, and therefore ran up embarrassing bills. At last, in 1875, she was officially declared insane, though by that time she had undergone the further shock of seeing her husband murdered at her side.

Lincoln was fond of the Bible and knew it well. He also was fond of Shakespeare. In private conversation he used many Shakespearean allusions, discussed problems of dramatic interpretation with considerable insight, and recited long passages from memory with rare feeling and understanding. He liked the works of John Stuart Mill, particularly *On Liberty*, but disliked heavy or metaphysical works.

EARLY POLITICS

When Lincoln first entered politics, Andrew Jackson was president. Lincoln shared the sympathies that the Jacksonians professed for the common man, but he disagreed with the Jacksonian view that the government should be divorced from economic enterprise. In Lincoln's view, Illinois and the West as a whole desperately needed government aid for economic development. Associating himself with the Whig party, he was elected four times to the Illinois State Legislature between 1834 and 1840. In 1847–49 he served a single term in Congress as the lone Whig from Illinois.

Lincoln devoted much of his time to presidential politics. He found an issue and a candidate in the Mexican War, challenging the statement of Pres. James K. Polk that Mexico had started the war by shedding American blood upon American soil. He later laboured for the nomination and election of the war hero Zachary Taylor. His criticisms of the war, however, had not been popular among the voters in his own congressional district. At the age of 40, frustrated in politics, he seemed to be at the end of his public career.

THE ROAD TO PRESIDENCY

For about five years Lincoln took little part in politics, and then a new sectional crisis gave him a chance to reemerge and rise to statesmanship. In 1856 he joined the new Republican Party, which had arisen out of opposition in Illinois and other states to the extension of slavery to the territories of the Louisiana Purchase. Determined to be the Republican leader of his state, Lincoln challenged the incumbent Illinois senator Stephen Douglas for his seat in 1858, and the series of debates they engaged in throughout Illinois was political oratory of the highest order. In their basic views, Lincoln and Douglas were not as far apart as they seemed in the heat of political argument. Neither was abolitionist or proslavery. But Lincoln, unlike Douglas, insisted that Congress must exclude slavery from the territories. In one of his most famous speeches, he said: "*A house divided against itself cannot stand.* I believe the government cannot endure permanently half slave and half free." He agreed with Thomas Jefferson and other founding fathers, however, that slavery should be merely contained, not directly attacked. Lincoln drove home the inconsistency between Douglas's "popular sovereignty" principle and the *Dred Scott* decision (1857), in which the U.S. Supreme Court held that Congress could not constitutionally exclude slavery from the territories.

In the end, however, Lincoln lost the election to Douglas. Lincoln had, nevertheless, gained national recognition and soon began to be mentioned as a presidential prospect for 1860.

On May 18, 1860, he was nominated on the third ballot at the Republican National Convention in Chicago. With the Republicans united, the Democrats divided, and a total of four candidates in the field, he carried the election on

This image of Abraham Lincoln was used in his 1860 bid to become the 16th president of the United States. Library of Congress, Washington, D.C.

November 6. Although he received no votes from the Deep South and no more than 40 out of 100 in the country as a whole, the popular votes were so distributed that he won a clear and decisive majority in the electoral college.

PRESIDENT LINCOLN

After Lincoln's election and before his inauguration, the state of South Carolina proclaimed its withdrawal from the Union. To forestall similar action by other Southern states, various compromises were proposed in Congress. From his home in Springfield he advised Republicans in Congress to vote against a proposal to divide the territories into slave and free. Six additional states then seceded and, with South Carolina, combined to form the Confederate States of America.

OUTBREAK OF WAR

On April 12, 1861, Confederate batteries opened fire on Fort Sumter, in Charleston Harbor, S.C., which was garrisoned with U.S. troops. "Then, and thereby," Lincoln informed Congress when it met on July 4, "the assailants of the Government, began the conflict of arms." Lincoln was determined to preserve the Union, and to do so he thought he must take a stand against the Confederacy. He concluded he might as well take this stand at Sumter.

After the firing on Fort Sumter, Lincoln called upon the state governors for troops (Virginia and three other states of the upper South responded by joining the Confederacy). He then proclaimed a blockade of the Southern ports. He ordered a direct advance on the Virginia front, which resulted in defeat and rout for the federal forces at Bull Run (July 21, 1861). After a succession of more or less sleepless nights, Lincoln produced a set of memorandums on military policy. His basic thought was that the armies should advance concurrently on several fronts and should move so as to hold and use the support of Unionists in Missouri, Kentucky, western Virginia, and eastern Tennessee.

LEADERSHIP IN WAR

As a war leader, Lincoln employed the style that had served him as a politician: he preferred to react to problems and to the circumstances that others had created rather than to originate policies and lay out long-range designs. It was the pragmatic approach of a practical, mentally nimble, and flexible man. If one action or decision proved unsatisfactory in practice, he was willing to experiment with another.

From 1861 to 1864, while hesitating to impose his ideas upon his generals, Lincoln experimented with command personnel and organization. After disappointing performances by a series of generals, he decided to appoint Ulysses S. Grant, the leader of the successful assault on Vicksburg, commander of all federal armies. At last Lincoln had found a man who, with such able subordinates as William T. Sherman, Philip Sheridan, and George H. Thomas, could put into effect those parts of Lincoln's concept of a large-scale, coordinated offensive that still remained to be carried out. Lincoln pioneered in the creation of a high command, an organization for amassing all the energies and resources of a people in the grand strategy of total war. He combined statecraft and the overall direction of armies with an effectiveness that increased year by year. His achievement is all the more

U.S. President Abraham Lincoln (seated centre) *and his cabinet, with Lieutenant General Winfield Scott, in the council chamber at the White House, lithograph, 1866.* Library of Congress, Washington, D.C.

remarkable in view of his lack of training and experience in the art of warfare.

As president, Lincoln was at first reluctant to adopt an abolitionist policy. There were several reasons for his hesitancy. He had been elected on a platform pledging no interference with slavery within the states, and in any case he doubted the constitutionality of federal action under the circumstances. He was concerned about the possible difficulties of incorporating nearly four million African Americans, once they had been freed, into the nation's social and political life. Above all, he felt that he must hold the border slave states in the Union, and he feared that an abolitionist program might impel them, in particular his native Kentucky, toward the Confederacy. So he held back.

Meanwhile, in response to the rising antislavery sentiment, Lincoln came forth with a gradual emancipation plan that called for the colonization of freedmen abroad.

While still hoping for the eventual success of his gradual plan, however, he took quite a different step by issuing his preliminary (Sept. 22, 1862) and his final (Jan. 1, 1863) Emancipation Proclamation. This famous decree, which he justified as an exercise of the president's war powers, applied only to those parts of the country actually under Confederate control, not to the loyal slave states nor to the federally occupied areas of the Confederacy. Directly or indirectly the proclamation brought freedom during the war to fewer than 200,000 slaves. Yet it had great significance as a symbol. It indicated that the Lincoln government had added freedom to reunion as a war aim, and it attracted liberal opinion in England and Europe to increased support of the Union cause.

Lincoln himself doubted the constitutionality of his step, except as a temporary war measure. After the war, the slaves freed by the proclamation would have risked re-enslavement had nothing else been done to confirm their liberty. But something else was done: the Thirteenth Amendment was added to the Constitution, Lincoln playing a large part in bringing about this change in the fundamental law. Through the chairman of the Republican National Committee, he urged the party to include a plank for such an amendment in its platform of 1864. When Lincoln was reelected on this platform and the Republican majority in Congress was increased, he was justified in feeling, as he apparently did, that he had a mandate from the people for the Thirteenth Amendment. The newly chosen Congress, with its overwhelming Republican majority, was not to meet until after the lame duck session of the old Congress during the winter of 1864–65. Lincoln did not wait. Using his resources of patronage and persuasion upon certain of the Democrats, he managed to get the necessary two-thirds vote before the session's end. He did not , however, live to see its ultimate adoption.

WARTIME POLITICS

During the war the opposition party remained alive and strong. Its membership included war Democrats and peace Democrats, often called "Copperheads," a few of whom collaborated with the enemy. Lincoln did what he could to cultivate the assistance of the war Democrats, and, as feasible, he conciliated the peace Democrats. In dealing with persons suspected of treasonable intent, however, Lincoln at times authorized his generals to make arbitrary arrests. He justified this action on the grounds that he had to allow some temporary sacrifice of parts of the Constitution in order to maintain the Union, thus preserving the Constitution as a whole. He let his generals suspend several newspapers, but only for short periods.

Considering the dangers and provocations of the time, Lincoln was quite liberal in his treatment of political opponents and the opposition press. He was by no means the dictator critics often accused him of being. Nevertheless, his abrogating of civil liberties, especially his suspension of the privilege of the writ of habeas corpus, disturbed Democrats, Republicans, and even members of his own cabinet.

By 1863 Lincoln was already the candidate of the "Union" (that is, the Republican) party for reelection to the presidency. In 1864, as in 1860, he was the chief strategist of his own electoral campaign. He was reelected with a large popular majority (55 percent) over his Democratic opponent, Gen. George B. McClellan.

On Feb. 3, 1865, he met personally with Confederate commissioners on a steamship in Hampton Roads, Va. He promised to be liberal with pardons if the South would quit the war, but he insisted on reunion as a precondition for any peace arrangement. In his second inaugural address he embodied the spirit of his policy in the famous words "with malice toward none; with charity for all." His terms satisfied neither the Confederacy nor the extremists in his own party, and so no peace was possible until the final defeat of the Confederacy.

POSTWAR POLICY

At the end of the war, Lincoln's policy for the defeated South was not clear in all its details, though he continued to believe that the main object should be to restore the "seceded States, so-called," to their "proper practical relation" with the Union as soon as possible. What Lincoln's reconstruction policy would have been, if he had lived to complete his second term, can only be guessed at.

On the evening of April 14, 1865, 26-year-old John Wilkes Booth—a rabid advocate of slavery with ties to the South and the flamboyant son of one of the most distinguished theatrical families of the 19th century—shot Lincoln as he sat in Ford's Theatre in Washington. Early the next morning Lincoln died.

REPUTATION AND CHARACTER

Lincoln deserves his reputation as the Great Emancipator. His claim to that honour, if it rests uncertainly upon his famous proclamation, has a sound basis in the support he gave to the antislavery amendment. It is well founded also in his greatness as the war leader who carried the nation safely through the four-year struggle that brought freedom in its train. And, finally, it is strengthened by the practical demonstrations he gave of respect for human worth and dignity, regardless of colour. During the last two years of his life he welcomed African Americans as visitors and friends in a way no president had done before. One of his friends was the distinguished former slave Frederick Douglass, who once wrote: "In all my interviews with Mr.

Lincoln I was impressed with his entire freedom from prejudice against the colored race."

"Now he belongs to the ages," Stanton is supposed to have said as Lincoln took his last breath. Many thought of Lincoln as a martyr. The assassination had occurred on Good Friday, and on the following Sunday, memorable as "Black Easter," hundreds of speakers found a sermon in the event. Some of them saw more than mere chance in the fact that assassination day was also crucifixion day.

Lincoln's best ideas and finest phrases were considered and written and rewritten with meticulous revisions. Some resulted from a slow gestation of thought and phrase through many years. One of his recurring themes—probably his central theme—was the promise and the problem of self-government. Again and again he returned to this idea, especially after the coming of the Civil War. In his first message to Congress after the fall of Fort Sumter, he declared that the issue between North and South involved more than the future of the United States.

It presents to the whole family of man, the question, whether a constitutional republic, or a democracy—a government of the people, by the same people—can, or cannot, maintain its territorial integrity, against its own domestic foes.

And finally at Gettysburg, Pa., he made the culminating, supreme statement, concluding with the words:

. . . that from these honored dead we take increased devotion to that cause for which they gave the last full measure of devotion—that we here highly resolve that these dead shall not have died in vain—that this nation, under God, shall have a new birth of freedom—and that government of the people, by the people, for the people, shall not perish from the earth.

ANDREW JOHNSON

(b. Dec. 29, 1808, Raleigh, N.C.—d. July 31, 1875, near Carter
Station, Tenn.)

Andrew Johnson was the 17th president of the United
States (1865–69), taking office upon the assassination of Pres. Abraham Lincoln during the closing
months of the American Civil War (1861–65). His lenient
Reconstruction policies toward the South embittered the
Radical Republicans in Congress and led to his political
downfall and impeachment, though he was acquitted.

EARLY LIFE AND CAREER

Johnson was the younger of two sons of Jacob and Mary
McDonough Johnson. Jacob Johnson, who served as a por-
ter in a local inn, as a sexton in the Presbyterian church,
and as town constable, died when Andrew was three years
old, leaving his family in poverty. His widow took in work
as a spinner and weaver to support her family and later
remarried. She bound Andrew as an apprentice tailor when
he was 14. In 1826, when he had just turned 17, having broken his indenture, he and his family moved to Greeneville,
Tenn. Johnson opened his own tailor shop, which bore the
simple sign "A. Johnson, tailor." He hired a man to read to
him while he worked with needle and thread. From a book
containing some of the world's great orations he began to
learn history. Another subject he studied was the
Constitution of the United States, which he was soon able
to recite from memory in large part.

Johnson never went to school and taught himself how
to read and spell. In 1827, now 18 years old, he married
16-year-old Eliza McCardle, whose father was a shoemaker. She taught her husband to read and write more

fluently and to do arithmetic. She, too, often read to him
as he worked. In middle age she contracted what was called
"slow consumption" (tuberculosis) and became an invalid.
She rarely appeared in public during her husband's presidency, the role of hostess usually being filled by their eldest
child, Martha, wife of David T. Patterson, U.S. senator
from Tennessee.

Johnson's lack of formal schooling and his homespun
quality were distinct assets in building a political base of
poor people seeking a fuller voice in government. His tailor shop became a kind of centre for political discussion
with Johnson as the leader; he had become a skillful orator
in an era when public speaking and debate was a powerful
political tool. Before he was 21, he organized a working-
man's party that elected him first an alderman and then
mayor of Greeneville. During his eight years in the state
legislature (1835–43), he found a natural home in the states'
rights Democratic Party of Andrew Jackson and emerged
as the spokesman for mountaineers and small farmers
against the interests of the landed classes. In that role, he
was sent to Washington for 10 years as a U.S. representative (1843–53), after which he served as governor of
Tennessee (1853–57). Elected a U.S. senator in 1856, he generally adhered to the dominant Democratic views
favouring lower tariffs and opposing antislavery agitation.
Johnson had achieved a measure of prosperity and owned
a few slaves himself. In 1860, however, he broke dramatically with the party when, after Lincoln's election, he
vehemently opposed Southern secession. When Tennessee
seceded in June 1861, he alone among the Southern senators remained at his post and refused to join the
Confederacy. In recognition of this unwavering support,
Lincoln appointed him (May 1862) military governor of
Tennessee, by then under federal control.

THE PRESIDENCY

To broaden the base of the Republican Party to include loyal "war" Democrats, Johnson was selected to run for vice president on Lincoln's reelection ticket of 1864. His first appearance on the national stage was a fiasco. On Inauguration Day, in order to counter the effects of a recent illness, he imbibed more whiskey than he should have. As he swayed on his feet and stumbled over his words, he embarrassed his colleagues in the administration and dismayed onlookers. Less than five weeks later he was president.

Thrust so unexpectedly into the White House (April 14, 1865), he was faced with the enormously vexing problem of reconstructing the Union and settling the future of the former Confederate states. Congressional Radical Republicans, who favoured severe measures toward the defeated yet largely impenitent South, were disappointed with the new president's program with its lenient policies begun by Lincoln and its readmission of seceded states into the Union with few provisions for reform or civil rights for freedmen.

Johnson's vetoing of two important pieces of legislation aimed at protecting former slaves, an extension of the Freedman's Bureau bill and the Civil Rights Act of 1866, united Moderate and Radical Republicans in outrage and further polarized a situation already filled with acrimony. Congress succeeded in overriding Johnson's veto of the Civil Rights Act; it was the first instance of a presidential veto's being overridden. In addition, Congress passed the Fourteenth Amendment to the Constitution, conferring citizenship on all persons born or naturalized in the United States and guaranteeing them equal protection under the law. Against Johnson's objections, the amendment was ratified.

Photographic portrait of Andrew Johnson. National Archives/ Getty Images

In the congressional elections of 1866, Johnson undertook an 18-day speaking tour into the Midwest, in order to explain and defend his policies and defeat congressional candidates opposing them. His effort proved a failure. A result was sweeping electoral victories everywhere for the Radicals.

In March 1867 the new Congress passed, over Johnson's veto, the first of the Reconstruction acts, providing for suffrage for male freedmen and military administration of the Southern states. He maintained that the Reconstruction acts were unconstitutional because they were passed without Southern representation in Congress. Aloof, gruff, and undiplomatic, Johnson constantly antagonized the Radicals, who became his sworn enemies.

IMPEACHMENT

Johnson played into the hands of his enemies by an imbroglio over the Tenure of Office Act, passed the same day as the Reconstruction acts. It forbade the chief executive from removing without the Senate's concurrence certain federal officers whose appointments had originally been made by and with the advice and consent of the Senate. The question of the power of the president in this matter had long been a controversial one. Johnson plunged ahead and dismissed from office Secretary of War Edwin M. Stanton—the Radicals' ally within his cabinet—to provide a court test of the act's constitutionality. In response, the House of Representatives voted articles of impeachment against the president—the first such occurrence in U.S. history. While the focus was on Johnson's removal of Stanton in defiance of the Tenure of Office Act, the president was also accused of bringing "into disgrace, ridicule, hatred, contempt, and reproach the Congress of the United States."

In a theatrical proceeding before the Senate, presided over by Chief Justice Salmon P. Chase, the charges proved weak, despite the passion with which they were argued, and the key votes (May 16 and 26, 1868) fell one short of the necessary two-thirds for conviction, seven Republicans voting with Johnson's supporters.

Despite his exoneration, Johnson's usefulness as a national leader was over. The vexing problem of African American suffrage was addressed by Congress's passage of the Fifteenth Amendment (ratified during the ensuing administration of Ulysses S. Grant), which forbade denial of suffrage on the basis of "race, color, or previous condition of servitude." At the 1868 Democratic National Convention, Johnson received a modest number of votes, but he did not actively seek renomination.

After returning to Tennessee, Johnson finally won reelection (1875) as a U.S. senator after unsuccessful bids for a Senate seat in 1869 and a House seat in 1872. He died a short time later.

ULYSSES S. GRANT

(b. April 27, 1822, Point Pleasant, Ohio—d. July 23, 1885, Mount McGregor, N.Y.)

Ulysses S. Grant commanded the Union armies during the late years (1864–65) of the American Civil War before becoming the 18th president of the United States (1869–77).

EARLY LIFE

Grant was the son of Jesse Root Grant, a tanner, and Hannah Simpson, and he grew up in Georgetown, Ohio. Detesting the work around the family tannery, Ulysses instead performed his share of chores on farmland owned by his father and developed considerable skill in handling horses. In 1839 Jesse secured for Ulysses an appointment to the United States Military Academy at West Point, N.Y., and pressured him to attend.

Grant ranked 21st in a class of 39 when he graduated from West Point in 1843. Upon graduation he was assigned as a brevet second lieutenant to the 4th U.S. Infantry, stationed near St. Louis, Mo., where he fell in love with and married Julia Boggs Dent, the sister of his roommate at West Point.

In the Mexican War (1846–48) Grant showed gallantry in campaigns under Gen. Zachary Taylor. He was then transferred to Gen. Winfield Scott's army, where he first served as regimental quartermaster and commissary. He subsequently distinguished himself in battle in September 1847, earning brevet commissions as first lieutenant and captain, though his permanent rank was first lieutenant.

On July 5, 1852, when the 4th Infantry sailed from New York for the Pacific coast, Grant left his growing family of Julia and their two sons behind. A promotion to captain in August 1853 brought an assignment to Fort Humboldt, Calif., a dreary post with an unpleasant commanding officer. On April 11, 1854, Grant resigned from the army. Whether this decision was influenced in any way by Grant's fondness for alcohol, which he reportedly drank often during his lonely years on the Pacific coast, remains open to conjecture.

Settling at White Haven, the Dents' estate in Missouri, Grant began to farm 80 acres (30 hectares) given to Julia by her father. This farming venture was a failure, as was a real estate partnership in St. Louis in 1859. The next year Grant joined the leather goods business owned by his father and operated by his brothers in Galena, Ill.

THE CIVIL WAR

At the outbreak of the Civil War in April 1861, Grant helped recruit, equip, and drill troops in Galena, then accompanied them to the state capital, Springfield, where Gov. Richard Yates appointed him colonel of an unruly regiment in June 1861. Before he had even engaged the enemy, Grant was appointed brigadier general through the influence of Elihu B. Washburne, a U.S. congressman from Galena.

In January 1862, dissatisfied with the use of his force for defensive and diversionary purposes, Grant received permission from Gen. Henry Wager Halleck to begin an offensive campaign. On February 16 he won the first major Union victory of the war, when Fort Donelson, on the Cumberland River in Tennessee, surrendered with about 15,000 troops.

Promoted to major general, Grant repelled an unexpected Confederate attack on April 6–7 at Shiloh Church, near Pittsburg Landing, Tenn. Before the end of the year, he began his advance toward Vicksburg, Miss., the last major Confederate stronghold on the Mississippi River. Displaying his characteristic aggressiveness, resilience, independence, and determination, Grant brought about the besieged city's surrender on July 4, 1863.

COMMAND OVER UNION ARMIES

Grant was appointed lieutenant general in March 1864 and was entrusted with command of all the U.S. armies. His

Ulysses S. Grant. Library of Congress, Washington, D.C.

basic plan for the 1864 campaign was to immobilize the army of Gen. Robert E. Lee near the Confederate capital at Richmond, Va., while Gen. William Tecumseh Sherman led the western Union army southward through Georgia. It worked. By mid-June, Lee was pinned down at Petersburg, near Richmond, while Sherman's army cut and rampaged through Georgia and cavalry forces under Gen. Philip Sheridan destroyed railroads and supplies in Virginia. On April 2, 1865, Lee was forced to abandon his Petersburg defensive line, and the surrender of Lee's army followed on April 9 at Appomattox Court House, effectively marking the end of the Civil War.

In 1867 Johnson removed Secretary of War Edwin M. Stanton and thereby tested the constitutionality of the Tenure of Office Act, and in August appointed Grant interim secretary of war. When Congress insisted upon Stanton's reinstatement, Grant resigned (January 1868), thus infuriating Johnson.

Johnson's angry charges brought an open break between the two men and strengthened Grant's ties to the Republican Party, which led to his nomination for president in 1868. Grant's Democratic opponent was Horatio Seymour, former governor of New York. The race was a close one, and Grant's narrow margin of victory in the popular vote (300,000 ballots) may have been attributable to newly enfranchised black voters. The vote of the electoral college was more one-sided, with Grant garnering 214 votes, compared with 80 for Seymour.

GRANT'S PRESIDENCY

Grant entered the White House on March 4, 1869, politically inexperienced and, at age 46, the youngest man theretofore elected president. Notably, Grant named Ely S. Parker, a Seneca Indian who had served with him as a staff officer, commissioner of Indian affairs.

Julia was not beautiful—she had a cast in her left eye and squinted—but Grant was attracted to her liveliness, and his devotion to her was unbounded. Photography was just becoming part of the political scene when Julia rose to prominence as first lady, and, self-conscious about her looks, she contemplated having surgery to correct her eyes. Grant vetoed the idea, saying he loved her as she was. Consequently, almost all pictures of her were taken in profile.

On March 18, 1869, Grant signed his first law, pledging to redeem in gold the greenback currency issued during the Civil War, thus placing himself with the financial conservatives of the day. Grant was unsuccessful when the Senate narrowly rejected a treaty of annexation with the Dominican Republic, which Grant had been persuaded would be of strategic importance to the building of a canal connecting the Atlantic and Pacific oceans.

Grant won reelection easily in 1872, defeating Horace Greeley, the editor of the *New York Tribune* and the candidate for the coalition formed by Democrats and Liberal Republicans, by nearly 800,000 votes in the popular election and capturing 286 of 366 electoral votes. During the campaign, newspapers discovered that prominent Republican politicians were involved in the Crédit Mobilier of America, a shady corporation designed to siphon profits of the Union Pacific Railroad. More scandal followed in 1875, when Secretary of the Treasury Benjamin Helm Bristow exposed the operation of the "Whiskey Ring," which had the aid of high-placed officials in defrauding the government of tax revenues. When the evidence touched the president's private secretary, Orville E. Babcock, Grant regretted his earlier statement, "Let no guilty man escape." Grant blundered in accepting the hurried resignation of Secretary of War William W. Belknap, who was impeached on charges of accepting bribes; because he was no longer a government official, Belknap escaped conviction.

LATER LIFE

After leaving office, Ulysses and Julia Grant set forth on a round-the-world trip in May 1877. Grant's reputation as the man who had saved the American Union having preceded him, he was greeted everywhere as a conquering hero.

In 1879 Grant found that a faction of the Republican Party was eager to nominate him for a third term. Although he did nothing to encourage support, he received more than 300 votes in each of the 36 ballots of the 1880 convention, which finally nominated James A. Garfield. In 1881 Grant bought a house in New York City and began to take an interest in the investment firm of Grant and Ward, in which his son Ulysses, Jr., was a partner. Grant put his capital at the disposal of the firm and encouraged others to follow. In 1884 the firm collapsed, swindled by Ferdinand Ward. This impoverished the entire Grant family and tarnished Grant's reputation.

In 1884 Grant began to write reminiscences of his campaigns for the *Century Magazine* and found this work so congenial that he began his memoirs. Despite excruciating throat pain, later diagnosed as cancer, he signed a contract with his friend Mark Twain to publish the memoirs and resolved grimly to complete them before he died. In June 1885 the Grant family moved to a cottage in Mount McGregor, N.Y., in the Adirondack Mountains, and a month later Grant died there.

RUTHERFORD B. HAYES

(b. Oct. 4, 1822, Delaware, Ohio—d. Jan. 17, 1893, Fremont, Ohio)

R utherford Birchard Hayes, the 19th president of the United States (1877–81), brought post–Civil War Reconstruction to an end in the South, trying to establish new standards of official integrity after eight years of corruption in Washington, D.C. He was the only president to hold office by decision of an extraordinary commission of congressmen and Supreme Court justices appointed to rule on contested electoral ballots.

Hayes was the son of Rutherford Hayes, a farmer, and Sophia Birchard. After graduating from Kenyon College at the head of his class in 1842, Hayes studied law at Harvard, where he took a bachelor of laws degree in 1845. Returning to Ohio, he established a successful legal practice in Cincinnati, where he represented defendants in several fugitive-slave cases and became associated with the newly formed Republican Party. In 1852 he married Lucy Ware Webb, a cultured and unusually well-educated woman for her time. After combat service with the Union army, Hayes was elected to Congress (1865–67) and then to the Ohio governorship (1868–76).

In 1875, during his third gubernatorial campaign, Hayes attracted national attention by his uncompromising advocacy of a sound currency backed by gold. The following year he became his state's favourite son at the national Republican nominating convention, where a shrewdly managed campaign won him the presidential nomination. Hayes's unblemished public record and high moral tone offered a

Rutherford B. Hayes, c. 1880.
Library of Congress/Hulton
Archive/Getty Images

striking contrast to widely publicized accusations of corruption in the administration of Pres. Ulysses S. Grant (1869–77). An economic depression, however, and Northern disenchantment with Reconstruction policies in the South combined to give Hayes's Democratic opponent, Samuel J. Tilden, a popular majority, and early returns indicated a Democratic victory in the electoral college as well. Hayes's campaign managers challenged the validity of the returns from South Carolina, Florida, and Louisiana, and as a result two sets of ballots were submitted from the three states. Eventually a bipartisan majority of Congress created a special Electoral Commission to decide which votes should be counted. While the commission was deliberating, Republican allies of Hayes engaged in secret negotiations with moderate Southern Democrats aimed at securing acquiescence to Hayes's election. On March 2, 1877, the commission voted along strict party lines to award all the contested electoral votes to Hayes, who was thus elected with 185 electoral votes to Tilden's 184.

As president, Hayes promptly made good on the secret pledges made during the electoral dispute. He withdrew federal troops from states still under military occupation, thus ending the era of Reconstruction (1865–77). His promise not to interfere with elections in the former Confederacy ensured a return there of traditional white Democratic supremacy. He appointed Southerners to federal positions and made financial appropriations for Southern improvements. These policies aroused the animosity of a conservative Republican faction known as the Stalwarts.

During the national railroad strikes of 1877, Hayes, at the request of state governors, dispatched federal troops to suppress rioting. In 1878 Congress overrode his veto of the Bland-Allison Act (1878), which provided for government purchase of silver bullion and restoration of the silver dollar as legal tender.

Hayes refused renomination by the Republican Party in 1880, contenting himself with one term as president. In retirement he devoted himself to humanitarian causes, notably prison reform and educational opportunities for African American youth in the South.

JAMES A. GARFIELD

(b. Nov. 19, 1831, near Orange [in Cuyahoga county], Ohio—d. Sept. 19, 1881, Elberon [now in Long Branch], N.J.)

James Abram Garfield was the 20th president of the United States (March 4–Sept. 19, 1881). He had the second shortest tenure in presidential history. When he was shot and incapacitated, serious constitutional questions arose concerning who should properly perform the functions of the presidency.

Garfield was the son of Abram Garfield and Eliza Ballou, who continued to run the family's impoverished Ohio farm after her husband's death in 1833. Always studious, James attended Western Reserve Eclectic Institute (later Hiram College) at Hiram, Ohio, and graduated (1856) from Williams College. He returned to the Eclectic Institute as a professor of ancient languages and in 1857, at age 25, became the school's president. A year later he married Lucretia Rudolph and began a family that included seven children (two died in infancy). Garfield also studied law and was ordained as a minister in the Disciples of Christ church, but he soon turned to politics.

An advocate of free-soil principles (opposing the extension of slavery), Garfield became a supporter of the newly organized Republican Party and in 1859 was elected to the Ohio legislature. During the Civil War he helped recruit the 42nd Ohio Volunteer Infantry and became its colonel. After commanding a brigade at the Battle of Shiloh (April 1862), he was elected to the U.S. House of Representatives. While waiting for Congress to begin its session, he served as chief of staff in the Army of the Cumberland, winning promotion to major general after distinguishing himself at the Battle of Chickamauga (September 1863).

For nine terms, until 1880, Garfield represented Ohio's 19th congressional district. As chairman of the House Committee on Appropriations, he became an expert on fiscal matters and advocated a high protective tariff; as a Radical Republican, he sought a firm policy of Reconstruction for the South. In 1880 the Ohio legislature elected him to the U.S. Senate.

At the Republican presidential convention the same year in Chicago, the delegates were divided into three principal camps: those who backed former president Ulysses S. Grant, those who supported Maine Sen. James G. Blaine, and those committed to Secretary of the Treasury John Sherman. Tall, bearded, affable, and eloquent, Garfield steered fellow Ohioan Sherman's campaign and impressed so many with his nominating speech that he, not the candidate, became the focus of attention. Grant led all other candidates for 35 ballots, but failed to command a majority; and on the 36th ballot the nomination went to a dark horse, Garfield, who was still trying to remove his name from nomination as the bandwagon gathered speed.

His Democratic opponent in November was Gen. Winfield Scott Hancock, like Garfield a Civil War veteran, so both could wrap themselves in the symbolic "bloody shirt" of the Union. But Garfield also capitalized on his rags-to-riches background, using a campaign biography literally written by Horatio Alger. In an era when it was still considered unseemly for a candidate to court voters actively, Garfield, aided by Lucretia (who remained an important adviser), conducted the first "front porch" campaign, from his home in Mentor, Ohio, where reporters and voters came to hear him speak. Notwithstanding allegations of involvement in the Crédit Mobilier Scandal and a forged letter that supposedly revealed Garfield's advocacy of unrestricted Chinese immigration,

James A. Garfield, 1880. Library of Congress, Washington, D.C.

he defeated Hancock (as well as the third-party Greenback candidate), though he won the popular election by fewer than 10,000 votes. The vote in the electoral college was less close: 214 votes for Garfield, 155 for Hancock.

By the time of his election, Garfield had begun to see education rather than the ballot box as the best hope for improving the lives of African Americans. He tried to put together a cabinet that would appease all factions of the Republican Party, but, prompted by his secretary of state, Blaine, he eventually challenged Sen. Roscoe Conkling's patronage machine in New York. Instead of appointing one of Conkling's friends as collector of the Port of New York, Garfield chose a Blaine protégé, prompting the resignation of an outraged Conkling and strengthening the independence and power of the presidency. So demanding were the office seekers and the pressures of the patronage system that at one point Garfield wondered why anyone would want to seek the presidency.

On July 2, 1881, after only four months in office, while on his way to visit his ill wife in Elberon, N.J., Garfield was shot in the back at the railroad station in Washington, D.C., by Charles J. Guiteau, a disappointed office seeker with messianic visions. For 80 days the president lay ill and performed only one official act—the signing of an extradition paper. It was generally agreed that, in such cases, the vice president was empowered by the Constitution to assume the powers and duties of the office of president. But should he serve merely as acting president until Garfield recovered, or would he receive the office itself and thus displace his predecessor? Because of an ambiguity in the Constitution, opinion was divided, and, because Congress was not in session, the problem could not be debated there. On Sept. 2, 1881, the matter came before a cabinet meeting, where it was finally agreed that no action would be taken without first consulting Garfield. But in the opinion of the doctors this was impossible, and no further action was taken before the death of the president, the result of slow blood poisoning, on September 19.

CHESTER A. ARTHUR

(b. Oct. 5, 1829, North Fairfield, Vt.—d. Nov. 18, 1886, New York, N.Y.)

Chester Alan Arthur was the 21st president of the United States (1881–85), acceding to the presidency upon the assassination of Pres. James A. Garfield.

Arthur was the son of William Arthur, a Baptist minister, and Malvina Stone. After graduating in 1848 from Union College in Schenectady, N.Y., where he was a member of Phi Beta Kappa, Arthur studied law and simultaneously taught school; he was admitted to the New York bar in 1854 and joined a law firm in New York City. One year later, he successfully represented Lizzie Jennings, an African American, in her suit against a Brooklyn streetcar company for forcing her off a car reserved for whites. The landmark victory led to a New York law forbidding discrimination in public transportation. An ardent abolitionist, Arthur also pleaded successfully the case of a slave who sued for his freedom on the ground that his master had brought him temporarily to the free state of New York.

Chester A. Arthur, c. 1880. Hulton Archive/Getty Images

Arthur joined the Republican Party in the 1850s, became active in local politics, and served as quartermaster general of New York State's troops during the Civil War. Resuming his law practice in 1863, he became closely associated with Sen. Roscoe Conkling, the Republican boss of New York. In 1871, with Conkling's backing, Arthur was appointed customs collector for the port of New York City by Pres. Ulysses S. Grant. The New York customhouse, which brought in the bulk of the nation's tariff revenue, had long been conspicuous for flagrant use of the spoils system, by which Conkling's political supporters were rewarded with government jobs.

In 1877 newly elected Pres. Rutherford B. Hayes, intent on reducing Conkling's patronage fiefdom, demanded the resignation of Arthur and others in the New York City customhouse. With Conkling's support, Arthur was able to

resist Hayes for a time, but in July 1878 Hayes finally suspended him, and Arthur returned to the practice of law.

Widely regarded as Conkling's protégé, Arthur worked
with his mentor at the Republican National Convention
of 1880 to secure the renomination of Grant for a third
term as president. When the convention deadlocked
between the conservative Stalwart and liberal Half-Breed
factions, delegates turned to dark-horse candidate James
A. Garfield, and Arthur was nominated vice president as a
conciliatory gesture to Conkling and the Stalwarts.

When Garfield was assassinated by a disappointed
office seeker who wanted Arthur to be president, public
apprehension increased markedly. Arthur took the presidential oath on Sept. 19, 1881, amid widespread belief that
he, the product of a corrupt spoils system with no experience in shaping public policy, was unworthy of the office
to which he had now tragically acceded. Said to have been
deeply wounded by the public's low regard for him, Arthur
proceeded to prove that he could rise above expectations.
In 1882 he displayed surprising independence when he
vetoed an $18 million rivers and harbours bill that con-
tained ample funds for projects that could be used for
political patronage. Yet it was Arthur's support for the
Pendleton Civil Service Act (1883) that clearly showed how
far he had come from his days as patronage purveyor at
the New York customhouse. The Pendleton Act at last
made a reality of civil-service reform, creating a merit-
based system of appointment and promotion for a limited
number of specified offices.

In 1882, soon after vetoing a bill that would have suspended Chinese immigration to the United States for 20
years, Arthur signed the Chinese Exclusion Act (1882),
which reduced the suspension to 10 years. In conjunction
with his secretary of the navy, William Eaton Chandler,

Arthur recommended appropriations that would later help to transform the United States Navy into one of the world's great fleets. During Arthur's final year as president, the United States acquired a naval coaling station at Pearl Harbor in the Hawaiian Islands.

Arthur had married Ellen ("Nell") Lewis Herndon on Oct. 25, 1859. She died of pneumonia shortly after the 1880 election, and when Arthur acceded to the presidency, his sister Mary Arthur McElroy acted as White House hostess.

At the Republican convention in 1884, Arthur allowed his name to be put forward for the party's presidential nomination even though he knew he was suffering from Bright's disease, a then-incurable kidney ailment. Defeated for the nomination by James G. Blaine, he finished his term, attended the inauguration of Democrat Grover Cleveland, and then returned to New York City, where he died at his home the following year.

GROVER CLEVELAND

(b. March 18, 1837, Caldwell, N.J.—d. June 24, 1908, Princeton)

G rover Cleveland was the 22nd and 24th president of the United States (1885–89 and 1893–97) and the only president ever to serve two discontinuous terms. Cleveland distinguished himself as one of the few truly honest and principled politicians of the Gilded Age.

Cleveland was the son of Richard Falley Cleveland, an itinerant Presbyterian minister, and Ann Neal. The death of Grover Cleveland's father in 1853 forced him to abandon school in order to support his mother and sisters. After clerking in a law firm in Buffalo, N.Y., he was admitted to the bar in 1859 and soon entered politics as a member of the Democratic Party. During the Civil War he was drafted but hired a substitute so that he could care for his mother—an altogether legal procedure but one that would make him vulnerable to political attack in the future. In 1863 he became assistant district attorney of Erie county, New York, and in 1870–73 he served as county sheriff.

In 1881, eight years after stepping down as sheriff, Cleveland was nominated for mayor by Buffalo Democrats who remembered his honest and efficient service in that office. In 1882, without the support of the Tammany Hall Democratic machine in New York City, Cleveland received his party's nomination for governor and went on to crush his Republican opponent by more than 200,000 votes.

Cleveland's devotion to principle and his unstinting opposition to Tammany Hall soon earned him a national reputation—particularly among Americans disgusted with the frequent scandals of Gilded Age politics.

In 1884 the Democrats sought a presidential candidate who would contrast sharply with Republican nominee James G. Blaine, a longtime Washington insider with a reputation for dishonesty and financial impropriety. Cleveland won the Democratic nomination with ease.

During the campaign, Cleveland's image as the clean alternative to the supposedly sullied Blaine suffered serious damage when Republicans charged that the Democratic candidate had fathered a child out of wedlock some 10 years earlier. Cleveland remained undaunted, and he instructed Democratic leaders to "Tell the truth." The truth, as Cleveland admitted, was that he had had an affair with the child's mother, Maria Halpin, and had agreed to provide financial support when she named him as the father, though he was uncertain whether the child was really his. Late in the campaign, Blaine experienced an embarrassment of his own, when a supporter at a rally in New York City described the Democrats as the party of "rum, Romanism, and rebellion"—a swipe at the city's

Irish Catholics, many of whom Blaine hoped to lure into his camp. The general election was determined by electoral votes from New York State, which Blaine lost to Cleveland by fewer than 1,200 votes.

As president, Cleveland continued to act in the same negative capacity that had marked his tenures as mayor and governor. He nullified fraudulent grants to some 80,000,000 acres (30,000,000 hectares) of Western public lands and vetoed hundreds of pension bills that would have sent federal funds to undeserving Civil War veterans. He also received credit for two of the more significant measures enacted by the federal

Grover Cleveland. Library of Congress, Washington, D.C.

government in the 1880s: the Interstate Commerce Act (1887), which established the Interstate Commerce Commission, the first regulatory agency in the United States, and the Dawes General Allotment Act (1887), which redistributed Indian reservation land to individual tribe members.

In 1886 Cleveland, a lifelong bachelor, married Frances Folsom, the daughter of his former law partner. Frances Cleveland, 27 years younger than her husband, proved to be a very popular first lady.

The major issue of the 1888 presidential campaign was the protective tariff. Cleveland, running for reelection, opposed the high tariff, calling it unnecessary taxation imposed upon American consumers, while Republican candidate Benjamin Harrison defended protectionism. On election day, Cleveland won about 100,000 more popular votes than Harrison, but Harrison won the election by capturing a majority of votes in the electoral college (233 to 168).

Cleveland spent the four years of the Harrison presidency in New York City, working for a prominent law firm. When the Republican-dominated Congress and the Harrison administration enacted the very high McKinley Tariff in 1890 and made the surplus in the treasury vanish in a massive spending spree, the path to a Democratic victory in 1892 seemed clear. Cleveland won his party's nomination for the third consecutive time and then soundly defeated Harrison and Populist Party candidate James B. Weaver by 277 electoral votes to Harrison's 145, making Cleveland the only president ever elected to discontinuous terms.

Early in Cleveland's second term the United States sank into the most severe economic depression the country had yet experienced. Cleveland believed that the Sherman Silver Purchase Act of 1890—which required the secretary of the treasury to purchase 4.5 million ounces of silver each month—had eroded confidence in the stability of the currency and was thus at the root of the nation's economic troubles. He called Congress into special session and, over considerable opposition from Southern and Western members of his own party, forced the repeal of the act. Yet the depression only worsened, and Cleveland's negative view of government began to diminish his popularity. He insisted the government could do nothing to alleviate the suffering of the many thousands of people who had lost jobs, homes, and farms. His popularity sank even lower when he negotiated with a syndicate of bankers headed by John Pierpont Morgan to sell government bonds abroad for gold. The deal was seen as an alliance between the president and one of the era's leading "robber barons."

Cleveland sent federal troops to Chicago to quell violence at Pullman's railroad car facility, the scene of the Pullman Strike, despite the objections of Illinois Gov. John P. Altgeld. The strike was broken within a week, and the president received the plaudits of the business community. However, he had severed whatever support he still had in the ranks of labour.

At the tumultuous Democratic convention in 1896, the party was divided between supporters of Cleveland and the gold standard and those who wanted a bimetallic standard of gold and silver designed to expand the nation's money supply. When William Jennings Bryan delivered his impassioned Cross of Gold speech, the delegates not only nominated the little-known Bryan for president but also repudiated Cleveland—the first and only president ever to be so repudiated by his own party.

Cleveland retired to Princeton, N.J., where he became active in the affairs of Princeton University as a lecturer in public affairs and as a trustee (1901–08).

BENJAMIN HARRISON

(b. Aug. 20, 1833, North Bend, Ohio—d. March 13, 1901, Indianapolis, Ind.)

Benjamin Harrison was the 23rd president of the United States (1889–93). A moderate Republican, he won an electoral majority while losing the popular vote by more than 100,000 to Democrat Grover Cleveland. Harrison signed into law the Sherman Antitrust Act (1890), the first legislation to prohibit business combinations in restraint of trade.

Harrison was the son of John Scott Harrison, a farmer, and Elizabeth Irwin Harrison. He was also the grandson of the ninth president, William Henry Harrison (elected 1840). In 1852 Benjamin graduated with distinction from Miami University in Oxford, Ohio, and the following year married Caroline Lavinia Scott, with whom he had two children. In 1854, after two years studying law, Harrison moved to Indianapolis, Ind., to establish his own practice. He served in the Civil War as an officer in the Union army, finally reaching the rank of brevet brigadier general. Resuming his law practice after the war, Harrison supported the Reconstruction policies of the Radical Republicans. He failed to win the governorship of Indiana in 1876, but in 1881 he was elected to the United States Senate.

Nominated for the presidency by the Republicans in 1888, he lost the popular vote by 5,439,853 to Cleveland's 5,540,309 but won the election by outpolling Cleveland in the electoral college by 233 electoral votes to Cleveland's 168.

Harrison's administration was marked by an innovative foreign policy and expanding American influence abroad. His secretary of state, James G. Blaine, presided over the First International Conference of American States, held in Washington, D.C. (1889–90), which established the International Union of American Republics (later called the Pan-American Union) for the exchange of cultural and scientific information. In addition, in February 1893, after an American-led coup toppled Queen Liliuokalani in the Hawaiian Islands, Harrison placed a treaty of annexation before the Senate, but Democrats blocked ratification for the remainder of Harrison's term.

In 1890 Republicans controlled both houses of Congress, but an economic depression in the agrarian West and South led to pressure for legislation that conservative Republicans normally resisted. The Sherman Antitrust Act (1890) outlawed "every contract, combination ... or conspiracy in restraint of trade or commerce," and the Sherman Silver Purchase Act of the same year, which required the government to buy 4.5 million ounces of the metal every month. Farmers and debtors in the Free Silver Movement had long advocated a bimetallic (gold and silver) standard for the nation's currency in the belief that an increase in the amount of money in circulation would raise crop prices and allow for easier debt repayment.

Benjamin Harrison, photograph by George Prince, 1888. Library of Congress, Washington, D.C.

Although the treasury had a surplus at the inception of Harrison's administration, Congress spent such enormous sums on soldiers' pensions and business subsidies that the surplus soon vanished. In the congressional elections of 1890, the Democrats recaptured the House of Representatives by a large majority, and during the remaining two years of his term Harrison had little, if any, influence on legislation. He was renominated at the party convention in Minneapolis (1892), but growing populist discontent and several major strikes late in his term largely accounted for his defeat by his old rival, Grover Cleveland, by an electoral vote of 145 to 277.

Having retired to his law practice in Indianapolis, Harrison, at 62, married his deceased wife's niece and caretaker, Mary Lord Dimmick; they had one daughter. He died of pneumonia in 1901 at his house in Indianapolis.

WILLIAM MCKINLEY

(b. Jan. 29, 1843, Niles, Ohio—d. Sept. 14, 1901, Buffalo, N.Y.)

William McKinley was the 25th president of the United States (1897–1901). Under his leadership, the United States went to war against Spain in 1898 and thereby acquired a global empire, including Puerto Rico, Guam, and the Philippines.

McKinley was the son of William McKinley, a manager of a charcoal furnace and a small-scale iron founder, and Nancy Allison. Eighteen years old at the start of the Civil War, McKinley enlisted in an Ohio regiment under the command of Rutherford B. Hayes, later the 19th president of the United States (1877–81). Promoted second lieutenant for his bravery in the Battle of Antietam (1862), he was discharged a brevet major in 1865. Returning to Ohio, he studied law, was admitted to the bar in 1867, and opened a law office in Canton, where he resided—except for his years in Washington, D.C.—for the rest of his life.

Drawn immediately to politics in the Republican Party, McKinley supported Hayes for governor in 1867 and Ulysses S. Grant for president in 1868. The following year he was elected prosecuting attorney for Stark county, and in 1877 he began his long career in Congress as representative from Ohio's 17th district. McKinley served in the House of Representatives until 1891, failing reelection only twice—in 1882, when he was temporarily unseated in an extremely close election, and in 1890, when Democrats gerrymandered his district.

The issue with which McKinley became most closely identified during his congressional years was the protective tariff, a high tax on imported goods that served to protect American manufacturers from foreign competition. As chairman of the House Ways and Means Committee, he was the principal sponsor of the McKinley

Tariff of 1890, which raised duties higher than they had been at any previous time. Yet by the end of his presidency McKinley had become a convert to commercial reciprocity among nations, recognizing that Americans must buy products from other countries in order to sustain the sale of American goods abroad.

William McKinley. Gramstorff

McKinley's loss in 1890 brought an end to his career in the House of Representatives, but with the help of wealthy Ohio industrialist Mark Hanna, he won two terms as governor of his home state (1892–96). During those years Hanna, a powerful figure in the Republican Party, laid plans to gain the party's presidential nomination for his good friend in 1896. McKinley went on to win the nomination easily.

The presidential campaign of 1896 was one of the most exciting in American history. The central issue was the nation's money supply. McKinley ran on a Republican platform emphasizing maintenance of the gold standard, while his opponent—William Jennings Bryan, candidate of both the Democratic and Populist parties—called for a bimetallic standard of gold and silver. McKinley won the election decisively, becoming the first president to achieve a popular majority since 1872 and bettering Bryan 271 to 176 in the electoral vote.

Inaugurated president March 4, 1897, McKinley promptly called a special session of Congress to revise customs duties upward. On July 24 he signed into law the

Dingley Tariff, the highest protective tariff in American history to that time. Yet domestic issues would play only a minor role in the McKinley presidency.

By the time McKinley took the oath of office as president, many Americans—influenced greatly by the sensationalistic yellow journalism of the Hearst and Pulitzer newspapers—were eager to see the United States intervene in Cuba, where Spain was engaged in brutal repression of an independence movement. Initially, McKinley hoped to avoid American involvement, but in February 1898 two events stiffened his resolve to confront the Spanish. First, a letter written by the Spanish minister to Washington, Enrique Dupuy de Lôme, was intercepted, and on February 9 it was published in American newspapers; the letter described McKinley as weak and too eager for public adulation. Then, six days after the appearance of the Dupuy de Lôme letter, the American battleship USS *Maine* suddenly exploded and sank as it sat anchored in Havana harbour, carrying 266 enlisted men and officers to their deaths. Although a mid-20th century investigation proved conclusively that the *Maine* was destroyed by an internal explosion, the yellow press convinced Americans of Spanish responsibility. The public clamoured for armed intervention, and congressional leaders were eager to satisfy the public demand for action.

In March McKinley gave Spain an ultimatum, including demands for an end to the brutality inflicted on Cubans and the start of negotiations leading toward independence for the island. Spain agreed to most of McKinley's demands but balked at giving up its last major New World colony. On April 20 Congress authorized the president to use armed force to secure the independence of Cuba, and five days later it passed a formal declaration of war.

In the brief Spanish-American War—"a splendid little war," in the words of Secretary of State John Hay—the

United States easily defeated Spanish forces in the Philippines, Cuba, and Puerto Rico. The subsequent Treaty of Paris, signed in December 1898 and ratified by the Senate in February 1899, ceded Puerto Rico, Guam, and the Philippines to the United States; Cuba became independent.

McKinley married Ida Saxton in 1871. Within two years, the future first lady witnessed the deaths of her mother and two daughters. She never recovered and spent the rest of her life as a chronic invalid, frequently suffering seizures and placing an enormous physical and emotional burden on her husband.

Renominated for another term without opposition, McKinley again faced Democrat William Jennings Bryan in the presidential election of 1900. McKinley's margins of victory in both the popular and electoral votes were greater than they were four years before, no doubt reflecting satisfaction with the outcome of the war and with the widespread prosperity that the country enjoyed. On Sept. 6, 1901, while McKinley was shaking hands with a crowd of well-wishers at the Pan-American Exposition in Buffalo, N.Y., Leon Czolgosz, an anarchist, fired two shots into the president's chest and abdomen. Rushed to a hospital in Buffalo, McKinley lingered for a week before dying in the early morning hours of September 14.

Chapter 3

Presidents of the United States: Theodore Roosevelt to Barack Obama

THEODORE ROOSEVELT

(b. Oct. 27, 1858, New York, N.Y.—d. Jan. 6, 1919, Oyster Bay)

Theodore Roosevelt was the 26th president of the United States (1901–09) and a writer, naturalist, and soldier. He expanded the powers of the presidency and of the federal government in support of the public interest in conflicts between big business and labour, also steering the nation toward an active role in world politics, particularly in Europe and Asia. He won the Nobel Prize for Peace in 1906 for mediating an end to the Russo-Japanese War, and secured the route and began construction of the Panama Canal (1904–14).

Portrait of Theodore Roosevelt.
Encyclopædia Britannica, Inc.

THE EARLY YEARS

Roosevelt was the second of four children born into a long-established, socially prominent family of Dutch and English ancestry; his mother, Martha Bulloch of

Georgia, came from a wealthy, slave-owning plantation family. In frail health as a boy, Roosevelt was educated by private tutors. He graduated from Harvard College, where he was elected to Phi Beta Kappa, in 1880. He then studied briefly at Columbia Law School but soon turned to writing and politics as a career. In 1880 he married Alice Hathaway Lee, by whom he had one daughter, Alice. After his first wife's death, in 1886 he married Edith Kermit Carow, with whom he lived for the rest of his life at Sagamore Hill, an estate near Oyster Bay, Long Island, N.Y.

Elected as a Republican to the New York State Assembly at 23, Roosevelt quickly made a name for himself as a foe of corrupt machine politics. In 1884, overcome by grief by the deaths of both his mother and his wife on the same day, he left politics to spend two years on his cattle ranch in the badlands of the Dakota Territory, where he became increasingly concerned about environmental damage to the West and its wildlife. His attempt to reenter

Theodore Roosevelt riding a horse. Encyclopædia Britannica, Inc.

public life in 1886 was unsuccessful; he was defeated in a bid to become mayor of New York City. Roosevelt remained active in politics and again battled corruption as a member of the U.S. Civil Service Commission (1889–95) and as president of the New York City Board of Police Commissioners. Appointed assistant secretary of the navy by Pres. William McKinley, Roosevelt vociferously championed a bigger navy and agitated for war with Spain. When war was declared in 1898, he organized the 1st Volunteer Cavalry, known as the Rough Riders, who were sent to fight in Cuba. Roosevelt was a brave and well-publicized military leader. The charge of the Rough Riders (on foot) up Kettle Hill during the Battle of Santiago made him the biggest national hero to come out of the Spanish-American War.

Elected governor of New York in 1898, Roosevelt became an energetic reformer, removing corrupt officials and enacting legislation to regulate corporations and the civil service. His actions irked the party's bosses so much that they conspired to get rid of him by drafting him for the Republican vice presidential nomination in 1900, assuming that his would be a largely ceremonial role.

Elected with McKinley, Roosevelt chafed at his powerless office until Sept. 14, 1901, when McKinley died after being shot by an assassin and he became president. Six weeks short of his 43rd birthday, Roosevelt was the youngest person ever to enter the presidency.

From what he called the presidency's "bully pulpit," Roosevelt gave speeches aimed at raising public consciousness about the nation's role in world politics, the need to control the trusts that dominated the economy, the regulation of railroads, and the impact of political corruption. Roosevelt recognized that he had become president by accident, and wanted above all to be elected in 1904. Knowing that conservative Republicans who were bitterly opposed to all reforms controlled both houses of Congress,

Roosevelt focused his activities on foreign affairs, using his executive power to address problems of business and labour and the conservation of natural resources.

THE SQUARE DEAL

Despite his caution, Roosevelt managed to do enough in his first three years in office to build a platform for election in his own right. He resurrected the nearly defunct Sherman Antitrust Act by bringing a successful suit to break up a huge railroad conglomerate, the Northern Securities Company. Roosevelt pursued this policy of "trust-busting" by initiating suits against 43 other major corporations during the next seven years.

Also in 1902 Roosevelt intervened in the anthracite coal strike when it threatened to cut off heating fuel for homes, schools, and hospitals. The president publicly asked representatives of capital and labour to meet in the White House and accept his mediation. He also talked about calling in the army to run the mines, and had Wall Street investment houses threaten to withhold credit to the coal companies and dump their stocks. The combination of tactics worked to end the strike and gain a modest pay hike for the miners. This was the first time that a president had publicly intervened in a labour dispute at least implicitly on the side of workers. Campaigning on a platform of a "Square Deal" between capital and labour, Roosevelt won the 1904 election, defeating the Democratic contender Alton B. Parker by 336 to 140 electoral votes. Roosevelt proceeded to put teeth into his Square Deal programs. He pushed Congress to grant powers to the Interstate Commerce Commission to regulate interstate railroad rates and to pass the Pure Food and Drug and Meat Inspection acts, which created agencies to assure protection to consumers.

Roosevelt's boldest actions came in the area of natural resources. At his urging, Congress created the Forest Service (1905) to manage government-owned forest reserves, appointing a fellow conservationist, Gifford Pinchot, to head the agency. Simultaneously, Roosevelt exercised existing presidential authority to designate millions of acres of public lands as national forests in order to make them off limits to commercial exploitation of lumber, minerals, and waterpower.

FOREIGN POLICY

Roosevelt knew that taking on the Philippine Islands as an American colony after the Spanish-American War had ended America's isolation from international power politics—a development that he welcomed. Every year he asked for bigger appropriations for the army and navy. Congress cut back on his requests, but by the end of his presidency he had built the U.S. Navy into a major force at sea and reorganized the army along efficient, modern lines.

In 1904 he framed a policy statement that became known as the Roosevelt Corollary to the Monroe Doctrine. It stated that the United States would not only bar outside intervention in Latin American affairs but would also police the area and guarantee that countries there met their international obligations. In 1905, without congressional approval, Roosevelt forced the Dominican Republic to install an American "economic advisor," who was in reality the country's financial director.

Quoting an African proverb, Roosevelt claimed that the right way to conduct foreign policy was to "speak softly and carry a big stick." Roosevelt resorted to big-stick diplomacy most conspicuously in 1903, when he helped

Panama to secede from Colombia and gave the United States a canal zone. Construction began at once on the Panama Canal, which Roosevelt visited in 1906, the first president to leave the country while in office.

Alarmed by Russian expansionism and by rising Japanese power, in 1904–05 Roosevelt worked to end the Russo-Japanese War by bringing both nations to the Portsmouth Peace Conference and mediating between them. Contrary to his bellicose image, Roosevelt privately came to favour withdrawal from the Philippines, judging it to be militarily indefensible, and renounced any hopes of exerting major power in Asia.

LAST YEARS AS PRESIDENT

The end of Roosevelt's presidency was tempestuous. From his bully pulpit, he crusaded against "race suicide," prompted by his alarm at falling birth rates among white Americans, and tried to get the country to adopt a simplified system of spelling. Especially after a financial panic in 1907, his already strained relations with Republican conservatives in Congress degenerated into a spiteful stalemate that blocked any further domestic reforms. Roosevelt's term ended in March 1909, just four months after his 50th birthday.

LATER YEARS

Immediately upon leaving office, Roosevelt embarked on a 10-month hunting safari in Africa and made a triumphal tour of Europe. On his return he became ineluctably drawn back into politics. Both policy differences and personal animosity eventually impelled Roosevelt to run against his handpicked successor, William Howard Taft, for the

Republican nomination in 1912. When that quest failed, he bolted to form the Progressive Party, nicknamed the Bull Moose Party.

In the presidential campaign as the Progressive candidate, Roosevelt espoused a "New Nationalism" that would inspire greater government regulation of the economy and promotion of social welfare. This effort failed because the Democrats had an attractive, progressive nominee in Woodrow Wilson, who won the election with an impressive 435 electoral votes to Roosevelt's 88. Roosevelt had been shot in the chest by a fanatic while campaigning in Wisconsin, but quickly recovered.

Although he had some slight hope for the 1916 Republican nomination, Roosevelt was ready to support almost any candidate who opposed Wilson; he abandoned the Progressives to support the Republican candidate, Charles Evans Hughes, who lost by a narrow margin. After the United States entered World War I, his anger at Wilson boiled over when his offer to lead a division to France was rejected. By 1918 Roosevelt's support of the war and his harsh attacks on Wilson reconciled Republican conservatives to him, and he was the odds-on favourite for the 1920 nomination. But he died in early January 1919, less than three months after his 60th birthday.

WILLIAM HOWARD TAFT

(b. Sept. 15, 1857, Cincinnati, Ohio—d. March 8, 1930, Washington, D.C.)

William Howard Taft was the 27th president of the United States (1909–13) and the 10th chief justice of the United States (1921–30). As the choice of Pres. Theodore Roosevelt to succeed him and carry on the progressive Republican agenda, Taft as president alienated the progressives—and later Roosevelt—thereby contributing greatly to the split in Republican ranks in 1912, to the formation of the Bull Moose Party, and to his humiliating defeat that year in his bid for a second term.

The son of Alphonso Taft, secretary of war and attorney general (1876–77) under Pres. Ulysses S. Grant, and Louisa Maria Torrey, Taft graduated second in his Yale class of 1878, studied law, and was admitted to the Ohio bar in 1880. Drawn to politics in the Republican Party, he served in several minor appointive offices until 1887, when he was named to fill the unfinished term of a judge of the superior court of Ohio. The following year he was elected to a five-year term of his own, the only time he ever attained office via popular vote other than his election to the presidency. From 1892 to 1900 he served as a judge of the United States Sixth Circuit Court of Appeals, where he made several decisions hostile to organized labour.

In 1901 Taft became the first civilian governor of the Philippines, concentrating in that post on the economic development of the islands. In 1904 he agreed to return to Washington to serve as Theodore Roosevelt's secretary of war, with the stipulation that he could continue to supervise Philippine affairs.

Taft and Roosevelt became close friends, and the president regarded his secretary of war as a trusted adviser. When Roosevelt

William Howard Taft, Kent professor of constitutional law at Yale University between 1913 and 1921. Library of Congress, Washington, D.C.

declined to run for reelection, he threw his support to Taft, who won the 1908 Republican nomination and defeated Democrat William Jennings Bryan in the electoral college by 321 votes to 162.

Despite his close relationship with Roosevelt, Taft as president aligned himself with the more conservative members in the Republican Party, disappointing progressive Republicans. He did prove to be a vigorous trustbuster, however, launching twice as many antitrust prosecutions as had his progressive predecessor. He also backed conservation of natural resources, another key component of the progressive reform program. But when he fired Gifford Pinchot—head of the Bureau of Forestry, ardent conservationist, and close friend of Roosevelt—Taft severed whatever support he still had among Republican progressives.

Roosevelt returned from an African safari in 1910, and by 1912 a breach between the former friends was clearly evident. When Roosevelt decided to challenge Taft for the Republican presidential nomination, the two attacked each other mercilessly in the Republican primary elections. The primary results proved beyond doubt that Republican voters wanted Roosevelt to be the party's standard-bearer in 1912, but Taft's forces controlled the convention and secured the nomination for the incumbent. Republican progressives then bolted their party to form the Bull Moose (or Progressive) Party and nominated Roosevelt as their presidential candidate.

The split in Republican ranks assured the election of Democrat Woodrow Wilson. Roosevelt came in a distant second, and Taft, capturing less than a quarter of the popular vote, won just two states—Utah and Vermont. In the electoral college, Taft set a record for the poorest performance by an incumbent president seeking reelection: He won a mere 8 electoral votes compared with 88 for Roosevelt and 435 for Wilson.

As president, Taft frequently claimed that "politics makes me sick." Never eager for the office, he had been prodded to pursue it by his wife, Helen Herron Taft, whom he had married in 1886. As first lady she was a key political adviser to her husband.

On his departure from the White House Taft returned to Yale, where he became a professor of constitutional law. In 1921 Pres. Warren G. Harding appointed Taft chief justice of the United States, launching what was probably the happiest period in Taft's long career in public service.

Although generally conservative in his judicial philosophy, Taft was no rigid ideologue. His most important contribution to constitutional law was his opinion in *Myers* v. *United States* (1926) upholding the authority of the president to remove federal officials, a much-belated endorsement of the position taken by Andrew Johnson with respect to the Tenure of Office Act in his impeachment trial in 1868.

Suffering from heart disease, perhaps brought on by obesity, Taft resigned as chief justice on Feb. 3, 1930, and died a little more than a month later.

WOODROW WILSON

(b. Dec. 28, 1856, Staunton, Va. — d. Feb. 3, 1924, Washington, D.C.)

Woodrow Wilson was the 28th president of the United States (1913–21). An American scholar and statesman, he is best remembered for his legislative accomplishments and his high-minded idealism. Wilson led his country into World War I and became the creator and leading advocate of the League of Nations, for which he was awarded the 1919 Nobel Prize for Peace.

Early Life, Education, and Governorship

Wilson's father, Joseph Ruggles Wilson, was a Presbyterian minister who had moved to Virginia from Ohio and was the son of Scotch-Irish immigrants; his mother, Janet Woodrow, the daughter of a Presbyterian minister, had been born in England of Scottish parentage. Wilson was the only president since Andrew Jackson to have a foreign-born parent.

Apparently dyslexic from childhood, Wilson did not learn to read until after he was 10 and never became a rapid reader. Nevertheless, he developed passionate interests in politics and literature. He attended Davidson College near Charlotte, N.C., for a year before entering what is now Princeton University in 1875. After graduation from Princeton in 1879, Wilson studied law at the University of Virginia, with the hope that law would lead to politics. Two years of humdrum legal practice in Atlanta, Ga., disillusioned him, and he abandoned his law career for graduate study in government and history at Johns Hopkins University, where in 1886 he received a Ph.D.; he was the only president to earn that degree.

In 1885 Wilson married Ellen Louise Axson, the daughter of a Presbyterian minister from Rome, Ga., with whom he had three daughters. Ellen's death in August 1914 devastated Wilson with grief, which lifted only when he met and courted Edith Bolling Galt, whom he married in December 1915.

Wilson began his career teaching history and political science at Bryn Mawr College in 1885 and moved to Wesleyan University in Connecticut in 1888. Two years later he went to Princeton, where he quickly became the most popular and highest-paid faculty member. In 1902 he was the unanimous choice to become president of Princeton.

Meanwhile, the publicity that Wilson had generated as Princeton's president attracted the attention of conservative kingmakers in the Democratic Party. In 1910 Wilson resigned from the university to run for governor of New Jersey, winning election with a dynamic, progressive campaign. Once in office he implemented a sweeping reform program that gave him a national reputation, making him a contender for the Democratic presidential nomination.

Prevailing at the 1912 convention after a hard struggle against better-entrenched rivals, Wilson entered into a three-way race for president with former president Theodore Roosevelt and the Republican incumbent William Howard Taft. Wilson was elected with only 42 percent of the popular vote but with an electoral college landslide of 435 votes to Roosevelt's 88 and Taft's 8.

FIRST TERM AS PRESIDENT

Wilson drew up a legislative program in advance and broke with previous presidential practice by appearing before Congress in person. His approach achieved spectacular results. After months of complicated debate and bargaining over banking and currency reform, Congress passed the act creating the Federal Reserve System, which remains the most powerful government agency in economic affairs. Another victory came with passage of the Clayton

President Woodrow Wilson at the 1915 baseball World Series. Encyclopædia Britannica, Inc.

Antitrust Act, which strengthened existing laws against anticompetitive business actions; accompanying this act was one creating the Federal Trade Commission, which remains a major agency overseeing business practices.

Wilson followed those legislative accomplishments with a second wave of reform measures in 1916, including laws to prohibit child labour, raise income and inheritance taxes, and mandate an eight-hour workday for railroad workers.

The outbreak of World War I in August 1914, which coincided with his wife's death, tried Wilson's mind and soul. Almost no one questioned American neutrality in the beginning, but both the British blockade of maritime trade and German U-boat attacks soon made neutrality painful. On May 7, 1915, when a U-boat sank the British liner *Lusitania*, killing more than 1,100 people, including 128 Americans, Wilson at first urged his countrymen to show restraint. A combination of patience and firmness on the president's part paid off when the Germans, for military reasons of their own, pledged to curtail submarine warfare in April 1916.

SECOND TERM AS PRESIDENT

Wilson prevailed in the 1916 election, becoming the first Democrat to win a second consecutive term since Andrew Jackson. His narrow victory by 277 to 254 electoral votes over Charles Evans Hughes, the nominee of the reunited and resurgent Republicans, was a great political feat.

His reelection assured, Wilson mounted a peace offensive in December 1916 and January 1917 aimed at ending the world war. Unfortunately, the Germans rendered Wilson's peace efforts moot by unleashing their submarines on February 1. Wilson finally decided to intervene, mainly because he could see no alternative and hoped to use American belligerency as a means to build a just, lasting peace. On April 2, 1917, he went before Congress to ask for a declaration of war so that the United States could strive to fulfill his injunction that "the world must be made safe for democracy."

Recognizing what he did not know, Wilson delegated military decisions to professional soldiers. The boost given to the Allies by American money, supplies, and manpower tipped the scales against the Germans, who sued for peace and laid down their arms with the Armistice of Nov. 11, 1918.

Diplomacy was the one job that Wilson kept to himself. He seized the initiative on war aims with his Fourteen Points speech of Jan. 8, 1918, in which he promised a liberal, nonpunitive peace and a league of nations. Determined to keep those promises, Wilson made the controversial decision to go in person to the Paris Peace Conference, where he spent seven months in wearying, often acrimonious negotiations with the British, French, and Italians. The final product, the Treaty of Versailles, was signed on June 28, 1919. The treaty included the Covenant of the League of Nations, which he believed would adjust international differences and maintain peace.

Wilson returned from the peace conference exhausted and in failing health. Republican senators, led by Henry Cabot Lodge, sought either to reject the treaty or to attach reservations that would gravely limit America's commitments to the League of Nations. After two months of frustrating talks with senators, Wilson took his case to the people, throwing himself into a whirlwind cross-country tour, giving 39 speeches in three weeks.

On Oct. 2, 1919, Wilson suffered a massive stroke that left him partially paralyzed on his left side. His intellectual capacity was not affected, but his emotional balance and judgment were badly impaired.

His wife, Edith, controlled access to him, made decisions by default, and engineered a cover-up of his condition, which included misleadingly optimistic reports from his doctors. Although he gradually recovered from the worst effects of the stroke, Wilson never again fully functioned as president.

The peace treaty went down to defeat in the Senate, as a consequence of Wilson's stroke-induced rigidity. The United States never joined the League of Nations.

In the 1920 election, which became a referendum on Wilson, the Republican candidate, Warren Harding, won a landslide victory, which Republicans interpreted as a mandate to reverse Wilson's progressive policies at home and his internationalism abroad.

Wilson lived in Washington for almost three years after leaving office in March 1921. He died in his sleep at his Washington home.

WARREN G. HARDING

(b. Nov. 2, 1865, Caledonia [now Blooming Grove], Ohio—d. Aug. 2, 1923, San Francisco, Calif.)

Warren Gamaliel Harding was the 29th president of the United States (1921–23). Harding won the presidency by the greatest popular vote margin to that time. However, a series of scandals soon after his death doomed his presidency to be judged among the worst in American history.

Born on a farm, Harding was the eldest of eight children of George Tryon Harding and Phoebe Dickerson Harding. Following a mediocre education at local schools in Ohio and three years at Ohio Central College, Harding tried his hand at several vocations until in 1884 he bought a struggling weekly newspaper in Marion, Ohio, to which he devoted himself. Seven years thereafter, he married Florence Kling De Wolfe, who proved instrumental in transforming the Marion *Star* into a financially successful daily paper.

Harding was elected a state senator (1899–1902) and lieutenant governor (1903–04), but was defeated in his bid for the governorship in 1910. On most issues he allied himself with the conservative ("Old Guard") wing of the Republican Party, standing firm against U.S. membership in the League of Nations and always supporting legislation friendly to business. He achieved national visibility when he was chosen to

Warren G. Harding. National Archives/Getty Images

nominate William Howard Taft at the 1912 Republican Convention, and in his next campaign was elected U.S. senator (1915–21).

When the 1920 Republican Convention deadlocked over its selection of a presidential nominee, party leaders turned—supposedly in a smoke-filled room in Chicago's Blackstone Hotel—to the handsome, genial Ohioan as a compromise candidate. Paired with vice presidential candidate Calvin Coolidge, the affable Harding called for a nostalgic return to "normalcy," which was well received by voters disillusioned by the country's involvement in World War I. Harding won the election by the largest landslide to date, capturing some 60 percent of the popular vote.

President-elect Harding appointed to his cabinet a mixture of outstanding leaders and unscrupulous politicians waiting for an opportunity to line their pockets. Harding was a notoriously poor judge of character who expected his appointees to repay his trust with integrity. He was to be deeply disappointed.

The administration got off to a good start when Congress completed an initiative begun in the Wilson administration and established a budget system for the federal government; Charles G. Dawes was appointed first director of the budget. Then in 1921–22, the United States hosted the Washington Naval Disarmament Conference, which succeeded in getting the world's major powers to agree to halt the arms race in the production of large naval vessels. It was by far the most important achievement of the Harding presidency.

Early in 1923, Attorney General Harry Daugherty disclosed to Harding that Charles Forbes, director of the Veterans Bureau, had been illegally selling government medical supplies to private contractors. Harding allowed him to leave the country to escape prosecution. Shortly thereafter Charles Cranmer, general counsel of the Veterans Bureau, committed suicide. Ten weeks later Jesse Smith, Daugherty's private secretary, also committed suicide—one day after a long conversation with Harding in the White House. Rumours had been circulating that Smith and a group known as the "Ohio Gang" had been profiting from a variety of corrupt activities.

By the spring of 1923, Harding was visibly distraught at what he regarded as the betrayal of his friends who were taking advantage of his kindliness and lax administration. He sought escape from Washington in mid-June by taking a trip to Alaska with his wife and a large entourage. On his way home at the end of July, he complained of abdominal pain, but seemed to rally as he rested at a San Francisco hotel. On the evening of August 2, however, as his wife read to him from a magazine, Harding suddenly died from either a heart attack or stroke.

Senate investigations after Harding's death uncovered Forbes's illegal financial dealings at the Veterans Bureau and pointed to Daugherty's collusion with the Ohio Gang. Far more serious was the unfolding of the Teapot Dome Scandal. In 1921 Interior Secretary Albert Fall had persuaded Harding to transfer authority over two of the nation's most important oil reserves—Elk Hills in California and Teapot Dome in Wyoming—from the Navy Department to the Department of the Interior. Fall then leased these reserves to private oil companies, netting for himself several hundreds of thousands of dollars in gifts and loans. Fall and Forbes later received jail sentences for their crimes; Daugherty twice went on trial, the first resulting in a hung jury and the second in a not guilty verdict.

Harding was never personally implicated in the scandals, but he was aware of the actions of Forbes, Smith, and the Ohio Gang and failed to bring their corruption to light. By the mid-1920s, the public began to regard Harding as a man who simply did not measure up to the responsibilities of his high office.

CALVIN COOLIDGE

(b. July 4, 1872, Plymouth, Vt.—d. Jan. 5, 1933, Northampton, Mass.)

Calvin Coolidge was the 30th president of the United States (1923–29). Coolidge acceded to the presidency after the death in office of Warren G. Harding, just as the Harding scandals were coming to light. He restored integrity to the executive branch of the federal government while continuing the conservative pro-business policies of his predecessor.

Coolidge was the only son of John Calvin Coolidge and Victoria Moor Coolidge. His father, whose forebears had immigrated to America about 1630, was a storekeeper who instilled in his son the New England Puritan virtues—honesty, industry, thrift, taciturnity, and piety—while his mother cultivated in him a love of nature and books. A graduate of Amherst College, Coolidge began practicing law in 1897. In 1905 he married Grace Anna Goodhue, a teacher in the Clarke Institute for the Deaf, with whom he had two sons.

A Republican, Coolidge entered politics as a city councilman in Northampton, Mass., in 1898. He was elected mayor of Northampton in 1909 and then served in the Massachusetts state government as senator (1911–15) and lieutenant governor (1915–18). Elected governor in 1918, Coolidge captured national attention the following year when he called out the state guard to quell violence and disorder resulting from a strike by the Boston police.

Calvin Coolidge. Encyclopædia Britannica, Inc.

Coolidge's strong stand against the Boston police at a time when many Americans viewed organized labour as too radical catapulted him onto the Republican Party's ticket in 1920 as Harding's vice presidential running mate. The personality of the taciturn Coolidge could not have provided a greater contrast to that of the gregarious Harding. In terms of policy, however, Harding and Coolidge were nearly identical. Both were members of the Old Guard Republicans, that conservative segment of the party that had remained with Pres. William Howard Taft in 1912 when Theodore Roosevelt left to form the Bull Moose Party. Harding and Coolidge achieved the greatest popular vote margin in presidential elections to that time, crushing the Democratic ticket of James Cox and Franklin Delano Roosevelt by 60 to 34 percent. The electoral vote was equally one-sided: 404 to 127.

Acceding to the presidency upon Harding's unexpected death (Aug. 2, 1923), Coolidge took the oath of office from his father, a notary public, by the light of a kerosene lamp at 2:47 AM on August 3 at the family home in Plymouth, Vt. Inheriting an administration mired in scandal, Coolidge skillfully rooted out the perpetrators and restored integrity to the executive branch. A model of personal rectitude himself, Coolidge convinced the American people that the presidency was once again in the hands of someone they could trust.

At the Republican convention in 1924 Coolidge was nominated virtually without opposition. He won a landslide victory over conservative Democrat John W. Davis and Progressive Party candidate Robert La Follette, gaining about 54 percent of the popular vote to Davis's 29 percent and La Follette's nearly 17 percent; in the electoral college Coolidge received 382 votes to Davis's 136 and La Follette's 13.

Coolidge captured the prevailing sentiment of the American people in the 1920s when he said, "The chief business of the American people is business." The essence of the Coolidge presidency was its noninterference in and bolstering of American business and industry. Most Americans, identifying their own prosperity with the growth of corporate profits, welcomed this reversal of progressive reforms.

Reflecting its focus on internal economic growth, the Coolidge administration showed little interest in events

outside the nation's borders. Coolidge adamantly opposed
U.S. membership in the League of Nations, though he did
increase unofficial American involvement in the international organization. Ironically for such an inward-looking
administration, two of its members received the Nobel
Prize for Peace: Vice Pres. Charles G. Dawes in 1925 for
his program to help Germany meet its war debt obligations, and Secretary of State Frank B. Kellogg in 1929 for
his role in negotiating the Kellogg-Briand Pact, a multinational agreement renouncing war as an instrument of
national policy.

In 1928, announcing, "I do not choose to run," Coolidge
turned his back on what surely would have been another
election victory and instead retired to Northampton. He
died of a heart attack a little less than four years later.

HERBERT HOOVER

(b. Aug. 10, 1874, West Branch, Iowa—d. Oct. 20, 1964,
New York, N.Y.)

Herbert Hoover was the 31st president of the United
States (1929–33). Hoover's reputation as a humanitarian—earned during and after World War I as he rescued
millions of Europeans from starvation—faded from public consciousness when his administration proved unable
to alleviate widespread joblessness, homelessness, and
hunger in his own country during the early years of the
Great Depression.

Hoover was the son of Jesse and Hulda Hoover. His
father was a blacksmith and farm-implement dealer and
his mother an extremely pious woman who eventually
adopted Quakerism. When the young Hoover was six
years old his father died from heart disease; his mother
died of pneumonia three years later. The orphaned
Herbert then left Iowa for Oregon, where he grew up in

the home of his maternal uncle and aunt. A member of the first class at Stanford University (1895), Hoover graduated with a degree in geology and became a mining engineer, working on a wide variety of projects on four continents and displaying exceptional business acumen. Within two decades of leaving Stanford, he had amassed a personal net worth of about $4 million.

Caught in China during the Boxer Rebellion (1900), Hoover organized relief for trapped foreigners. He drew on his China experience in 1914, when he helped Americans stranded in Europe at the outbreak of World War I. For the next three years,

Herbert Hoover. Library of Congress, Washington, D.C. (digital. id. cph.3c21855)

he headed the Commission for Relief in Belgium, overseeing what he called "the greatest charity the world has ever seen" and exhibiting impressive executive ability in helping to procure food for some nine million people whose country had been overrun by the German army. So skilled was Hoover's performance that Pres. Woodrow Wilson appointed him U.S. food administrator for the duration of the war. His success in that post led to his appointment as the American Relief Administration, which sent shiploads of food and other life-sustaining supplies to war-ravaged Europe.

In 1921 President-elect Warren G. Harding chose Hoover to serve as secretary of commerce. In the Harding cabinet Hoover proved to be one of the few progressive voices in a Republican administration that generally saw little role for government other than assisting the growth of business. Continuing as commerce secretary under Pres. Calvin Coolidge, Hoover spearheaded efforts that ultimately led to the construction of Hoover Dam and the St. Lawrence Seaway.

When Coolidge decided not to run for another term in 1928, Hoover received the Republican presidential nomination, despite the objections of conservatives opposed to his departure from the party's traditional laissez-faire philosophy. In the ensuing campaign Hoover ran against New York Governor Alfred E. Smith in a contest that focused on Prohibition and religion. Smith opposed Prohibition, while Hoover remained equivocal. Smith's Roman Catholicism proved a liability, but the election outcome chiefly reflected the close identification in the public mind of the Republican Party with the enormous prosperity of the 1920s. Hoover captured 21 million votes to Smith's 15 million, 444 electoral votes to his Democratic opponent's 87.

One year later the Stock Market Crash of 1929 plunged the country into the worst economic collapse in its history. Pres. Hoover parted ways with those leaders of the Republican Party—including Secretary of the Treasury Andrew Mellon—who believed there was nothing for the government to do but wait for the next phase of the business cycle. Hoover took prompt action. He called business leaders to the White House to urge them not to lay off workers or cut wages. He urged state and local governments to join private charities in caring for Americans made destitute by the Depression. He asked Congress to appropriate money for public-works projects to expand government employment. In 1931 he backed the creation of the Reconstruction Finance Corporation (RFC, established 1932), a large-scale lending institution

intended to help banks and industries and thereby promote a general recovery.

The nation's economy failed to respond to Hoover's
initiatives. As the Depression worsened, banks and other
businesses collapsed and poverty stalked the land, and
the American people began to blame Hoover for the
calamity. The homeless began calling their shantytowns
"Hoovervilles."

Hoover made some critical mistakes in his handling of
the Depression. In 1930, for example, he signed into law
(against the advice of many leading economists) the
Smoot-Hawley Tariff Act, which raised many import duties
so high that foreign countries could not sell goods in the
United States; as a result, those countries could not—or
would not—purchase American goods at a time when the
need for sales abroad had never been greater.

More problems arose in 1932, when Hoover authorized
Gen. Douglas MacArthur to evict from Washington, D.C.,
the Bonus Army, a group of World War I veterans who had
camped in the nation's capital to pressure Congress into
awarding a promised bonus many years in advance of the
scheduled payout date. The result was a public relations
nightmare for the president.

By the 1932 presidential campaign, Hoover was blam-
ing the Depression on events abroad and predicting that
election of his Democratic challenger, Franklin Delano
Roosevelt, would only intensify the disaster. The electorate obviously thought differently, as Roosevelt captured
nearly 23 million votes (and 472 electoral votes) to Hoover's
slightly less than 16 million (59 electoral votes). When he
left the White House on March 4, 1933, Hoover was a
defeated and embittered man.

Hoover and his wife—the former Lou Henry, also a
Stanford-trained geologist—moved first to Palo Alto, Calif.,

and then to New York City, where they took up residence
at the Waldorf Astoria Hotel. For the next 30 years, Hoover
was closely identified with the most conservative elements
in the Republican Party, condemning what he regarded as
the radicalism of the New Deal and opposing Roosevelt's
attempts to take a more active role against German and
Japanese aggression. His last major activity was heading
the Hoover Commission, under presidents Harry Truman
and Dwight D. Eisenhower, which aimed at streamlining
the federal bureaucracy. The research-oriented Hoover
Institution on War, Revolution, and Peace at Stanford
University—founded in 1919 as the Hoover War Collection,
a library on World War I—is named in his honour.

FRANKLIN D. ROOSEVELT

(b. Jan. 30, 1882, Hyde Park, N.Y.—d. April 12, 1945,
Warm Springs, Ga.)

Franklin Delano Roosevelt, also known as FDR, was
the 32nd president of the United States (1933–45). The
only president elected to the office four times, Roosevelt
led the United States through two of the greatest crises of
the 20th century: the Great Depression and World War
II. In so doing, he greatly expanded the powers of the federal government through a series of programs and reforms
known as the New Deal, and served as the principal architect of the successful effort to rid the world of German
National Socialism and Japanese militarism.

EARLY LIFE

Roosevelt was the only child of James and Sara Delano
Roosevelt. Young Roosevelt was educated privately at home
until age 14, when he entered Groton Preparatory School
in Groton, Mass.

In 1900 Roosevelt entered Harvard University, where he spent most of his time on extracurricular activities and a strenuous social life; his academic record was undistinguished. It was during his Harvard years that he fell under the spell of his fifth cousin, Pres. Theodore Roosevelt, the progressive champion who advocated a vastly increased role for the government in the nation's economy. It was also during this time that he fell in love with Theodore Roosevelt's niece, Eleanor Roosevelt, who was then active in charitable work for the poor in New York City. The distant cousins became engaged during Roosevelt's final year at Harvard and were married on March 17, 1905.

Roosevelt attended Columbia University Law School but was not much interested in his studies. After passing the New York bar exam, he went to work as a clerk for the distinguished Wall Street firm of Carter, Ledyard, and Milburn, but he displayed the same attitude of indifference toward the legal profession as he had toward his education.

EARLY POLITICAL ACTIVITIES

Inspired by his cousin Theodore, Roosevelt looked for an opportunity to launch a career in politics. That opportunity came in 1910, when Democratic leaders of Dutchess county, New York, persuaded him to undertake an apparently futile attempt to win a seat in the state senate. Roosevelt campaigned strenuously and won.

In the New York Senate Roosevelt learned much of the give-and-take of politics, and came to champion the full program of progressive reform. In 1912 Roosevelt was reelected to the state senate, despite an attack of typhoid fever that prevented him from making public appearances during the campaign.

Having worked for the successful presidential campaign of Woodrow Wilson, Roosevelt was appointed assistant secretary of the navy in March 1913. After war broke out in Europe in 1914, Roosevelt became a vehement advocate of military preparedness, and following U.S. entry into the war in 1917, built a reputation as an effective administrator. In the summer of 1918 he made an extended tour of naval bases and battlefields overseas. Upon his return, Eleanor Roosevelt discovered that her husband had been romantically involved with her social secretary, Lucy Mercer. She offered him a divorce; he refused and promised never to see Mercer again (a promise he would break in the 1940s). Although the Roosevelts agreed to remain together, their relationship ceased to be an intimate one.

PARALYSIS TO PRESIDENCY

At the 1920 Democratic convention Roosevelt won the nomination for vice president on a ticket with presidential nominee James M. Cox. Roosevelt campaigned vigorously on behalf of American entry into the League of Nations, but the Democrats lost in a landslide to the Republican ticket of Warren G. Harding and Calvin Coolidge.

In August 1921, while on vacation at Campobello Island, New Brunswick, Canada, Roosevelt's life was transformed when he was stricken with poliomyelitis. He suffered intensely, and for some time he was almost completely paralyzed. Unable to pursue an active political career as he recovered, Roosevelt depended on his wife to keep his name alive in Democratic circles. Although initially very shy, Eleanor Roosevelt became an effective public speaker and an adroit political analyst. As a result of her speaking engagements all over New York State, Roosevelt never faded entirely from the political scene, despite what seemed to be a career-ending affliction.

In 1928 he ran for governor of New York, winning the election by 25,000 votes despite the fact that the state went

Republican in the presidential election, contributing to Herbert Hoover's landslide victory over Alfred E. Smith.

During his first term, Gov. Roosevelt concentrated on tax relief for farmers and cheaper public utilities for consumers. The appeal of his programs, particularly in upstate New York, led to his reelection in 1930 by 725,000 votes. As the Depression worsened during his second term, Roosevelt moved farther to the political left, mobilizing the state government to provide relief and to aid in economic recovery. His aggressive approach to the economic problems of his state, along with his overwhelming electoral victory in 1930, boosted Roosevelt into the front ranks of contenders for the Democratic presidential nomination in 1932.

On the fourth ballot at the 1932 Democratic convention, Roosevelt captured the required two-thirds vote to win the presidential nomination. John Nance Garner received the vice presidential nomination. In his speech before the delegates, he said, "I pledge you, I pledge myself, to a new deal for the American people."

With the Depression the only issue of consequence in the presidential campaign of 1932, the American people had a choice between the apparently unsuccessful policies of the incumbent Hoover and the vaguely defined New Deal program presented by Roosevelt. While Roosevelt avoided specifics, he made clear that his program for economic recovery would make extensive use of the power of the federal government. On election day, Roosevelt received nearly 23 million popular votes to Hoover's nearly 16 million; the electoral vote was 472 to 59.

In the four months between the election and Roosevelt's inauguration the economy continued to decline. By inauguration day—March 4, 1933—most banks had shut down, industrial production had fallen to just 56 percent of its 1929 level, at least 13 million wage earners were unemployed, and farmers were in desperate straits.

THE FIRST TERM

In his inaugural address Roosevelt promised prompt, decisive action, conveying some of his own unshakable self-confidence to millions of Americans listening on radios throughout the land. "This great nation will endure as it has endured, will revive and prosper," he asserted, adding, "the only thing we have to fear is fear itself."

"THE HUNDRED DAYS"

Roosevelt followed up on his promise of prompt action with "The Hundred Days"—the first phase of the New Deal, in which his administration presented Congress with a broad array of measures intended to achieve economic recovery, provide relief to the millions of poor and unemployed, and reform aspects of the economy that Roosevelt believed had caused the collapse.

His first step was to order all banks closed until Congress, meeting in special session on March 9, could pass legislation allowing banks in sound condition to reopen; this "bank holiday," as Roosevelt euphemistically called it, was intended to end depositors' runs, which were threatening to destroy the nation's entire banking system. When banks finally did reopen, the much-feared runs did not materialize.

Two key recovery measures of The Hundred Days were the Agricultural Adjustment Act (AAA) and the National Industrial Recovery Act (NIRA). The AAA established the Agricultural Adjustment Administration, which was charged with increasing prices of agricultural commodities and expanding the proportion of national income going to farmers. Its strategy was to grant subsidies to producers of seven basic commodities in return for reduced production, thereby reducing the surpluses that kept commodity prices low. The AAA program gradually succeeded in raising farmers' incomes, though it was not until 1941 that farm income reached even the inadequate level of 1929.

The NIRA was a two-part program. One part consisted of a $3.3-billion appropriation for public works, to be spent by the Public Works Administration (PWA).

The other part of the NIRA was the National Recovery Administration (NRA), whose task was to establish and administer industrywide codes that prohibited unfair trade practices, set minimum wages and maximum hours, guaranteed workers the right to bargain collectively, and imposed controls on prices and production. In May 1935 the Supreme Court invalidated the NRA.

Another important recovery measure was the Tennessee Valley Authority (TVA), a public corporation created in 1933 to build dams and hydroelectric power plants and to improve navigation and flood control in the vast Tennessee River basin. The constitutionality of the agency was challenged immediately after its establishment but was upheld by the Supreme Court in 1936.

The Hundred Days also included relief and reform measures, the former referring to short-term payments to individuals to alleviate hardship, the latter to long-range programs aimed at eliminating economic abuses. The Civilian Conservation Corps (CCC) employed hundreds of thousands of young men in reforestation and flood-control work, and the Home Owners' Refinancing Act provided mortgage relief for millions of unemployed Americans in danger of losing their homes. The Federal Securities Act provided government oversight of stock trading, and the Glass-Steagall Banking Reform Act prohibited commercial banks from making risky investments and established the Federal Deposit Insurance Corporation (FDIC) to protect depositors' accounts.

THE "SECOND NEW DEAL"

By 1935 Roosevelt knew he had to do more. Although the economy had begun to rise from its nadir during the winter of 1932–33, it was still far below its level before the Stock Market Crash of 1929. Roosevelt asked Congress to pass additional New Deal legislation—sometimes called the "Second New Deal"—in 1935, the key measures of which were the Social Security Act, the Works Progress Administration (WPA), and the Wagner Act. The Social Security Act for the first time established an economic "safety net" for all Americans, providing unemployment and disability insurance and old-age pensions. The WPA aimed to provide the unemployed with useful work that would help to maintain their skills and bolster their self-respect. The Wagner Act (officially the National Labor Relations Act) reestablished labour's right to bargain collectively (which had been eliminated when the Supreme Court had invalidated the NRA), and created the National Labor Relations Board (NLRB) to adjudicate labour disputes.

THE SECOND TERM

Roosevelt ran for reelection in 1936 with the firm support of farmers, labourers, and the poor. He faced the equally firm opposition of conservatives, but the epithets hurled at him from the right merely helped to unify his following. The Republican nominee, Gov. Alfred M. Landon of Kansas, a moderate, could do little to stem the Roosevelt tide. Landon received fewer than 17 million votes to Roosevelt's nearly 28 million; Roosevelt carried every state except Maine and Vermont.

SUPREME COURT FIGHT

Roosevelt was determined to push forward with further New Deal reforms. With large Democratic majorities in both houses of Congress, there remained only one obstacle to his objectives: the Supreme Court. During Roosevelt's first term, the court, which consisted entirely of pre-Roosevelt appointees, had invalidated several key New Deal measures. To make the court more supportive of reform legislation, Roosevelt proposed a reorganization plan that would have allowed him to appoint one new justice for every sitting justice aged 70 years or older. Widely viewed as a court-packing scheme (even by Roosevelt's supporters), the reorganization bill was eventually voted down, handing Roosevelt his first major legislative defeat.

END OF THE NEW DEAL

By 1937 the economy had recovered substantially, and Roosevelt, seeing an opportunity to return to a balanced budget, drastically curtailed government spending. The result was a sharp recession, during which the economy began plummeting toward 1932 levels. Chastened by the recession, Roosevelt now began to pay more attention to advisers who counseled deficit spending as the best way to counter the depression. Late in 1937 he backed another massive government spending program, and by the middle of 1938 the crisis had passed. By 1938, however, the New Deal was drawing to a close. In the congressional elections that year the Republicans gained 80 seats in the House and 7 in the Senate, resulting in an alliance of Republicans and conservative Democrats that blocked any further reform legislation.

FOREIGN POLICY

In the 1930s Congress was dominated by isolationists who believed that American entry into World War I had been mistaken; they were determined to prevent the United States from being drawn into another European war. Beginning with the Neutrality Act of 1935, Congress passed a series of laws designed to minimize American involvement with belligerent nations. Roosevelt accepted the neutrality laws but at the same time warned Americans of the danger of remaining isolated from a world increasingly menaced by the dictatorial regimes in Germany, Italy, and Japan.

When World War II broke out in Europe in September 1939, Roosevelt called Congress into special session to revise the neutrality acts to permit belligerents—i.e., Britain and France—to buy American arms on a "cash-and-carry" basis. When France fell to the Germans in the spring and early summer of 1940, and Britain was left alone to face the Nazi war machine, Roosevelt convinced Congress to intensify defense preparations and to support Britain with "all aid short of war." In the fall of that year Roosevelt sent 50 older destroyers to Britain, which feared an imminent German invasion, in exchange for eight naval bases.

THE THIRD AND FOURTH TERMS

The swap of ships for bases took place during the 1940 presidential election campaign. Earlier in the year the Democrats had nominated Roosevelt for a third term, even though his election would break the two-term tradition honoured since the presidency of George Washington. The Republican nominee, Wendell L. Willkie, represented a departure from the isolationist-dominated Republican Party, and the two candidates agreed on most foreign-policy issues, including increased military aid to Britain. On election day, Roosevelt defeated Willkie soundly—by 27 million to 22 million popular votes—though his margin of victory was less than it had been in 1932 and 1936.

In March 1941, Roosevelt obtained passage of the Lend-Lease Act, which enabled the United States to accept noncash payment for military and other aid to Britain and its allies. Later that year he authorized the United States Navy to provide protection for lend-lease shipments, and in the fall he instructed the navy to "shoot on sight" at German submarines. All these actions moved the United States closer to actual belligerency with Germany.

In August 1941 Roosevelt and British Prime Minister Winston Churchill issued a joint statement, the Atlantic Charter, in which they pledged their countries to the goal of achieving "the final destruction of the Nazi tyranny." Reminiscent of the Four Freedoms that Roosevelt outlined in his annual message to Congress in January 1941—freedom of speech and expression, the freedom of every person to worship God in his own way, freedom from want, and freedom from fear—the statement affirmed a commitment to national self-determination, freedom of the seas, freedom from want and fear, greater economic opportunities, and disarmament of all aggressor nations.

ATTACK ON PEARL HARBOR

Yet it was in the Pacific rather than the Atlantic that war came to the United States. When Japan joined the Axis powers of Germany and Italy, Roosevelt began to restrict exports to Japan of supplies essential to making war. Throughout 1941, Japan negotiated with the United States, seeking restoration of trade in those supplies, particularly petroleum products. When the negotiations failed to produce agreement, Japanese military leaders began to plan an attack on the United States.

By the end of November, Roosevelt knew that an attack was imminent (the United States had broken the Japanese code), but was uncertain where it would take place. To his great surprise, the Japanese bombed Pearl

Harbor, Hawaii, on Dec. 7, 1941, destroying nearly the entire U.S. Pacific fleet and hundreds of airplanes and killing about 2,500 military personnel and civilians. On December 8, at Roosevelt's request, Congress declared war on Japan; on December 11 Germany and Italy declared war on the United States. Full economic recovery, which had resisted Roosevelt's efforts throughout the 1930s, suddenly came about as a consequence of massive government spending on war production in the early 1940s.

RELATIONS WITH THE ALLIES

From the start of American involvement in World War II, Roosevelt took the lead in establishing a grand alliance

(From left, seated) *Canadian Prime Minister W.L. Mackenzie King, U.S. President Franklin D. Roosevelt, and British Prime Minister Winston Churchill at an Allied conference in Quebec, 1943.* Encyclopædia Britannica, Inc.

among all countries fighting the Axis powers. Relations with the Soviet Union, however, posed a difficult problem for Roosevelt because the Soviet Union seldom divulged its military plans or acted in coordination with its Western allies. Roosevelt, Joseph Stalin, and Churchill seemed to get along well when they met at Tehrān in November 1943. At the Yalta Conference in the Crimea, U.S.S.R., in February 1945, Roosevelt secured Stalin's commitment to enter the war against Japan soon after Germany's surrender and to establish democratic governments in the nations of eastern Europe occupied by Soviet troops. Stalin kept his pledge concerning Japan but proceeded to impose Soviet satellite governments throughout eastern Europe.

DECLINING HEALTH AND DEATH

Despite suffering from advanced arteriosclerosis for more than a year before the Yalta Conference, Roosevelt ran for a fourth term in 1944 against Gov. Thomas E. Dewey of New York, winning the election by a popular vote of 25 million to 22 million and an electoral college vote of 432 to 99. Early in April 1945 he traveled to his cottage in Warm Springs, Ga., to rest. On the afternoon of April 12, while sitting for a portrait, he suffered a massive cerebral hemorrhage and died a few hours later.

HARRY S. TRUMAN

(b. May 8, 1884, Lamar, Mo. — d. Dec. 26, 1972, Kansas City)

Harry S. Truman was the 33rd president of the United States (1945–53). He led his nation through the final stages of World War II and through the early years of the Cold War, vigorously opposing Soviet expansionism in Europe and sending U.S. forces to turn back a communist invasion of South Korea.

EARLY LIFE AND CAREER

Truman was the eldest of three children of John A. and
Martha E. Truman; his father was a mule trader and farmer.
After graduating from high school in 1901 in Independence,
Mo., he went to work as a bank clerk in Kansas City. In
1906 he moved to the family farm near Grandview, and
took over the farm management after his father's death in
1914. When the United States entered World War I in 1917,
Truman—nearly 33 years old and with two tours in the
National Guard (1905–11) behind him—immediately vol-
unteered. He was sent overseas a year later and served in
France as the captain of a field artillery unit that saw action
at St. Mihiel and the Meuse-Argonne.

Returning to the United States in 1919, Truman married Elizabeth Wallace, known as Bess, whom he had
known since childhood. With the backing of Thomas
Pendergast, Democratic boss of Kansas City, Truman
launched his political career in 1922, running successfully
for county judge. He lost his bid for reelection in 1924, but
he was elected presiding judge of the county court in 1926,
serving two four-year terms.

In 1934 Pendergast offered Truman the chance to run in
the Democratic primary for a seat in the U.S. Senate, and
Truman quickly accepted. He won the primary with a
40,000-vote plurality, assuring his election in solidly Democratic Missouri. In January 1935 Truman was sworn in as
Missouri's junior senator by Vice Pres. John Nance Garner.

Following a tough Democratic primary victory in 1940,
he won a second term in the Senate. It was during this
term that he gained national recognition for leading an
investigation into fraud and waste in the U.S. military.

Respected by his Senate colleagues and admired by the
public at large, Truman was selected to run as Franklin

Delano Roosevelt's vice president on the 1944 Democratic ticket, replacing Henry A. Wallace. The Roosevelt-Truman ticket garnered 53 percent of the vote to 46 percent for their Republican rivals, and Truman took the oath of office as vice president on Jan. 20, 1945. His term lasted just 82 days, however, during which time he met with the president only twice. Roosevelt, who apparently did not realize how ill he was, made little effort to inform Truman about the administration's programs and plans, nor did he prepare Truman for dealing with the heavy responsibilities that were about to devolve upon him.

Harry S. Truman, c. 1950.
Library of Congress/Hulton Archive/Getty Images

SUCCESSION TO THE PRESIDENCY

Roosevelt's sudden death on April 12, 1945, left Truman and the public in shock. Truman began his presidency with great energy, making final arrangements for the San Francisco meeting to draft a charter for the United Nations, helping to arrange Germany's unconditional surrender on May 8, and traveling to Potsdam in July for a meeting with Allied leaders to discuss the fate of postwar Germany. While in Potsdam Truman received word of the successful test of an atomic bomb at Los Alamos, N.M., and it was from Potsdam that Truman sent an ultimatum to Japan to surrender or face "utter devastation." When Japan did not surrender and his advisers estimated that up to 500,000

Americans might be killed in an invasion of Japan, Truman authorized the dropping of atomic bombs on the cities of Hiroshima (August 6) and Nagasaki (August 9), which killed more than 100,000 men, women, and children. Japan surrendered August 14, the Pacific war ending officially on Sept. 2, 1945.

Scarcely had the guns of World War II been silenced than Truman faced the threat of Soviet expansionism in eastern Europe. In 1947 Truman put the world on notice through his Truman Doctrine that the United States would oppose communist aggression everywhere; specifically, he called for economic aid to Greece and Turkey to help those countries resist communist takeover. Later in 1947, the president backed Secretary of State George Marshall's strategy for undercutting communism's appeal in western Europe by sending enormous amounts of financial aid (ultimately about $13 billion) to rebuild devastated European economies.

WINNING A SECOND TERM

In 1948 Truman launched a cross-country whistle-stop campaign for the presidency, blasting the "do-nothing, good-for-nothing Republican Congress." As he hammered away at Republican support for the antilabour Taft-Hartley Act (passed over Truman's veto) and other conservative policies, crowds responded with "Give 'em hell, Harry!" Truman defeated the Republican candidate Thomas E. Dewey by a comfortable margin, 49 percent to 45 percent.

Energized by his victory, Truman presented his program for domestic reform in 1949. The Fair Deal included proposals for expanded public housing, increased aid to education, a higher minimum wage, federal protection for civil rights, and national health insurance. Despite

Democratic majorities in the House and Senate, most Fair Deal proposals either failed to gain legislative majorities or passed in much weakened form.

In 1950 Truman led the United States into a collective security agreement with noncommunist European nations—the North Atlantic Treaty Organization (NATO)—to resist Soviet expansionism. In 1950 he authorized development of the hydrogen bomb in order to maintain an arms lead over the Soviets, who by then had successfully tested a nuclear bomb. By the end of the decade, the United States and the Soviet Union had embarked on an arms race of potentially world-destroying dimensions.

OUTBREAK OF THE KOREAN WAR

In June 1950 military forces of communist North Korea suddenly plunged southward across the 38th parallel boundary in an attempt to seize noncommunist South Korea. Determined to intervene, Truman did not ask Congress for a declaration of war; instead, he sent to South Korea, with UN sanction, U.S. forces under Gen. Douglas MacArthur to repel the invasion. Ill-prepared for combat, the Americans were pushed back to the southern tip of the Korean peninsula before MacArthur's Inchon offensive drove the communists north of the 38th parallel. South Korea was liberated, but MacArthur wanted a victory over the communists. When MacArthur insisted on extending the war to China and using nuclear weapons to defeat the communists, Truman removed him from command—a courageous assertion of civilian control over the military. The war, however, dragged on inconclusively past the end of Truman's presidency, eventually claiming the lives of more than 33,000 Americans.

As the nation's second "Red Scare" (the fear that communists had infiltrated key positions in government and society) took hold in the late 1940s and early '50s, Truman's popularity began to plummet. In March 1952 he announced he was not going to run for reelection. By the time he left the White House in January 1953, his approval rating was just 31 percent; it had peaked at 87 percent in July 1945.

His life in retirement was modest but active. In the mid-1960s his health began to decline, and he died on the morning of Dec. 26, 1972.

DWIGHT D. EISENHOWER

(b. Oct. 14, 1890, Denison, Texas—d. March 28, 1969, Washington, D.C.)

D wight David Eisenhower was the 34th president of the United States (1953–61) and supreme commander of the Allied forces in western Europe during World War II.

EARLY CAREER

Eisenhower was the third of seven sons of David Jacob and Ida Elizabeth (Stover) Eisenhower. In the spring of 1891 the Eisenhowers left Denison, Texas, and returned to Abilene, Kan., where their forebears had settled as part of a Mennonite colony.

"Ike," as Dwight was called, graduated from Abilene High School in 1909, worked for more than a year to support a brother's college education, and then entered the U.S. Military Academy at West Point, N.Y. In the remarkable class of 1915—which was to produce 59 generals—he ranked 61st academically and 125th in discipline out of the total of 164 graduates.

Commissioned a second lieutenant, he was sent to San Antonio, Texas, where he met Mamie Geneva Doud, daughter of a successful Denver, Colo., meat packer. They were married in 1916 and had two sons.

During World War I, Eisenhower commanded a tank training centre, was promoted to captain, and received the Distinguished Service Medal. Eisenhower attended the army's Command and General Staff School at Fort Leavenworth, Kan., and two years later graduated from the Army War College. He became an aide to Army Chief of Staff Gen. Douglas MacArthur in 1933. Gradually promoted through the ranks, he was eventually made chief of staff of the Third Army, and soon won the attention of Army Chief of Staff Gen. George C. Marshall for his role in planning war games involving almost 500,000 troops.

SUPREME COMMANDER

When the United States entered World War II in December 1941, Marshall appointed Eisenhower to the army's war plans division in Washington, D.C., where he prepared strategy for an Allied invasion of Europe. In June 1942 Marshall selected him to be commander of U.S. troops in Europe.

Eisenhower was promoted to lieutenant general in July 1942 and named to head Operation Torch, the Allied invasion of French North Africa, which was successfully completed in May 1943. A full general since that February,

Brigadier General Dwight D. Eisenhower, c. 1941–42. Encyclopædia Britannica, Inc.

Eisenhower then directed the amphibious assault of Sicily and the Italian mainland, which resulted in the fall of Rome on June 4, 1944.

Appointed supreme commander of the Allied Expeditionary Force, Eisenhower gave the order to launch the Normandy Invasion on June 6, 1944. On August 25 Paris was liberated, and Germany surrendered on May 7, 1945, ending the war in Europe. In the meantime, in December 1944, Eisenhower had been made a five-star general.

Eisenhower was given a hero's welcome upon returning to the United States for a visit in June 1945. In May 1948 he left active duty the most popular and respected soldier in the United States and became president of Columbia University in New York City.

In 1950 Pres. Truman asked him to become supreme commander of the North Atlantic Treaty Organization (NATO), and in early 1951 he flew to Paris to assume his new position, which he held for the next 15 months.

FIRST TERM AS PRESIDENT

As early as 1943 Eisenhower was mentioned as a possible presidential candidate. As the campaign of 1952 neared, Eisenhower, a Republican, decided to run. Retiring from the army in June 1952, he began to campaign actively. At the party convention in July, he won the nomination on the first ballot. His running mate was Sen. Richard M. Nixon of California. The Democrats nominated Gov. Adlai E. Stevenson of Illinois for president and Sen. John Sparkman of Alabama for vice president. The Eisenhower-Nixon ticket won handily, carrying 39 states, winning the electoral vote 442 to 89, and collecting more than 33 million popular votes. The Republican Party won control of Congress by a slim margin but lost both houses two years later.

Dwight D. Eisenhower (second from right), *the Republican Party nominee for U.S. president, with running mate Richard Nixon* (left, holding daughter Julie) *at campaign headquarters in Washington, D.C., September 10, 1952.* Encyclopædia Britannica, Inc.

Eisenhower's domestic program, which came to be labeled "modern Republicanism," called for reduced taxes, balanced budgets, a decrease in government control over the economy, and the return of certain federal responsibilities to the states. But there was no sharp break with policies inherited from previous Democratic administrations.

The right wing of the Republican Party clashed with the president more often than the Democrats did during his first term. By far the largest challenge came from Sen. Joseph R. McCarthy of Wisconsin. Although Eisenhower refused to publicly condemn McCarthy's charges of

communist influence within the government, hundreds of
federal employees were fired under his expanded loyalty-
security program, and with his approval Congress passed a
law designed to outlaw the American Communist Party.

Foreign affairs drew much of Eisenhower's attention.
He and his secretary of state, John Foster Dulles, constructed collective defense agreements and threatened
the Soviet Union with "massive retaliatory power" in order
to check the spread of communism. Another strategy was
unknown to the public at the time but was heavily criticized in later years: the use of the Central Intelligence
Agency in covert operations to overthrow governments in
Iran (1953) and Guatemala (1954).

Eisenhower was able to negotiate a truce for the
Korean War in July 1953. In December of that year he proposed to the United Nations that the countries of the
world pool atomic information and materials under the
auspices of an international agency. This Atoms for Peace
speech bore fruit in 1957, when 62 countries formed the
International Atomic Energy Agency.

Second Term

A heart attack in September 1955 and an operation for ileitis
in June 1956 raised considerable doubt about Eisenhower's
ability to serve a second term. But he recovered quickly,
and the Republican convention unanimously endorsed the
Eisenhower-Nixon ticket on the first ballot. The Democrats
again selected Adlai E. Stevenson and named Sen. Estes
Kefauver of Tennessee as his running mate, but Eisenhower's
great personal popularity turned the election into a landslide victory, the most one-sided race since 1936, as the
Republican ticket garnered more than 57 percent of the
popular vote and won the electoral vote 457 to 73.

The election campaign of 1956, however, had been complicated by a crisis in the Middle East over Egypt's seizure of the Suez Canal. The subsequent attack on Egypt by Great Britain, France, and Israel and the Soviet Union's support of Egypt prompted the president to go before Congress in January 1957 to urge adoption of what came to be called the Eisenhower Doctrine, a pledge to send U.S. armed forces to any Middle Eastern country requesting assistance against communist aggression.

In September 1957 Eisenhower dispatched 1,000 federal troops to Little Rock, Ark., to halt Gov. Orval E. Faubus's attempt to obstruct a federal court order integrating a high school. Significantly, the Civil Rights Act of 1957 was the first such law passed since 1875.

The administration again came under fire in the fall of 1957 for an economic recession that lasted through the following summer. For fear of fueling inflation, Eisenhower refused to lower taxes or increase federal spending to ease the slump.

Following the Soviet Union's launch of Sputnik I, the first man-made satellite to orbit the Earth, on Oct. 4, 1957, the administration quickly took steps to boost space research and provide funds to increase the study of science. The result was the creation of the National Aeronautics and Space Administration (NASA) in July 1958.

Although his administrations had a great many critics, Eisenhower himself remained extraordinarily popular. In his farewell address he offered a prescient warning against the rise and power of "the military-industrial complex," but his successors ignored him amid the perceived demands of the Cold War. When he left office, Congress restored his rank as general of the army. Eisenhower retired to his farm in Gettysburg, Pa., and devoted much of his time to his memoirs.

PRIMARY DOCUMENT: DWIGHT D. EISENHOWER: FAREWELL ADDRESS

My Fellow Americans:

Three days from now, after half a century in the service of our country, I shall lay down the responsibilities of office as, in traditional and solemn ceremony, the authority of the presidency is vested in my successor.

This evening I come to you with a message of leavetaking and farewell, and to share a few final thoughts with you, my countrymen.

We now stand ten years past the midpoint of a century that has witnessed four major wars among great nations. Three of these involved our own country. Despite these holocausts, America is today the strongest, the most influential, and most productive nation in the world. Understandably proud of this preeminence, we yet realize that America's leadership and prestige depend not merely upon our unmatched material progress, riches, and military strength but on how we use our power in the interests of world peace and human betterment.

A vital element in keeping the peace is our military establishment. Our arms must be mighty, ready for instant action, so that no potential aggressor may be tempted to risk his own destruction.

Until the latest of our world conflicts, the United States had no armaments industry. American makers of plowshares could, with time and as required, make swords as well. But now we can no longer risk emergency improvisation of national defense; we have been compelled to create a permanent armaments industry of vast proportions. Added to this, 3.5 million men and women are directly engaged in the defense establishment. We annually spend on military security more than the net income of all United States corporations.

This conjunction of an immense military establishment and a large arms industry is new in the American experience. The total influence—economic, political, even spiritual—is felt in every city, every statehouse, every office of the federal government. We recognize the imperative need for this development. Yet we must not fail to comprehend its grave implications. Our toil, resources, and livelihood are all involved; so is the very structure of our society.

In the councils of government we must guard against the acquisition of unwarranted influence, whether sought or unsought, by the military-industrial complex. The potential for the disastrous rise of misplaced power exists and will persist.

We must never let the weight of this combination endanger our liberties or democratic processes. We should take nothing for granted. Only an alert and knowledgeable citizenry can compel the proper meshing of the huge industrial and military machinery of defense with our peaceful methods and goals so that security and liberty may prosper together.

You and I, my fellow citizens, need to be strong in our faith that all nations, under God, will reach the goal of peace with justice. May we be ever unswerving in devotion to principle, confident but humble with power, diligent in pursuit of the nation's great goals.

JOHN F. KENNEDY

(b. May 29, 1917, Brookline, Mass.—d. Nov. 22, 1963, Dallas, Texas)

John Fitzgerald Kennedy, also known as JFK, was the 35th president of the United States (1961–63). As president he faced a number of foreign crises, especially in Cuba and Berlin. He was assassinated while riding in a motorcade in Dallas.

EARLY LIFE

The second of nine children, Kennedy was reared in a family that demanded intense physical and intellectual competition among the siblings, and was schooled in both the religious teachings of the Roman Catholic church and the political precepts of the Democratic Party. His father, Joseph Patrick Kennedy, had acquired a multimillion-dollar fortune in banking, bootlegging, shipbuilding, and the film industry, and as a skilled player of the stock market. His mother, Rose, was the daughter of John F. ("Honey Fitz") Fitzgerald, onetime mayor of Boston.

In the fall of 1941 Kennedy joined the U.S. Navy and two years later was sent to the South Pacific. By the time

Kennedy family photo c. 1931: (left to right) *Rosemary; Joseph, Jr.;
Kathleen; Patricia; Rose; Joseph, Sr.; Jean; Eunice; John; Robert.*
Encyclopædia Britannica, Inc.

he was discharged in 1945, his older brother, Joe, who their
father had expected would be the first Kennedy to run for
office, had been killed in the war, and the family's political
standard passed to John, who had planned to pursue an
academic or journalistic career.

John Kennedy himself had barely escaped death in
battle. Commanding a patrol torpedo (PT) boat, he was
gravely injured when a Japanese destroyer sank it in the
Solomon Islands. Marooned far behind enemy lines, he
led his men back to safety and was awarded the U.S. Navy
and Marine Corps Medal for heroism.

CONGRESSMAN AND SENATOR

Kennedy did not disappoint his family; in fact, he never
lost an election. His first opportunity came in 1946, when
he ran for Congress. In the Democratic primary he
received nearly double the vote of his nearest opponent;

in the November election he overwhelmed the Republican candidate. He was only 29.

Kennedy served three terms in the House of Representatives (1947–53) as a bread-and-butter liberal. His congressional district in Boston was a safe seat, but Kennedy was too ambitious to remain long in the House of Representatives. In 1952 he ran for the U.S. Senate against the popular incumbent, Henry Cabot Lodge, Jr. ; Kennedy defeated Lodge by 70,000 votes. Less than a year later, on Sept. 12, 1953, Kennedy married Jacqueline Lee Bouvier. Twelve years younger than Kennedy and from a socially prominent family, the beautiful "Jackie" was the perfect complement to the handsome politician; they made a glamorous couple.

Back in the Senate, Kennedy led a fight against a proposal to abolish the electoral college, crusaded for labour reform, and became increasingly committed to civil rights legislation. As a member of the Senate Committee on Foreign Relations in the late 1950s, he advocated extensive foreign aid to the emerging nations in Africa and Asia, and surprised his colleagues by calling upon France to grant Algerian independence.

During these years Kennedy's political outlook was moving leftward. Possibly because of their father's dynamic personality, the sons of Joseph Kennedy matured slowly. Gradually John's stature among Democrats grew, until he had inherited the legions that had once followed Gov. Adlai E. Stevenson of Illinois, the two-time presidential candidate who, by appealing to idealism, had transformed the Democratic Party and made Kennedy's rise possible.

PRESIDENTIAL CANDIDATE AND PRESIDENT

Kennedy had nearly become Stevenson's vice presidential running mate in 1956. Overnight he became one of the best-known political figures in the country. Already his campaign for the 1960 nomination had begun. Kennedy felt that he had to redouble his efforts because of the widespread conviction that no Roman Catholic candidate could be elected president, making his 1958 race for reelection to the Senate a test of his popularity in Massachusetts. His margin of victory was 874,608 votes — the largest ever in Massachusetts politics and the greatest of any senatorial candidate that year.

In January 1960 John F. Kennedy formally announced his presidential candidacy. His chief rivals were the senators Hubert H. Humphrey of Minnesota and Lyndon B. Johnson of Texas. Nominated on the first ballot, he balanced the Democratic ticket by choosing Johnson as his running mate. In his acceptance speech Kennedy declared, "We stand on the edge of a New Frontier." Thereafter the phrase "New Frontier" was associated with his presidential programs.

Another phrase — "the Kennedy style" — encapsulated the candidate's emerging identity. It was glamorous and elitist, an amalgam of his charisma and easy wit, his father's wealth, Jacqueline Kennedy's beauty and fashion sense (the suits and pillbox hats she wore became widely popular), the charm of their children and relatives, and the erudition of the Harvard advisers who surrounded him.

Kennedy won the general election, narrowly defeating the Republican candidate, Vice Pres. Richard M. Nixon, by a margin of less than 120,000 out of some 70,000,000 votes cast. A major factor in the campaign was a unique series of four televised debates between the two men; an estimated 85–120 million Americans watched one or more of the debates. Both men showed a firm grasp of the issues, but Kennedy's poise in front of the camera, his tony Harvard accent, and his good looks (in contrast to Nixon's "five o'clock shadow") convinced many viewers that he had won the debate. As president, Kennedy continued to exploit the new medium, sparkling in precedent-setting televised weekly press conferences.

JFK was the youngest man and first Roman Catholic ever elected to the presidency of the United States. In his memorable inaugural address, he called upon Americans "to bear the burden of a long twilight struggle ... against the common enemies of man: tyranny, poverty, disease, and war itself."

John F. Kennedy, 1961. AP

The administration's first brush with foreign affairs was a disaster. In the last year of the Eisenhower presidency, the Central Intelligence Agency (CIA) had equipped and trained a brigade of anticommunist Cuban exiles for an invasion of their homeland. The Joint Chiefs of Staff unanimously advised the new president that this force, once ashore, would spark a general uprising against the Cuban leader, Fidel Castro. But the April 1961 Bay of Pigs invasion was a fiasco; every man on the beachhead was either killed or captured. Kennedy assumed "sole responsibility" for the setback.

The Soviet premier, Nikita Khrushchev, thought he had taken the young president's measure when the two leaders met in Vienna in June 1961. Khrushchev ordered a wall built between East and West Berlin and threatened to sign a separate peace treaty with East Germany. The president activated National Guard and reserve units, and Khrushchev backed down on his separate peace threat.

PRIMARY DOCUMENT: JOHN F. KENNEDY: INAUGURAL ADDRESS

Vice President Johnson, Mr. Speaker, Mr. Chief Justice, President Eisenhower, Vice President Nixon, President Truman, reverend clergy, fellow citizens, we observe today not a victory of party, but a celebration of freedom—symbolizing an end, as well as a beginning—signifying renewal, as well as change. For I have sworn before you and Almighty God the same solemn oath our forebears prescribed nearly a century and three quarters ago.

Let every nation know, whether it wishes us well or ill, that we shall pay any price, bear any burden, meet any hardship, support any friend, oppose any foe, in order to assure the survival and the success of liberty.

This much we pledge—and more.

To those old allies whose cultural and spiritual origins we share, we pledge the loyalty of faithful friends.

To those new States whom we welcome to the ranks of the free, we pledge our word that one form of colonial control shall not have passed away merely to be replaced by a far more iron tyranny.

To those peoples in the huts and villages across the globe struggling to break the bonds of mass misery, we pledge our best efforts to help them help themselves, for whatever period is required—not because the Communists may be doing it, not because we seek their votes, but because it is right.

To our sister republics south of our border, we offer a special pledge—to convert our good words into good deeds in a new alliance for progress—to assist free men and free governments in casting off the chains of poverty.

Finally, to those nations who would make themselves our adversary, we offer not a pledge but a request: that both sides begin anew the quest for peace, before the dark powers of destruction unleashed by science engulf all humanity in planned or accidental self-destruction.

In your hands, my fellow citizens, more than in mine, will rest the final success or failure of our course. Since this country was founded, each generation of Americans has been summoned to give testimony to its national loyalty. The graves of young Americans who answered the all to service surround the globe.

And so, my fellow Americans: ask not what your country can do for you—ask what you can do for your country.

My fellow citizens of the world: ask not what America will do for you, but what together we can do for the freedom of man.

Finally, whether you are citizens of America or citizens of the world, ask of us the same high standards of strength and sacrifice which we ask of you.

Kennedy then made a dramatic visit to West Berlin, where he told a cheering crowd, "Today, in the world of freedom, the proudest boast is 'Ich bin ein [I am a] Berliner.'" In October 1962 a buildup of Soviet short- and intermediate-range nuclear missiles was discovered in Cuba. Kennedy demanded that the missiles be dismantled; he ordered a "quarantine" of Cuba—in effect, a blockade that would stop Soviet ships from reaching that island. For 13 days nuclear war seemed near; then the Soviet premier announced that the offensive weapons would be withdrawn. Ten months later Kennedy scored his greatest foreign triumph when Khrushchev and Prime Minister Harold Macmillan of Great Britain joined him in signing the Nuclear Test-Ban Treaty. Yet Kennedy's commitment to combat the spread of communism led him to escalate American involvement in the conflict in Vietnam, where he sent not just supplies and financial assistance, as Pres. Eisenhower had, but 15,000 military advisers as well.

Congress was largely indifferent to Kennedy's legislative program. It approved his Alliance for Progress (Alianza) in Latin America and his Peace Corps, which won the enthusiastic endorsement of thousands of college students. But his two most cherished projects, massive income tax cuts and a sweeping civil rights measure, were not passed until after his death. In May 1961 Kennedy committed the United States to land a man on the Moon by the end of the decade.

Kennedy was an immensely popular president, both at home and abroad. The charm and optimism of the Kennedy family seemed contagious, sparking the idealism of a generation for whom the Kennedy White House became, in journalist Theodore White's famous analogy, Camelot—the magical court of Arthurian legend. But if the first family had become American royalty, its image of perfection would be tainted years later by allegations that the president had an affair with the motion-picture icon Marilyn Monroe.

ASSASSINATION

On Friday, Nov. 22, 1963, Pres. Kennedy and Jacqueline Kennedy rode in an open limousine in a slow motorcade through downtown Dallas. At 12:30 PM the president was struck by two rifle bullets, one at the base of his neck and one in the head. He was pronounced dead shortly after arrival at Parkland Memorial Hospital. Texas Gov. John B. Connally, though also gravely wounded, recovered. Vice Pres. Johnson took the oath as president at 2:38 PM. Lee Harvey Oswald, a 24-year-old Dallas citizen, was accused of the slaying. Two days later Oswald was shot to death by Jack Ruby, a local nightclub owner with connections to the criminal underworld, in the basement of a Dallas police station. A presidential commission headed by the chief justice of the United States, Earl Warren, later found that neither the sniper nor his killer "was part of any conspiracy, domestic or foreign, to assassinate President Kennedy," but that Oswald had acted alone. The Warren Commission, however, was not able to convincingly explain all the particular circumstances of Kennedy's murder. In 1979 a special committee of the U.S. House of Representatives declared that although the president had undoubtedly been slain by Oswald, acoustic analysis suggested the presence of a second gunman who had missed. But this declaration did little to squelch the theories that Oswald was part of a conspiracy involving either CIA agents angered over Kennedy's handling of the Bay of Pigs fiasco or members of organized crime seeking revenge for relentless criminal investigations by the president's younger brother, Attorney General Robert F. Kennedy.

John Kennedy was dead, but the Kennedy mystique was still alive. Both Robert and his brother Edward M. Kennedy ran for president (in 1968 and 1980, respectively). Yet tragedy would become nearly synonymous with the Kennedys when Robert, too, was assassinated on the campaign trail in 1968.

LYNDON B. JOHNSON

(b. Aug. 27, 1908, Gillespie county, Texas—d. Jan. 22, 1973, San Antonio)

Lyndon Baines Johnson, also known as LBJ, was the 36th president of the United States (1963–69). A moderate Democrat and a vigorous leader in the United States Senate, Johnson was elected vice president in 1960 and acceded to the presidency in 1963 upon the assassination of Pres. John F. Kennedy. During his administration he signed into law the Civil Rights Act (1964), the most comprehensive civil rights legislation since the Reconstruction era, initiated major social service programs, and bore the brunt of national opposition to his vast expansion of American involvement in the Vietnam War.

Lyndon B. Johnson, c. 1963.
White House Collection

EARLY LIFE

Johnson, the first of five children, was born in a three-room house in the hills of south-central Texas to Sam Ealy Johnson, Jr., a businessman and member of the Texas House of Representatives, and Rebekah Baines Johnson, daughter of state legislator Joseph Baines and a graduate of Baylor College. After graduating from high school in 1924, Johnson spent three years in a series of odd jobs before enrolling at Southwest Texas State Teachers College at San Marcos. While pursuing his studies there in 1928–29, he took a teaching job at a predominantly Mexican American school in Cotulla, Texas, where the extreme poverty of his students made a profound impression on him. Through his later work in state politics, Johnson developed close and enduring ties to the Mexican American community in Texas—a factor that would later help the Kennedy-Johnson ticket carry Texas in the presidential election of 1960.

CAREER IN CONGRESS

After graduating from college in 1930, Johnson participated in the congressional campaign of Democrat Richard Kleberg, and upon Kleberg's election he accompanied the new congressman to Washington, D.C., in 1931 as his legislative assistant.

In 1934, in San Antonio, Texas, Johnson married Claudia Alta Taylor, known from childhood as "Lady Bird." A recent graduate of the University of Texas, where she finished near the top of her class, Lady Bird Johnson was a much-needed source of stability in her husband's life as well as a shrewd judge of people.

In Washington, Johnson's political career blossomed rapidly after he was befriended by fellow Texan Sam

Rayburn, the powerful chairman of the Committee on Interstate and Foreign Commerce and later Democratic leader of the House of Representatives. In 1938 he ran successfully for a seat in the House as a supporter of the New Deal policies of Democratic Pres. Franklin D. Roosevelt. He represented his district in the House for most of the next 12 years, interrupting his legislative duties for six months in 1941–42 to serve as lieutenant commander in the navy.

Johnson won the Democratic primary (which in Texas was tantamount to election) for the United States Senate in 1948, after a vicious campaign that included vote fraud on both sides. He remained in the Senate for 12 years, becoming Democratic whip in 1951 and minority leader in 1953. With the return of a Democratic majority in 1955, Johnson, age 46, became the youngest majority leader in that body's history.

During his years in the Senate, Johnson developed a talent for negotiating and reaching accommodation among divergent political factions. By methods sometimes tactful but often ruthless, he transformed the Senate Democrats into a remarkably disciplined and cohesive bloc.

VICE PRESIDENCY

At the Democratic convention in 1960, Johnson lost the presidential nomination to John F. Kennedy on the first ballot. He then surprised many both inside and outside the party when he accepted Kennedy's invitation to join the Democratic ticket as the vice presidential candidate. Many observers felt that without his presence Kennedy could not have carried Texas, Louisiana, and the Carolinas, states that were essential to his victory over the Republican candidate, Richard M. Nixon.

Johnson was generally uncomfortable in his role as vice president. His legendary knowledge of Congress went largely unused, despite Kennedy's failure to push through his own legislative program. His frustration was compounded by the apparent disdain with which he was regarded by some prominent members of the Kennedy administration—including the president's brother, Attorney General Robert F. Kennedy.

ACCESSION TO THE PRESIDENCY

In Dallas on Nov. 22, 1963, during a political tour of Johnson's home state, Pres. Kennedy was assassinated. At 2:38 PM that day, Johnson took the oath of office aboard the presidential plane, Air Force One, as it stood on the tarmac at Love Field, Dallas, waiting to take Kennedy's

Jacqueline Kennedy and Lady Bird Johnson standing by U.S. President Lyndon B. Johnson as he takes the oath of office aboard Air Force One after the assassination of John F. Kennedy, November 22, 1963. Lyndon B. Johnson Library Photo

remains back to Washington. One of the new president's first acts was to appoint a commission to investigate the assassination of Kennedy and the shooting of Lee Harvey Oswald, the alleged assassin, two days later.

IN FOCUS: THE WARREN COMMISSION

The Warren Commission, formally called the President's Commission on the Assassination of Pres. John F. Kennedy, was appointed by Lyndon B. Johnson on Nov. 29, 1963, to investigate the circumstances surrounding the assassination of his predecessor and the shooting of Lee Harvey Oswald, the alleged assassin, two days later. The chairman of the commission was the chief justice of the United States, Earl Warren; the other members were two U.S. senators, Richard B. Russell of Georgia and John Sherman Cooper of Kentucky; two members of the U.S. House of Representatives, Hale Boggs of Louisiana and Gerald R. Ford of Michigan; and two private citizens, Allen W. Dulles, former director of the Central Intelligence Agency, and John J. McCloy, former president of the International Bank for Reconstruction and Development.

After months of investigation the commission submitted its findings to Pres. Johnson in September 1964, and they were immediately made public. The commission reported that the bullets that had killed Pres. Kennedy were fired by Oswald from a rifle pointed out a sixth-floor window of the Texas School Book Depository. The commission also reported that it had found no evidence that either Oswald or Jack Ruby, a Dallas nightclub operator charged with Oswald's murder, was part of any conspiracy, foreign or domestic, to assassinate Pres. Kennedy. This conclusion of the commission was later questioned in a number of books and articles and in a special congressional committee report in 1979.

The commission described in detail its investigation of Oswald's life but did not itself attempt to analyze his motives. The commission also proposed the strengthening of the Secret Service organization; the adoption of improved procedures for protecting the president; and the enactment of legislation to make killing the president or vice president a federal offense. The report was published by the U.S. Government Printing Office under the title *Report of the President's Commission on the Assassination of President John F. Kennedy* (1964).

On November 27 Johnson addressed a joint session of Congress and, invoking the memory of the martyred president, urged the passage of Kennedy's legislative agenda, which had been stalled in congressional committees. In February 1964, after a series of amendments by civil rights supporters, the House passed a much stronger civil rights bill than the one that Kennedy had proposed, and the measure was finally passed by the Senate in June.

The Civil Rights Act, which Johnson signed into law on July 2, 1964, was the most comprehensive and far-reaching legislation of its kind in American history. Among its provisions were a prohibition of racial segregation and discrimination in places of public accommodation, a prohibition of discrimination by race or sex in employment and union membership, and new guarantees of equal voting rights. The law also authorized the Justice Department to bring suit against local school boards to

President Lyndon B. Johnson talking with Martin Luther King, Jr., in the Oval Office at the White House, Washington, D.C., 1963. Yoichi Okamoto/Lyndon B. Johnson Library Photo

end allegedly discriminatory practices, thereby speeding up school desegregation. The constitutionality of the law was immediately challenged but was upheld by the Supreme Court in 1964.

Johnson's "Great Society" program of social legislation, beginning with the Civil Rights Act and continuing with other important measures passed during Johnson's second term, was the most impressive body of social legislation since the New Deal of the 1930s. It encompassed legislation establishing the Job Corps for the unemployed and the Head Start program for preschool children; new civil rights legislation, such as the Voting Rights Act (1965); and Medicare and Medicaid, which provided health benefits for the elderly and the poor, respectively. Other legislation addressed problems in education, housing and urban development, transportation, environmental conservation, and immigration. Johnson saw these measures as building on and completing the New Deal vision of Franklin D. Roosevelt.

ELECTION AND THE VIETNAM WAR

In the presidential elections of 1964, Johnson was opposed by conservative Republican Barry Goldwater. During the campaign Johnson portrayed himself as level-headed and reliable and suggested that Goldwater was a reckless extremist who might lead the country into a nuclear war. On election day Johnson defeated Goldwater easily, receiving more than 61 percent of the popular vote; the vote in the electoral college was 486 to 52.

In early August 1964, after North Vietnamese gunboats allegedly attacked U.S. destroyers in the Gulf of Tonkin near the coast of North Vietnam without provocation, Johnson ordered retaliatory bombing raids on North Vietnamese naval installations. Two days later, at Johnson's request, Congress overwhelmingly passed the Gulf of Tonkin Resolution, which authorized the president to take "all necessary measures to repel any armed attack against the forces of the United States and to prevent further aggression." In effect, the measure granted Johnson the constitutional authority to conduct a war in Vietnam without a formal declaration from Congress.

Johnson soon increased the number of U.S. troops in that country and expanded their mission. In July 1965 he sent 50,000 additional troops to Vietnam. The number increased steadily over the next two years, peaking at about 550,000 in 1968.

As no end to the combat appeared in sight and U.S. casualties mounted (reaching nearly 500 a week in 1967), the president's public support declined steeply. Moreover, the enormous financial cost of the war diverted money from Johnson's cherished Great Society programs and began to fuel inflation. Beginning in 1965, student demonstrations grew larger and more frequent, and from 1967 onward antiwar sentiment gradually spread among other segments of the population, including liberal Democrats, intellectuals, and civil rights leaders. To avoid the demonstrations, Johnson eventually restricted his travels, becoming a virtual "prisoner" in the White House.

DOMESTIC PROBLEMS

Meanwhile, the lives of the nation's poor, particularly African Americans, failed to show significant improvement. Expectations of prosperity arising from the promise of the Great Society failed to materialize, and discontent and alienation grew accordingly. Beginning in the mid-1960s, violence erupted in several cities as the country suffered through "long, hot summers" of riots or the threat of riots.

LAST DAYS

On Jan. 30, 1968, North Vietnamese and Viet Cong forces in South Vietnam began the Tet Offensive, which embarrassed the Johnson administration and shocked the country. Although the attack was a failure in military terms, the news coverage completely undermined the administration's claim that the war was being won. On March 31, 1968, Johnson startled television viewers with a national address that included three announcements: he had just ordered major reductions in the bombing of North Vietnam, he was requesting peace talks, and he would neither seek nor accept his party's renomination for the presidency.

Johnson retired to his home in Texas, the LBJ Ranch near Johnson City, where he worked on plans for his presidential library (dedicated May 1971) and wrote his memoirs. In January 1973, less than one week before all the belligerents in Vietnam signed an agreement in Paris to end the war, Johnson suffered a heart attack and died.

RICHARD M. NIXON

(b. Jan. 9, 1913, Yorba Linda, Calif.—d. April 22, 1994, New York, N.Y.)

Richard Milhous Nixon was the 37th president of the United States (1969–74). Faced with almost certain impeachment for his role in the Watergate Scandal, he became the first American president to resign from office. He was also vice president (1953–61) under Pres. Dwight D. Eisenhower.

Early Life and Congressional Career

Nixon was the second of five children born to Frank Nixon, a service station owner and grocer, and Hannah Milhous Nixon, whose devout Quakerism would exert a strong influence on her son. Nixon graduated from Whittier College in Whittier, Calif., in 1934 and from Duke University Law School in Durham, N.C., in 1937. Returning to Whittier to practice law, he met Thelma Catherine ("Pat") Ryan, a teacher and amateur actress. The couple married in 1940.

In August 1942 Nixon joined the navy, serving as an aviation ground officer in the Pacific and rising to the rank of lieutenant commander. Following his return to civilian life in 1946, he was elected to the U.S. House of Representatives. Running for reelection in 1948, Nixon entered and won both the Democratic and Republican primaries, thus eliminating the need to participate in the general election. As a member of the House Un-American Activities Committee (HUAAC) in 1948–50, he took a leading role in the investigation of Alger Hiss, a former State Department official accused of spying for the Soviet Union. Nixon's hostile questioning of Hiss during the committee hearings did much to make his national reputation as a fervent anticommunist. In 1950 Nixon successfully ran for the United States Senate against Democratic Representative Helen Gahagan Douglas.

Vice Presidency

At the Republican convention in 1952, Nixon won nomination as vice president on a ticket with Eisenhower, largely because of his anticommunist credentials. The Eisenhower-Nixon ticket defeated the Democratic candidates, Adlai

E. Stevenson and John Sparkman, with just under 34 million popular votes to their 27.3 million; the vote in the electoral college was 442 to 89.

During his two terms as vice president, Nixon campaigned actively for Republican candidates but otherwise did not assume significant responsibilities. Nevertheless, his performance in office helped to make the role of vice president more prominent and to enhance its constitutional importance. Nixon's vice presidency was also noteworthy for his many well-publicized trips abroad, including a 1958 tour of Latin America and a 1959 visit to the Soviet Union, highlighted by an impromptu (and profanity-filled) "kitchen debate" in Moscow with Soviet Premier Nikita Khrushchev.

ELECTION OF 1960

Nixon received his party's presidential nomination in 1960 and was opposed in the general election by Democrat John F. Kennedy. The campaign was memorable for an unprecedented series of four televised debates between the two candidates. Although Nixon performed well rhetorically, Kennedy managed to convey an appealing image of youthfulness, energy, and physical poise, which convinced many that he had won the debates. In the closest presidential contest since Grover Cleveland defeated James G. Blaine in 1884, Nixon lost to Kennedy by fewer than 120,000 popular votes.

In 1962 Nixon reluctantly decided to run for governor of California but lost to incumbent Democrat Edmund G. ("Pat") Brown. In a memorable postelection news conference, Nixon announced his retirement from politics and attacked the press, declaring that it would not "have Dick Nixon to kick around anymore."

PRESIDENCY

Richard M. Nixon, 1969. U.S. Department of Defense

Nixon won the Republican nomination for president in 1968 by putting together a coalition that included Southern conservatives. In exchange for Southern support, Nixon promised to appoint "strict constructionists" to the federal judiciary, to name a Southerner to the Supreme Court, to oppose court-ordered busing, and to choose a vice presidential candidate acceptable to the South. With Maryland Gov. Spiro Agnew as his running mate, Nixon campaigned against Democrat Hubert H. Humphrey and third-party candidate George Wallace. Humphrey, as Lyndon B. Johnson's vice president, was heavily burdened by the latter's unpopular Vietnam policies. Nixon won the election by a narrow margin, 31.7 million popular votes to Humphrey's nearly 30.9 million; the electoral vote was 301 to 191.

DOMESTIC POLICIES

The Nixon administration undertook a number of important reforms in welfare policy, civil rights, law enforcement, the environment, and other areas. In the area of civil rights, Nixon's administration instituted so-called "set aside" policies to reserve a certain percentage of jobs for minorities on federally funded construction projects — the first "affirmative action" program. In addition, funding for many federal civil rights agencies, in particular the

Equal Employment Opportunity Commission (EEOC), was substantially increased while Nixon was in office. In response to pressure from consumer and environmental groups, Nixon proposed legislation that created the Occupational Safety and Health Administration (OSHA) and the Environmental Protection Agency (EPA).

Nixon's New Economic Policy, announced in August 1971 in response to continuing inflation and increasing unemployment, included an 8 percent devaluation of the dollar, new surcharges on imports, and unprecedented peacetime controls on wages and prices. These policies produced temporary improvements in the economy by the end of 1972, but, once price and wage controls were lifted, inflation returned with a vengeance.

Foreign Affairs

Vietnam War

Aiming to achieve so-called "peace with honor" in the Vietnam War, Nixon gradually reduced the number of U.S. military personnel in Vietnam. Under his policy of "Vietnamization," combat roles were transferred to South Vietnamese troops, who nevertheless remained heavily dependent on American supplies and air support. At the same time, however, Nixon resumed the bombing of North Vietnam (suspended by Pres. Johnson in October 1968) and expanded the air and ground war to neighbouring Cambodia and Laos.

After intensive negotiations between National Security Adviser Henry Kissinger and North Vietnamese Foreign Minister Le Duc Tho, a peace agreement was finally reached in January 1973 and signed in Paris. It included an immediate cease-fire, the withdrawal of all American military personnel, the release of all prisoners of war, and an international force to keep the peace. For their work on the accord, Kissinger and Tho were awarded the 1973 Nobel Prize for Peace (though Tho declined the honour).

CHINA AND THE SOVIET UNION

Nixon's most significant achievement in foreign affairs may have been the establishment of direct relations with the People's Republic of China after a 21-year estrangement. Nixon's visit to China in February–March 1972, the first by an American president while in office, concluded with the Shanghai Communiqué, in which the United States formally recognized the "one-China" principle — that there is only one China, and that Taiwan is a part of China.

The rapprochement with China gave Nixon more leverage in his dealings with the Soviet Union. In May 1972 Nixon paid a state visit to Moscow to sign 10 formal agreements, the most important of which were the nuclear-arms limitation treaties known as SALT I (based on the Strategic Arms Limitation Talks conducted between the United States and the Soviet Union beginning in 1969).

WATERGATE AND OTHER SCANDALS

Renominated with Agnew in 1972, Nixon defeated his Democratic challenger, the liberal Sen. George S. McGovern, in one of the largest landslide victories in the history of American presidential elections: 46.7 million to 28.9 million in the popular vote and 520 to 17 in the electoral vote. Despite his resounding victory, Nixon would soon be forced to resign in disgrace in the worst political scandal in United States history.

The Watergate Scandal stemmed from illegal activities by Nixon and his aides related to the burglary and wiretapping of the national headquarters of the Democratic Party at the Watergate office complex in Washington, D.C.;

eventually it came to encompass allegations of other loosely related crimes committed both before and after the break-in. The five men involved in the burglary, who were hired by the Republican Party's Committee to Re-elect the President, were arrested and charged on June 17, 1972. In the days following the arrests, Nixon secretly directed the White House counsel, John Dean, to oversee a cover-up to conceal the administration's involvement. Nixon also obstructed the Federal Bureau of Investigation (FBI) in its inquiry and authorized secret cash payments to the Watergate burglars in an effort to prevent them from implicating the administration.

In February 1973 a special Senate committee—the Select Committee on Presidential Campaign Activities, chaired by Senator Sam Ervin—was established to look into the Watergate affair. In televised committee hearings, Dean accused the president of involvement in the cover-up, and others testified to illegal activities by the administration and the campaign staff.

In July the committee learned that in 1969 Nixon had installed a recording system in the White House and that all the president's conversations in the Oval Office had been recorded. When the tapes were subpoenaed by Archibald Cox, the special prosecutor appointed to investigate the Watergate affair, Nixon refused to comply, offering to provide summary transcripts instead. Cox rejected the offer. Nixon then ordered Attorney General Elliot Richardson to fire Cox, and Richardson resigned rather than comply. Nixon then fired Richardson's assistant, William Ruckelshaus, when he too refused to fire Cox. Cox was finally removed by Solicitor General Robert Bork, though a federal district court subsequently ruled the action illegal.

Amid calls for his impeachment, Nixon agreed to the appointment of another special prosecutor, Leon Jaworski, and released seven of the nine tapes requested by Cox, one of which contained a suspicious gap of 18 and one-half minutes. Jaworski later subpoenaed 64 tapes that Nixon continued to withhold on grounds of "executive privilege," and in July 1974 the Supreme Court ruled unanimously that Nixon's claims of executive privilege were invalid. By that time the House Judiciary Committee had already voted to recommend three articles of impeachment, relating to obstruction of justice, abuse of power, and failure to comply with congressional subpoenas. On August 5 Nixon submitted transcripts of a conversation taped on June 23, 1972, in which he discussed a plan to use the Central Intelligence Agency to block the FBI's investigation of the Watergate break-in.

Faced with the near-certain prospect of impeachment by the House and conviction in the Senate, Nixon announced his resignation on the evening of Aug. 8, 1974, effective at noon the next day. Nixon was pardoned by Pres. Ford on Sept. 8, 1974.

Retirement and Death

Nixon retired with his wife to the seclusion of his estate in San Clemente, Calif. He wrote several books on international affairs and American foreign policy, modestly rehabilitating his public reputation and earning a role as an elder statesman and foreign-policy expert. He died of a massive stroke in New York City in April 1994.

GERALD R. FORD

(b. July 14, 1913, Omaha, Neb.—d. Dec. 26, 2006, Rancho Mirage, Calif.)

Gerald Rudolph Ford was the 38th president of the United States (1974–77), who, as 40th vice president, succeeded to the presidency on the resignation of Pres.

**PRIMARY DOCUMENT: THE CONSTITUTION OF THE
UNITED STATES: TWENTY-FIFTH AMENDMENT,
SECTIONS 1 AND 2**

Section 1—In case of the removal of the President from office or of
his death or resignation, the Vice President shall become President.

Section 2—Whenever there is a vacancy in the office of the Vice
President, the President shall nominate a Vice President who shall
take office upon confirmation by a majority vote of both Houses
of Congress.

Richard M. Nixon under the process decreed by the
Twenty-fifth Amendment to the Constitution. He thereby
became the country's only chief executive who was not
elected as either president or vice president.

While Ford was still an infant, his parents, Dorothy
Ayer Gardner and Leslie Lynch King, were divorced, and
his mother moved to Grand Rapids, Mich., where in 1916
she married Gerald R. Ford, Sr., who adopted the boy and
gave him his name. (For Ford's first three years his name
had been Leslie Lynch King, Jr.) After graduating from the
University of Michigan (1935), where he was a star gridiron-
football player, Ford worked as an assistant coach while
he earned a law degree from Yale University (1941). He
joined the navy during World War II and served in the
South Pacific, attaining the rank of lieutenant commander. In 1948, the year he won his first elective office as
Republican congressman from Michigan, he married
Elizabeth Anne Bloomer, known as Betty, with whom he
had four children.

Ford served in Congress for 25 years. He won the role
of House minority leader in 1965 and held this position
until Nixon named him vice president in 1973 after Spiro
T. Agnew was forced to resign from office in disgrace. Ford

Gerald R. Ford. Courtesy
Gerald R. Ford Library

was seen as the only Republican whom the Democratic leadership of Congress would approve.

In 1974, when it became clear that Nixon would face impeachment and conviction for his role in the Watergate Scandal, Nixon resigned, effective August 9. On that day, Ford took the oath of office and became president, stating, "Our long national nightmare is over."

On Sept. 8, 1974, declaring that in the end "it is not the ultimate fate of Richard Nixon that most concerns me" but rather "the immediate future of this great country," Ford pardoned Nixon "for all offenses against the United States" that he had committed "or may have committed" while in office. The pardon effectively squelched any criminal prosecutions to which Nixon might have been liable. In another startling move, Ford annoyed members of his own party by naming Nelson A. Rockefeller, both a party liberal and a representative of the so-called "Eastern establishment," as his vice president.

Ford's administration attempted to cope with the high rate of inflation, which he inherited from the Nixon administration, by slowing down the economy. The result was a very severe recession in 1974–75, which succeeded in lowering inflation but at the cost of an unemployment rate that rose to nearly 9 percent. Despite his WIN (Whip Inflation Now) program, he could do little to stop the country's economic problems. Ford's relations with the Democrat-controlled Congress were perhaps typified by his more than 50 vetoes of legislation by the end of 1976; more than 40 were sustained. Legislative gridlock had set in.

Twice in September 1975, Ford was the target of assassination attempts. In the first instance, Secret Service agents intervened before shots were fired; in the second, the would-be assassin fired one shot at Ford but missed by several feet.

In a close contest at the Republican convention in August 1976, Ford won his party's nomination, despite a serious challenge by Ronald Reagan, the former governor of California. That fall Ford became the first incumbent president to agree to public debates with a challenger—Jimmy Carter, the Democratic nominee. Ford ran substantially behind from the beginning of the campaign, owing in large part to negative fallout from the Nixon pardon, but also to the general public's perception of his ineptitude. Ford was defeated in the November 1976 election by a popular vote of 40.8 million to 39.1 million and an electoral vote of 297 to 240. After leaving the White House, Ford happily retired from public life, golfed and skied at his leisure, and ultimately joined the boards of directors of numerous corporations. His autobiography, *A Time to Heal*, was published in 1979.

JIMMY CARTER

(b. Oct. 1, 1924, Plains, Ga.)

Jimmy Carter was the 39th president of the United States (1977–81). His perceived inability to deal successfully with serious problems at home and abroad led to his overwhelming defeat in his bid for reelection. After leaving office he embarked on a career of diplomacy and advocacy, for which he was awarded the Nobel Prize for Peace in 2002.

The son of Earl Carter, a peanut warehouser who had served in the Georgia state legislature, and Lillian Gordy Carter, a registered nurse who went to India as a Peace Corps volunteer at age 68, Carter attended Georgia Southwestern College and the Georgia Institute of Technology before graduating from the U.S. Naval Academy at Annapolis, Md., in 1946. After marrying Rosalynn Smith—who came from Carter's small home-town, Plains, Ga.—he embarked on a seven-year career in the U.S. Navy, serving submarine duty for five years. He was preparing to become an engineering officer for the submarine *Seawolf* in 1953 when his father died. Carter resigned his commission and returned to Georgia to manage the family peanut farm operations.

Carter won election as a Democrat to the Georgia State Senate in 1962 and was reelected in 1964. In 1966 he failed in a bid for the governorship and, depressed by this experience, found solace in evangelical Christianity, becoming a born-again Baptist. Prior to running again for governor and winning in 1970, Carter at least tacitly adhered to a segregationist approach; however, in his inaugural address he announced that "the time for racial discrimination is over" and proceeded to open Georgia's government offices to African Americans—and to women. As governor he reorganized the existing maze of state agencies and consolidated them into larger units while introducing stricter budgeting procedures. In the process he came to national attention, finding his way onto the cover of *Time* magazine as a symbol of both good government and the "New South."

In 1974, just before his term as governor ended, Carter announced his candidacy for the Democratic nomination for president. Although lacking a national political base or major backing, he managed through tireless and systematic campaigning to assemble a broad constituency. In the aftermath of the Watergate Scandal, which had raised widespread concern about the power of the presidency and the integrity of the executive branch, Carter styled himself as an outsider to Washington, D.C., a man of strong principles who could restore the faith of the American people in their leaders.

Winning the Democratic nomination in July 1976, Carter chose liberal Sen. Walter F. Mondale of Minnesota as his running mate. Carter's opponent was the unelected incumbent Republican president, Gerald R. Ford, who had come into office in 1974 when Richard Nixon resigned in the wake of Watergate. In November 1976 the Carter-Mondale ticket won the election, capturing 51 percent of the popular vote and garnering 297 electoral votes to Ford's 240.

Beginning with his inaugural walk with Rosalynn down Pennsylvania Avenue, Carter tried to reinforce his image as a man of the people. He adopted an informal style of dress and speech in public appearances, held frequent press conferences, and reduced the pomp of the presidency. Early on in his administration, Carter introduced an array of ambitious programs for social, administrative, and economic reform. Most of those programs, however, met with opposition in Congress despite the Democratic majorities in both the House of Representatives and the Senate. On one hand, Congress, in the post-Watergate environment, was more willing to challenge the executive branch; on the other, Carter the populist was quick to criticize Congress and to take his agenda to the American people. In either case, Carter's difficulties with Congress undermined the success of his administration, and by 1978 his initial popularity had dissipated in the face of his inability to convert his ideas into legislative realities.

Two scandals also damaged Carter's credibility. In summer 1977 Bert Lance, the director of the Office of

Management and Budget and one of Carter's closest friends, was accused of financial improprieties as a Georgia banker. In the summer of 1980, Carter's younger brother, Billy was accused of acting as an influence peddler for the Libyan government of Muammar al-Qaddafi. Senate investigators concluded that, while Billy had acted improperly, he had no real influence on the president.

In foreign affairs, Carter received accolades for championing international human rights, though critics charged that his vision of the world was naive. Carter's idealism notwithstanding, his major achievements were on the more pragmatic level of patient diplomacy. In 1977 he obtained two treaties between the United States and Panama that gave the latter control over the Panama Canal at the end of 1999 and guaranteed the neutrality of that waterway thereafter. In 1978 Carter brought together Egyptian Pres. Anwar el-Sādāt and Israeli Prime Minister Menachem Begin at the presidential retreat in Camp David, Md., and secured their agreement to the Camp David Accords, which ended the state of war that had existed between the two countries since Israel's founding in 1948. The difficult negotiations were salvaged only by Carter's tenacious intervention. In 1979, in Vienna, Carter and Soviet leader Leonid Brezhnev signed a new bilateral strategic arms limitation treaty (SALT II), though Carter removed the treaty from consideration by the Senate in January 1980 after the Soviet Union invaded Afghanistan. He also placed an embargo on the shipment of American grain to the Soviet Union and pressed for a U.S. boycott of the 1980 Summer Olympics due to be held in Moscow.

Carter's substantial foreign policy successes were overshadowed by a serious crisis in foreign affairs and by a groundswell of popular discontent over his economic policies. On Nov. 4, 1979, a mob of Iranian students stormed the U.S. embassy in Tehrān and took the diplomatic staff there hostage. Their actions were sanctioned by Iran's revolutionary government, led by Shī'ite cleric Ayatollah Ruhollah Khomeini. A standoff developed between the United States and Iran over the issue of the captive diplomats. Carter responded by trying to negotiate the hostages' release, but, as the crisis wore on, his inability to obtain the release of the hostages became a major political liability. The failure of a secret U.S. military mission to rescue the hostages (which ended almost before it began with a crash in the desert of a plane and helicopter) in April 1980 seemed to typify the inefficacy and misfortune of the Carter administration.

Jimmy Carter. Courtesy: Jimmy Carter Library

During Carter's years in office the inflation rate climbed steadily, from 6 percent in 1976 to more than 12 percent by 1980; unemployment remained high at 7.5 percent; and volatile interest rates reached a high of 20 percent or more twice during 1980. Both business leaders and the public at large blamed Carter for the nation's economic woes.

The faltering economy was due in part to the energy crisis that had originated in the early 1970s as a result of the country's overdependence on foreign oil. In 1977 the president, whose mistrust of special interest groups such as the oil companies was well known, proposed an energy program that included an oil tax, conservation, and the use of alternative sources of energy. The House supported the program but the Senate quashed it.

In July 1979 Carter met with a wide cross section of American leaders at Camp David. In the nationally televised speech that followed that meeting, Carter spoke of a "crisis of spirit" in the country, but most Americans were ultimately no more interested in rising to the challenge of a national "malaise" than they were in Carter's suggestion that they needed to lower some of their expectations. Still, Carter was able to fend off the challenge of Massachusetts Sen. Edward Kennedy to win the Democratic presidential nomination in 1980. However, the public's confidence in Carter's executive abilities had fallen to an irretrievable low. In the elections held that November, Carter was overwhelmingly defeated by the Republican nominee, a former actor and governor of California, Ronald W. Reagan. In the landslide, Carter won only 41 percent of the popular vote and 49 votes in the electoral college (third-party candidate John Anderson captured 7 percent of the vote). In the late 1980s, allegations surfaced that the Reagan campaign had made a secret agreement with the government of Iran to ensure that the hostages were not released before the election (thus preventing an "October Surprise" that might boost Carter's election chances); in 1993 a congressional subcommittee found the evidence inconclusive. The hostages were released on Jan. 21, 1981, one day after Reagan's inauguration.

In his final months in office, Carter was able to push through important legislation that created Superfund to clean up abandoned toxic waste dumps and that set aside some 100 million acres (40 million hectares) of land in Alaska to protect it from development. Carter would also be remembered for his inclusion of women and minorities in his cabinet, including Andrew Young, the African American former mayor of Atlanta, who played a prominent though controversial role as the U.S. ambassador to the United Nations.

At the conclusion of the president's term, the Carters returned to their hometown. Rosalynn joined her husband in establishing the Carter Presidential Center in Atlanta, which included a presidential library and museum.

Carter served as a sort of diplomat without portfolio in various conflicts in a number of countries—including Nicaragua, Panama, and Ethiopia. He was particularly active in this role in 1994, negotiating with North Korea to end nuclear weapons development there, with Haiti to effect a peaceful transfer of power, and with Bosnian Serbs and Muslims to broker a short-lived cease-fire. His efforts on behalf of international peace and his participation in building homes for the poor through Habitat for Humanity established in the public mind a much more favourable image of Carter than had been the case during his presidency.

After leaving office, Carter also became a prolific author, writing on a variety of topics. He was also the author of *The Hornet's Nest: A Novel of the Revolutionary War* (2003) and a collection of poetry.

RONALD W. REAGAN

(b. Feb. 6, 1911, Tampico, Ill., —d. June 5, 2004, Los Angeles, Calif.)

Ronald Wilson Reagan was the 40th president of the United States (1981–89). He was noted for his conservative Republicanism, his fervent anticommunism, and his appealing personal style, characterized by a jaunty affability and folksy charm. The only movie actor ever to become president, he had a remarkable skill as an orator that earned him the title "the Great Communicator." His policies have been credited with contributing to the demise of Soviet communism.

EARLY LIFE AND ACTING CAREER

Reagan was the second child of John Edward ("Jack") Reagan, a shoe salesman, and Nelle Wilson Reagan. After several years of moving from town to town, the family settled in Dixon, Ill., in 1920. At Eureka College in Eureka, Ill., Reagan was elected class president in his senior year. Graduating in 1932 with a bachelor's degree in economics and sociology, he decided to enter radio broadcasting. At station WHO in Des Moines he became popular throughout the state for his broadcasts of Chicago Cubs baseball games. Because the station could not afford to send him to Wrigley Field in Chicago, Reagan was forced to improvise a running account of the games based on sketchy details delivered over a teletype machine.

Ronald Reagan on the television series *General Electric Theater,* c. 1954–62. Courtesy Ronald Reagan Library

In 1937 Reagan followed the Cubs to their spring training camp in southern California, a trip he undertook partly in order to try his hand at movie acting. After a successful screen test at Warner Brothers, he was soon typecast in a series of mostly B movies as a sincere, wholesome, easygoing "good guy." (As many observers have noted, the characters that Reagan portrayed in the movies were remarkably like Reagan himself.) During the next 27 years, he appeared in more than 50 films. In 1938, while filming *Brother Rat*, Reagan became engaged to his costar Jane Wyman, and the couple married in Hollywood two years later. They had a daughter, Maureen, in 1941 and adopted a son, Michael, a few days after his birth in 1945. Their marriage ended in divorce in 1948. Reagan was the only president to have been divorced.

Commissioned a cavalry officer at the outbreak of World War II, Reagan was assigned to an army film unit based in Los Angeles, where he spent the rest of the war making training films. Although he never left the country and never saw combat, he and Wyman cooperated with the efforts of Warner Brothers to portray him as a real soldier to the public, and in newsreels and magazine photos he acted out scenes of "going off to war" and "coming home on leave." After leaving Hollywood, Reagan became known for occasionally telling stories about his past that were actually based on fictional episodes in movies.

Reagan had absorbed the liberal Democratic opinions of his father and became a great admirer of Franklin D. Roosevelt after his election in 1932. From 1947 to 1952 Reagan served as president of the union of movie actors, the Screen Actors Guild. Much to the disgust of union members, he testified as a friendly witness before the House Un-American Activities Committee and cooperated in the blacklisting of actors, directors, and writers suspected of leftist sympathies. Although Reagan was still a Democrat at the time, his political opinions were gradually growing more conservative. After initially supporting Democratic senatorial candidate Helen Douglas in 1950, he switched his allegiance to Republican Richard M. Nixon midway through the campaign. He supported Republican Dwight D. Eisenhower in the presidential elections of 1952 and 1956 and Nixon in the election of 1960. Reagan officially changed his party affiliation to Republican in 1962.

Reagan met Nancy Davis, a relatively unknown actress, at a dinner party in 1949, and the two were married in 1952.

After his acting career began to decline in the 1950s, Reagan became the host of a television drama series, *General Electric Theater*, as well as a spokesman for the General Electric Company. In the latter capacity he toured GE plants around the country, delivering inspirational speeches with a generally conservative, pro-business message. Eventually, however, his speeches became too controversial for the company's taste, and he was fired as both spokesman and television host in 1962.

GOVERNORSHIP OF CALIFORNIA

Reagan campaigned actively for Nixon in his run for governor of California in 1962 and supported the presidential candidacy of conservative Republican Barry Goldwater in 1964. In the last week of the campaign, he delivered a 30-minute nationally televised address, "A Time for Choosing," that catapulted him onto the national political stage and made him an instant hero of the Republican right.

Reagan announced his candidacy for governor of California in 1966. The incumbent, Democrat Edmund G. ("Pat") Brown (who had defeated Nixon's challenge in 1962), ridiculed Reagan's lack of experience. But Reagan turned this apparent liability into an asset by portraying himself as an ordinary citizen who was fed up with a state government that had become inefficient and unaccountable. The public also reacted well to Reagan's personality, in particular to his apparent genuineness, affability, and self-deprecating sense of humour. Reagan won the election by nearly one million votes. During his two terms as governor (1966–74), he erased a substantial budget deficit inherited from the Brown administration (through the largest tax increase in the history of any state to that time) and instituted reforms in the state's welfare programs.

Reagan made a halfhearted bid for the Republican presidential nomination in 1968 as a favourite-son candidate, finishing third behind Nixon and former New York governor Nelson Rockefeller. During his remaining years as governor, he made plans for a more serious run for the presidency, but Nixon's resignation in 1974 put Vice Pres. Gerald Ford in the Oval Office. Unwilling to wait another eight years, Reagan challenged Ford with a blistering critique of Ford's policies and appointments, but lost the nomination by 60 votes.

ELECTION OF 1980

Reagan dominated the Republican primary elections in 1980. Although his strongest opponent, George Bush, won an upset victory in the Iowa caucuses, Reagan went on to win New Hampshire and most of the other major primaries and entered the convention with a commanding lead, winning the nomination on the first ballot. Reagan chose Bush as his running mate, and the two men campaigned against Democratic incumbents Jimmy Carter and Walter Mondale on a platform promising steep tax cuts, increased defense spending, a balanced budget, and a constitutional amendment to ban abortion.

Carter began the campaign in a vulnerable position. Inflation had increased from 6 percent to more than 12 percent since his first year in office, and unemployment and interest rates were also high. An even more important factor than the economy, however, was Carter's apparent inability to resolve the Iran hostage crisis, which had continued for almost a year at the time of the election. In their only debate of the campaign, Reagan memorably reminded his national television audience of the country's economic problems by asking, "Are you better off now than you were four years ago?" Carter, for his part, tried to make the most of Reagan's image among some of the electorate as an extremist and a warmonger, charging that as president Reagan would eliminate cherished social programs and threaten world peace. On election day Reagan defeated Carter and John Anderson (who ran as an independent) with slightly more than half the popular vote, against Carter's 41 percent and Anderson's 7 percent. The vote in the electoral college was 489 to Carter's 49.

PRIMARY DOCUMENT: RONALD REAGAN: FIRST INAUGURAL ADDRESS

Tuesday, Jan. 20, 1981

Senator Hatfield, Mr. Chief Justice, Mr. President, Vice President Bush, Vice President Mondale, Senator Baker, Speaker O'Neill, Reverend Moomaw, and my fellow citizens: To a few of us here today, this is a solemn and most momentous occasion; and yet, in the history of our Nation, it is a commonplace occurrence. The orderly transfer of authority as called for in the Constitution routinely takes place as it has for almost two centuries and few of us stop to think how unique we really are. In the eyes of many in the world, this every-four-year ceremony we accept as normal is nothing less than a miracle.

The business of our nation goes forward. These United States are confronted with an economic affliction of great proportions. We suffer from the longest and one of the worst sustained inflations in our national history. It distorts our economic decisions, penalizes thrift, and crushes the struggling young and the fixed-income elderly alike. It threatens to shatter the lives of millions of our people.

In this present crisis, government is not the solution to our problem.

This administration's objective will be a healthy, vigorous, growing economy that provides equal opportunity for all Americans, with no barriers born of bigotry or discrimination. Putting America back to work means putting all Americans back to work.

It is no coincidence that our present troubles parallel and are proportionate to the intervention and intrusion in our lives that result from unnecessary and excessive growth of government.

In the days ahead I will propose removing the roadblocks that have slowed our economy and reduced productivity. Steps will be taken aimed at restoring the balance between the various levels of government. It is time to reawaken this industrial giant, to get government back within its means, and to lighten our punitive tax burden. And these will be our first priorities, and on these principles, there will be no compromise.

And as we renew ourselves here in our own land, we will be seen as having greater strength throughout the world. We will again be the exemplar of freedom and a beacon of hope for those who do not now have freedom.

To those neighbors and allies who share our freedom, we will strengthen our historic ties and assure them of our support and firm commitment.

As for the enemies of freedom, those who are potential adversaries, they will be reminded that peace is the highest aspiration of the American people. We will negotiate for it, sacrifice for it; we will not surrender for it—now or ever.

PRESIDENCY

FIRST DAYS

Reagan's presidency began on a dramatic note when, after the inaugural ceremony, he announced at a luncheon that Iran had agreed to release the remaining American hostages. The timing of Iran's decision led to suspicions, which were never substantiated, that the Reagan campaign had made a secret deal with the Iranians to prevent the Carter administration from arranging the release of the hostages in October 1980, before election day.

*Ronald and Nancy Reagan waving to crowds on the day of his first
inauguration, January 20, 1981.*Courtesy Ronald Reagan Library

Then, on March 30, 1981, a mentally disturbed drifter
named John W. Hinckley, Jr., fired six shots from a .22-cali-
bre revolver at Reagan as he left a Washington, D.C., hotel.
One of the bullets entered Reagan's chest, puncturing a
lung and lodging one inch from his heart; another criti-
cally wounded Press Secretary James Brady. After his
release from George Washington University Hospital 12
days later, Reagan made a series of carefully staged public
appearances designed to give the impression that he was
recovering quickly, though in fact he remained seriously
weakened for months and his workload was sharply
curtailed.

DOMESTIC POLICIES

Following the so-called "supply-side" economic program
he propounded in his campaign, Reagan proposed massive

tax cuts—30 percent reductions in both individual and corporate income taxes over a three-year period—which he believed would stimulate the economy and eventually increase revenues from taxes as income levels grew. At the same time, he proposed large increases in military expenditures ($1.5 trillion over a five-year period) and significant cuts in spending on education, food stamps, low-income housing, school lunches for poor children, Medicaid (the major program of health insurance for the poor), and Aid to Families with Dependent Children (AFDC). In 1981 Congress passed most of the president's budget proposals, though the tax cut was scaled back slightly, to 25 percent.

The results were mixed. A severe recession in 1982 pushed the nation's unemployment rate to nearly 11 percent, the highest it had been since the Great Depression. In addition, the huge increases in military spending, combined with insufficient cuts in other programs, produced massive budget deficits, the largest in the country's history. In order to address the deficit problem, Reagan backed away from strict supply-side theories to support a $98.3 billion tax increase in 1982. By early 1983 the economy had begun to recover, and by the end of that year unemployment and inflation were significantly reduced, and economic growth continued through the remainder of Reagan's presidency.

In keeping with his aim of reducing the role of government in the country's economic life, Reagan cut the budgets of many government departments and relaxed or ignored the enforcement of laws and regulations administered by the Environmental Protection Agency (EPA), the Department of the Interior, the Department of Transportation, and the Civil Rights Division of the Department of Justice, among other agencies. After the administration and Congress reduced regulations governing the savings and loan industry in the early 1980s, many savings institutions expanded recklessly through the decade and eventually collapsed, requiring bailouts by the federal government that cost taxpayers some $500 billion.

During his tenure in office, Reagan appointed more than half the federal judiciary and three new justices of the Supreme Court: Sandra Day O'Connor, the first woman appointed to the Supreme Court; Anthony Kennedy; and Antonin Scalia. He also elevated William Rehnquist to chief justice in 1986 upon the retirement of Warren Burger.

FOREIGN AFFAIRS

When he entered office in 1980, Reagan believed that the United States had grown weak militarily and had lost the respect it once commanded in world affairs. He called for massive increases in the defense budget to expand and modernize the military and urged a more aggressive approach to combating communism and related forms of leftist totalitarianism.

Relations with the Soviet Union

Reagan's militant anticommunism combined with his penchant for harsh anti-Soviet rhetoric was one of many factors that contributed to a worsening of relations with the Soviet Union in the first years of his presidency. The behaviour of the Soviet Union itself also strained relations—especially in December 1981, when the communist government of Poland, under intense pressure from Moscow, imposed martial law on the country to suppress the independent labour movement Solidarity. Reagan's massive military spending program, the largest in American peacetime history, was undoubtedly another factor, though some observers argued that the buildup—through the strain it imposed on the Soviet economy—was actually responsible

for a host of positive develop-
ments in Reagan's second term,
including a more accommodating
Soviet position in arms negotiations, a weakening of the influence
of hard-liners in the Soviet leadership, making possible the
glasnost ("openness") and *pere-
stroika* ("restructuring") policies of
moderate Soviet leader Mikhail
Gorbachev after 1985, and even the
dissolution of the Soviet Union
itself in 1990–91.

A significant component of
Reagan's military buildup was his
1983 proposal for a space-based
missile defense system that would
use lasers and other as-yet-unde-
veloped killing technologies to
destroy incoming Soviet nuclear

Ronald Reagan, 1983. U.S.
Department of Defense

missiles well before they could reach their targets in the
United States. The Strategic Defense Initiative (SDI),
dubbed "Star Wars" after the popular science-fiction
movie of the late 1970s, was eventually reconceived as a
much smaller and more conventional defensive system
than the one he originally proposed.

U.S.-Soviet relations improved considerably during
Reagan's second term, not least because Reagan softened
his anticommunist rhetoric and adopted a more encouraging tone toward the changes then taking place in the Soviet
Union. At a dramatic summit meeting in Reykjavík,
Iceland, in October 1986, Gorbachev proposed a 50 percent reduction in the nuclear arsenals of each side, but the
summit ended in failure owing to differences over SDI.

The Middle East and Central America

Following the Israeli invasion of Lebanon in June 1982, Reagan dispatched 800 Marines to join an international force to oversee the evacuation of Palestinian guerrillas from West Beirut, then surrounded by Israeli troops. After Israel withdrew its troops from the Beirut area in September 1983, the Marine contingent remained—along with forces from Italy, France, and Britain—to protect the fragile Lebanese government. On the morning of Oct. 23, 1983, a suicide bomber drove a truck laden with explosives into the Marine compound at the Beirut airport, killing 241 Marines and wounding 100 others. Reagan withdrew the Marines from Lebanon in February 1984.

Meanwhile, in the Caribbean island nation of Grenada, Prime Minister Maurice Bishop was deposed and executed in a bloody coup by radical elements of his leftist New Jewel Movement. Less than a week later, and only one day after the bombing of the Marine compound in Lebanon, Reagan ordered an invasion, which he justified as necessary to prevent the country from becoming a dangerous Soviet outpost and to protect American students at the medical school there.

In keeping with Reagan's belief that the United States should do more to prevent the spread of communism, his administration expanded military and economic assistance to friendly Third World governments battling leftist insurgencies, and he actively supported guerrilla movements and other opposition forces in countries with leftist governments. This policy, which became known as the Reagan Doctrine, was applied with particular zeal in Latin America. During the 1980s the United States supported military-dominated governments in El Salvador, providing the country with some $4 billion in military and economic aid and helping to organize and train elite units of the Salvadoran army. In 1981 Reagan authorized $20 million to recruit and train a band of guerillas to overthrow the new leftist government of Nicaragua. Numbering about 15,000 by the mid-1980s, the "Contras," as they came to be called, were never a serious military threat, though they did cause millions of dollars in damage to the Nicaraguan economy through their attacks on farms and cooperatives, infrastructure, and other civilian targets.

THE IRAN-CONTRA AFFAIR

At the time of the presidential election of 1984, Reagan was at the height of his popularity. He and Bush easily defeated their Democratic opponents, Walter Mondale and Geraldine Ferraro, by 59 percent to 41 percent of the popular vote; in the electoral college Reagan received 525 votes to Mondale's 13, the largest number of electoral votes of any candidate in history.

In early November 1985 Reagan authorized a secret initiative to sell antitank and antiaircraft missiles to Iran in exchange for that country's help in securing the release of Americans held hostage by terrorist groups in Lebanon. The plan directly contradicted the administration's publicly stated policy of refusing to negotiate with terrorists or to aid countries—such as Iran—that supported international terrorism. News of the arms-for-hostages deal, first made public in November 1986, proved intensely embarrassing to the president. Even more damaging, however, was the announcement later that month by Attorney General Edwin Meese that a portion of the $48 million earned from the sales had been diverted to a secret fund to purchase weapons and supplies for the Contras in Nicaragua. The diversion was undertaken by a National Security Council (NSC) aide, U.S. Marine Corps Lieutenant Colonel Oliver North with the approval of the head of the NSC, Rear Admiral John Poindexter. These activities constituted a violation of a law passed by Congress in 1984 (the second Boland Amendment) that forbade direct or indirect American military aid to the Contra insurgency.

In response to the crisis, by this time known as the Iran-Contra Affair, Reagan fired both North and Poindexter and appointed a special commission, headed by former senator John Tower of Texas (the Tower Commission), to investigate the matter. After investigations by an independent counsel, North and Poindexter were convicted on charges of obstructing justice and related offenses, but their convictions were overturned on the ground that testimony given at their trials had been influenced by information they had supplied to Congress under a limited grant of immunity. Reagan accepted responsibility for the arms-for-hostages deal but denied any knowledge of the diversion.

RETIREMENT AND DECLINING HEALTH

In the presidential election of 1988, Reagan campaigned actively for the Republican nominee, Vice Pres. Bush, who defeated Democratic candidate Michael Dukakis in large part because of Reagan's continued popularity. Reagan retired to his home in Los Angeles, where he wrote his autobiography, *An American Life* (1990). In 1994, in a letter to the American people, Reagan disclosed that he had been diagnosed with Alzheimer disease, a degenerative brain disorder.

GEORGE BUSH

(b. June 12, 1924, Milton, Mass.)

George Bush was a politician and businessman who was vice president of the United States (1981–89) and the 41st president of the United States (1989–93). As president, Bush assembled a multinational force to compel the withdrawal of Iraq from Kuwait in the Persian Gulf War.

EARLY LIFE AND CAREER

Bush was the son of Prescott Sheldon Bush, an investment banker and U.S. senator from Connecticut, and Dorothy Walker Bush, scion of a prominent St. Louis, Missouri, family. The young Bush grew up in Greenwich, Conn., and attended private schools there and in Andover, Mass. Upon graduation from Phillips Academy in Andover he joined the U.S. Naval Reserve. He served from 1942 to 1944 as a torpedo bomber pilot on aircraft carriers in the Pacific during World War II, flying some 58 combat missions; he was shot down by the Japanese in 1944. For his service he won the Distinguished Flying Cross. In January 1945 he married Barbara Pierce.

Following the family tradition, Bush attended Yale University, graduating in 1948. His membership in the Skull and Bones secret society there later became an issue that his critics used as evidence of elitism. Rejecting a position in his father's firm, he moved with his young family to Texas and became a salesman of oil-field supplies. He cofounded the Bush-Overbey Oil Development Company (1951), the Zapata Petroleum Corporation (1953), and the Zapata Off-Shore Company (1954). In 1959 he became active in the Republican Party in Houston, and after losing a campaign for the U.S. Senate to Democrat Ralph Yarborough in 1964, Bush was elected in 1966 to a safely Republican seat in the U.S. House of Representatives. He gave up the seat in 1970 to run again for the Senate. He was defeated again, this time by Democrat Lloyd Bentsen, Jr. Shortly after his defeat, Bush was appointed by Pres. Richard M. Nixon to serve as U.S. ambassador to the

United Nations (UN; 1971–72). In 1973, as the Watergate Scandal was erupting, Bush became chairman of the Republican National Committee. In this post, he stood by Pres. Nixon until August 1974, when he joined a growing chorus of voices calling on the president to resign. Later that year, Pres. Gerald R. Ford, who had nominated Nelson Rockefeller as his vice president, named a disappointed Bush chief of the U.S. Liaison Office in Beijing—which was then the senior U.S. representative in China, because relations between the two countries did not permit the exchange of ambassadors. He served in this capacity until he was asked to head the Central Intelligence Agency (CIA) in 1976. As CIA director, Bush took steps to ensure that the agency's activities did not exceed congressional authorization. When Jimmy Carter took office in 1977, Bush resigned and returned to Texas, where in 1979 he announced his candidacy for president.

VICE PRESIDENCY

After declaring that his opponent, the more popular and conservative Ronald W. Reagan, would have to practice "voodoo economics" in order to increase federal revenue by lowering taxes, Bush abandoned his campaign for the Republican Party's presidential nomination in May 1980 and threw his support behind Reagan, who then chose Bush as his running mate. The Reagan-Bush ticket defeated the Democratic ticket of Jimmy Carter and Walter Mondale by a wide margin in the 1980 presidential election. Bush won Reagan's loyalty, and the two were reelected in 1984 for a second term in an even greater landslide than that of 1980.

As vice president, Bush traveled more than a million miles as the administration's representative. When asked about his involvement in the Iran-Contra Affair—in which the Reagan administration, in violation of congressional edict, used funds from the illegal sale of arms to Iran to fund Contra rebels fighting the Marxist government of Nicaragua—Bush claimed that he was "out of the loop," though he did admit knowing about the arms sale to Iran. In 1987 he published an autobiography, *Looking Forward* (written with Victor Gold).

An early and leading candidate for the Republican Party's nomination for the presidency in 1988, he secured the nomination and, together with his running mate, Dan Quayle, defeated the Democratic candidate, Michael Dukakis, winning 53 percent of the popular vote to Dukakis's 46 percent.

George Bush, 1989. White House photo/Library of Congress, Washington, D.C.

Although Bush had called for "a kinder, and gentler, nation" in his speech accepting the nomination, his campaign was negative, at one point criticizing Dukakis with a phrase—"card-carrying member of the American Civil Liberties Union"—reminiscent of that used by Senator Joe McCarthy. Bush also won supporters with his pledge to continue the Reagan economic program, repeatedly stating: "Read my lips, no new taxes!"

PRESIDENCY

Upon assuming office, Bush made a number of notable senior staff appointments, among them that of Gen. Colin Powell to chairman of the U.S. Joint Chiefs of Staff. His other important policy makers included James Baker as

secretary of state and William Bennett as director of the
Office of National Drug Control Policy. In the course of
his presidency, he also nominated two Supreme Court justices, David H. Souter (to replace the retiring William J.
Brennan) and the more controversial Clarence Thomas
(to replace Thurgood Marshall).

From the outset of his presidency, however, Bush demonstrated far more interest in foreign than domestic policy.
In December 1989, he ordered a military invasion of
Panama in order to topple that country's leader, Gen.
Manuel Antonio Noriega, who—though at one time of
service to the U.S. government—had become notorious
for his brutality and his involvement in the drug trade.
The invasion, which lasted four days, resulted in hundreds
of deaths, mostly of Panamanians, and the operation was
denounced by both the Organization of American States
and the UN General Assembly.

Bush's presidency coincided with world events of large
proportion, including the collapse of communism in eastern Europe and the Soviet Union and the reunification of
Germany. In November 1990 Bush met with Soviet leader
Mikhail Gorbachev in Paris and signed a mutual nonag-
gression pact, a symbolic conclusion to the Cold War.
They signed treaties sharply reducing the number of weapons that the two superpowers had stockpiled over the
decades of Cold War hostility.

In August 1990, Iraq invaded and occupied Kuwait.
Bush led a worldwide UN-approved embargo against Iraq
to force its withdrawal and sent a U.S. military contingent
to Saudi Arabia to counteract Iraqi pressure and intimida-
tion. Perhaps his most significant diplomatic achievement
was the skillful construction of a coalition of western
European and Arab states against Iraq. Over the objections of those who favoured restraint, Bush increased the
U.S. military presence in the Persian Gulf region to about

500,000 troops within a few months. When Iraq failed to withdraw from Kuwait, he authorized a U.S.-led air offensive that began on Jan. 16–17, 1991. The ensuing Persian Gulf War culminated in an Allied ground offensive in late February that decimated Iraq's armies and restored Kuwait's independence.

On the strength of his victory over Iraq and his competent leadership in foreign affairs, Bush's approval rating soared to about 90 percent. This popularity soon waned, however, as an economic recession that began in late 1990 persisted into 1992. Throughout this period, Bush showed much less initiative in domestic affairs, though he initially worked with Congress in efforts to reduce the federal government's continuing large budget deficits. A moderate conservative, he made no drastic departures from Reagan's policies—except in taxes. In 1990, in a move that earned him the enmity of his conservative supporters and the distrust of many voters who had backed him in 1988, he reneged on his "read my lips" pledge and raised taxes in an attempt to cope with the soaring budget deficit.

Bush's policy reversal on taxation and his inability to turn around the economy—his failure to put across what he called "the vision thing" to the American public—ultimately proved his downfall. Bush ran a lacklustre campaign for reelection in 1992. He faced a fierce early challenge from Patrick Buchanan in the Republican primary and then lost votes in the general election to third-party candidate Ross Perot. Meanwhile, Bush's Democratic opponent, Bill Clinton of Arkansas, hammered away at the issue of the deteriorating economy. Bush, the first vice president since Martin Van Buren in 1836 to succeed directly to the presidency via an election rather than the death of the incumbent, lost to Clinton by a popular vote of 37 percent to Clinton's 43 percent; Perot garnered an impressive 19 percent of the vote.

In his last weeks in office, Bush ordered a U.S. military-led mission to feed the starving citizens of war-torn Somalia, thereby placing U.S. marines in the crossfire of warring factions and inadvertently causing the deaths of 18 soldiers. Equally as controversial was his pardoning of six Reagan administration officials charged with illegal actions associated with the Iran-Contra Affair.

RETIREMENT

Bush and his wife, Barbara, returned to Houston on the day of Clinton's inauguration and had little formal involvement with the Republican Party thereafter. His son George W. Bush, a popular two-term governor of Texas, successfully ran for president in 2000, becoming only the second son of a president to win the White House; the first was John Quincy Adams in 1824. Another son, Jeb, was elected governor of Florida in 1998.

BILL CLINTON

(b. Aug. 19, 1946, Hope, Ark., U.S.)

B ill Clinton was the 42nd president of the United States (1993–2001). As president he oversaw the country's longest peacetime economic expansion. In 1998 he became the second U.S. president to be impeached; he was acquitted by the Senate in 1999.

EARLY LIFE

Bill Clinton's father was a traveling salesman who died in an automobile accident three months before his son was born. His widow, Virginia Dell Blythe, married Roger Clinton, and, despite their unstable union (they divorced and then remarried) and her husband's alcoholism, her son eventually took his stepfather's name. (His name at birth was William Jefferson Blythe III.) Reared in part by his maternal grandmother, Bill Clinton developed political aspirations at an early age; they were solidified (by his own account) in July 1963, when he met and shook hands with Pres. John F. Kennedy.

Clinton enrolled at Georgetown University in Washington, D.C., in 1964 and graduated in 1968 with a degree in international affairs. During his freshman and sophomore years he was elected student president, and during his junior and senior years he worked as an intern for Sen. J. William Fulbright, the Arkansas Democrat who chaired the U.S. Senate Committee on Foreign Relations. Fulbright was a vocal critic of the Vietnam War, and Clinton, like many young men of his generation, opposed the war as well. He received a draft deferment for the first year of his studies as a Rhodes Scholar at the University of Oxford in 1968 and later attempted to extend the deferment by applying to the Reserve Officers' Training Corps (ROTC) program at the University of Arkansas School of Law. Although he soon changed his plans and returned to Oxford, thus making himself eligible for the draft, he was not chosen. While at Oxford, Clinton wrote a letter to the director of the Arkansas ROTC program thanking the director for "saving" him from the draft and explaining his concern that his opposition to the war could ruin his future "political viability." During this period Clinton also experimented with marijuana; his later claim that he "didn't inhale" would become the subject of much ridicule.

After graduating from Yale University Law School in 1973, Clinton joined the faculty of the University of Arkansas School of Law, where he taught until 1976. In 1974 he ran unsuccessfully for a seat in the U.S. House of Representatives. In 1975 he married a fellow Yale Law graduate, attorney Hillary Rodham, who thereafter took

an active role in his political career. In the following year
he was elected attorney general of Arkansas, and in 1978
he won the governorship, becoming the youngest governor the country had seen in 40 years.

GOVERNOR OF ARKANSAS

After an eventful two-year term as governor, Clinton failed
in his reelection bid in 1980, the year his daughter and only
child, Chelsea, was born. After apologizing to voters for
unpopular decisions he had made as governor (such as
highway-improvement projects funded by increases in the
state gasoline tax and automobile licensing fees), he
regained the governor's office in 1982 and was successively
reelected three more times by substantial margins. A
pragmatic, centrist Democrat, he imposed mandatory
competency testing for teachers and students and encouraged investment in the state by granting tax breaks to
industries. He became a prominent member of the
Democratic Leadership Council, a group that sought to
recast the party's agenda away from its traditional liberal-
ism and move it closer to what it perceived as the centre of
American political life.

Clinton declared his candidacy for president while still
governor of Arkansas. Just before the New Hampshire
presidential primary, his campaign was nearly derailed by
widespread press coverage of his alleged 12-year affair with
an Arkansas woman, Gennifer Flowers. In a subsequent
interview watched by millions of viewers on the television
news program *60 Minutes*, Clinton and his wife admitted
to having marital problems. Clinton's popularity soon
rebounded, and he scored a strong second-place showing
in New Hampshire. On the strength of his middle-of-the-
road approach, his apparent sympathy for the concerns
of ordinary Americans (his statement "I feel your pain"

became a well-known phrase), and his personal warmth, he eventually won the Democratic presidential nomination in 1992. Facing incumbent Pres. George Bush, Clinton and his running mate, Tennessee Sen. Al Gore, argued that 12 years of Republican leadership had led to political and economic stagnation. In November the Clinton-Gore ticket defeated both Bush and independent candidate Ross Perot with 43 percent of the popular vote to 37 percent for Bush and 19 percent for Perot; Clinton defeated Bush in the electoral college by a vote of 370 to 168.

PRESIDENCY

The Clinton administration got off to a shaky start. His attempt to fulfill a campaign promise to end discrimination against gay men and lesbians in the military was met with criticism from conservatives and some military leaders—including Gen. Colin Powell, the chairman of the Joint Chiefs of Staff. In response, Clinton proposed a compromise policy—summed up by the phrase "Don't ask, don't tell"— that failed to satisfy either side of the issue. Clinton's first two nominees for attorney general withdrew after questions were raised about domestic workers they had hired. Clinton's efforts to sign campaign-finance reform legislation were quashed by a Republican filibuster in the Senate, as was his economic-stimulus package.

Bill Clinton, 1992. White House photo/Library of Congress, Washington, D.C.

Clinton had promised during the campaign to institute a system of universal health insurance. His appointment of his wife to chair the Task Force on National Health Care Reform, a novel role for the country's first lady, was criticized by conservatives, who objected both to the propriety of the arrangement and to Hillary Rodham Clinton's feminist views. They joined lobbyists for the insurance industry, small-business organizations, and the American Medical Association to campaign vehemently against the task force's eventual proposal, the Health Security Act. Despite protracted negotiations with Congress, all efforts to pass compromise legislation failed.

Despite these early missteps, Clinton's first term was marked by numerous successes, including the passage by Congress of the North American Free Trade Agreement, which created a free-trade zone for the United States, Canada, and Mexico. Clinton also appointed several women and minorities to significant government posts throughout his administration, including Janet Reno as attorney general, Donna Shalala as secretary of Health and Human Services, Joycelyn Elders as surgeon general, Madeleine Albright as the first woman secretary of state, and Ruth Bader Ginsburg as the second woman justice on the United States Supreme Court. During Clinton's first term, Congress enacted a deficit-reduction package—which passed the Senate with a tie-breaking vote from Gore—and some 30 major bills related to education, crime prevention, the environment, and women's and family issues, including the Violence Against Women Act and the Family and Medical Leave Act.

In January 1994 Attorney General Reno approved an investigation into business dealings by Clinton and his wife with an Arkansas housing development corporation known as Whitewater. Led from August by independent counsel Kenneth Starr, the Whitewater inquiry consumed several years and more than $50 million but did not turn up conclusive evidence of wrongdoing by the Clintons.

The renewal of the Whitewater investigation under Starr, the continuing rancorous debate in Congress over Clinton's health care initiative, and the liberal character of some of Clinton's policies—which alienated significant numbers of American voters—all contributed to Republican electoral victories in November 1994, when the party gained a majority in both houses of Congress for the first time in 40 years. A chastened Clinton subsequently tempered some of his policies and accommodated some Republican proposals, eventually embracing a more aggressive deficit-reduction plan and a massive overhaul of the country's welfare system while continuing to oppose Republican efforts to cut government spending on social programs. Ultimately, most American voters found themselves more alienated by the uncompromising and confrontational behaviour of the new Republicans in Congress than they had been by Clinton, who won considerable public sympathy for his more moderate approach.

Clinton's initiatives in foreign policy during his first term included a successful effort in September–October 1994 to reinstate Haitian Pres. Jean-Bertrand Aristide, who had been ousted by a military coup in 1991; the sponsorship of peace talks and the eventual Dayton Accords (1995) aimed at ending the ethnic conflict in Bosnia and Herzegovina; and a leading role in the ongoing attempt to bring about a permanent resolution of the dispute between Palestinians and Israelis. In 1993 he invited Israeli Prime Minister Yitzhak Rabin and Palestine Liberation Organization chairman Yāsir 'Arafāt to Washington to sign a historic agreement that granted limited Palestinian self-rule in the Gaza Strip and Jericho.

Clinton was handily reelected in 1996, buoyed by a recovering and increasingly strong economy. He captured 49 percent of the popular vote to Republican Bob Dole's

41 percent and Perot's 8 percent; the electoral vote was 379 to 159. Strong economic growth continued during Clinton's second term, eventually setting a record for the country's longest peacetime expansion. By 1998 the Clinton administration was overseeing the first balanced budget since 1969 and the largest budget surpluses in the country's history. The vibrant economy also produced historically high levels of home ownership and the lowest unemployment rate in nearly 30 years.

In 1998 Starr was granted permission to expand the scope of his continuing investigation to determine whether Clinton had encouraged a 24-year-old White House intern, Monica Lewinsky, to state falsely under oath that she and Clinton had not had an affair. Clinton repeatedly and publicly denied that the affair had taken place. His compelled testimony, which appeared evasive and disingenuous even to Clinton's supporters, prompted renewed criticism of Clinton's character from conservatives and liberals alike. After conclusive evidence of the affair came to light, Clinton apologized to his family and to the American public. On the basis of Starr's 445-page report and supporting evidence, the House of Representatives in 1998 approved two articles of impeachment, for perjury and obstruction of justice. Clinton was acquitted of the charges by the Senate in 1999. Despite his impeachment, Clinton's job-approval rating remained high.

In foreign affairs, Clinton ordered a four-day bombing campaign against Iraq in December 1998 in response to Iraq's failure to cooperate fully with United Nations weapons inspectors (the bombing coincided with the start of full congressional debate on Clinton's impeachment). In 1999 U.S.-led forces of the North Atlantic Treaty Organization (NATO) conducted a successful three-month bombing campaign against Yugoslavia designed to end Serbian attacks on ethnic Albanians in the province of

Kosovo. In 1998 and 2000 Clinton was hailed as a peace-maker in visits to Ireland and Northern Ireland, and in 2000 he became the first U.S. president to visit Vietnam since the end of the Vietnam War. He spent the last weeks of his presidency in an unsuccessful effort to broker a final peace agreement between the Israelis and the Palestinians. Shortly before he left office, Clinton was roundly criticized by Democrats as well as by Republicans for having issued a number of questionable pardons, including one to the former spouse of a major Democratic Party contributor.

LIFE AFTER THE PRESIDENCY

Bill Clinton remained active in political affairs and was a popular speaker on the lecture circuit. In 2001 he founded the William J. Clinton Foundation, a philanthropic organization that addressed various global issues through such programs as the Clinton HIV/AIDS Initiative (established 2002), the Clinton Economic Opportunity Initiative (2002), the Clinton Global Initiative (2005), and the Clinton Climate Initiative (2006). In 2004 the William J. Clinton Presidential Library and Museum opened in Little Rock. The following year, after a tsunami in the Indian Ocean had caused widespread death and devastation, Clinton was appointed by United Nations Secretary-General Kofi Annan to serve as a special envoy for relief efforts, a position he held until 2007. In 2009 Clinton succeeded former president George H.W. Bush as chairman of the National Constitution Center, a history museum in Philadelphia. Later that year he was named a UN special envoy to Haiti. Clinton's writings include an autobiography, *My Life* (2004).

Bill Clinton once again entered the international spotlight in August 2009, when he made an unannounced visit to North Korea, securing the release of two U.S.

Bill Clinton, Laura Ling, Al Gore, and Euna Lee in Burbank, Calif., August 5, 2009, the day after the two Current TV journalists were released by North Korean authorities. Ann Johansson/Getty Images

journalists who had been captured and imprisoned by the North Koreans for illegally entering the country in March of 2009. On August 4, Clinton was able to obtain a pardon for the two women from North Korean leader Kim Jong Il. Clinton escorted the journalists back to the United States the following day.

GEORGE W. BUSH

(b. July 6, 1946, New Haven, Conn.)

George Walker Bush was the 43rd president of the United States (2001–09). As president he led his country's response to the terrorist September 11 attacks in 2001 and initiated the Iraq War in 2003. Narrowly winning the electoral college vote over Vice Pres. Al Gore in one of the closest and most controversial elections in

American history, George W. Bush became the first person since Benjamin Harrison in 1888 to be elected president despite having lost the nationwide popular vote. Before his election as president, Bush was a businessman and served as governor of Texas (1995–2000).

EARLY LIFE

Bush was the oldest of six children of George Bush, who served as the 41st president of the United States (1989–93), and Barbara Bush. The younger Bush grew up largely in Midland and Houston, Texas. From 1961 to 1964 he attended Phillips Academy in Andover, Mass., the boarding school from which his father had graduated. He received a bachelor's degree in history from Yale University, his father's and grandfather's alma mater, in 1968. Bush was president of his fraternity and, like his father, a member of Yale's secretive Skull and Bones society; unlike his father, he was only an average student and did not excel in athletics.

In May 1968, two weeks before his graduation from Yale and the expiration of his student draft deferment, Bush applied as a pilot trainee in the Texas Air National Guard, whose members were less likely than regular soldiers to fight in the Vietnam War. Commissioned a second lieutenant in July 1968, he became a certified fighter pilot in June 1970. In the fall of 1970, he applied for admission to the University of Texas law school but was rejected. Although Bush apparently missed at least eight months of duty between May 1972 and May 1973, he was granted an early discharge so that he could start Harvard Business School in the fall of 1973. His spotty military record resurfaced as a campaign issue in both the 2000 and 2004 presidential elections.

After receiving his M.B.A. from Harvard in 1975, Bush returned to Midland, where he began working for a

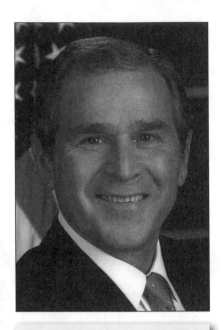

George W. Bush. Eric Draper/
White House Photo

Bush family friend, an oil and gas attorney, and later started his own oil and gas firm. He married Laura Welch, a teacher and librarian, in Midland in 1977. After an unsuccessful run for Congress in 1978, Bush devoted himself to building his business. With help from his uncle, who was then raising funds for Bush's father's campaign for the Republican presidential nomination, Bush was able to attract numerous prominent investors. The company struggled through the early 1980s until the eventual collapse of oil prices in 1986, when it was purchased by the Harken Energy Corporation. Bush received Harken stock, a job as a consultant to the company, and a seat on the company's board of directors.

In the same year, shortly after his 40th birthday, Bush gave up drinking alcohol. "I realized," he later explained, "that alcohol was beginning to crowd out my energies and could crowd, eventually, my affections for other people." His decision was partly the result of a self-described spiritual awakening and a strengthening of his Christian faith that had begun the previous year, after a conversation with the Rev. Billy Graham, a Bush family friend.

After the sale of his company, Bush spent 18 months in Washington, D.C., working as an adviser and speechwriter in his father's presidential campaign. Following the election, he moved to Dallas, where he and a former business partner organized a group of investors to purchase the Texas Rangers professional baseball team. Although Bush's investment, which he made with a loan he obtained by using his Harken stock as collateral, was relatively small, his role as managing partner of the team brought him much exposure in the media and earned him a reputation as a successful businessman. When Bush's partnership sold the team in 1998, Bush received nearly $15 million.

GOVERNOR OF TEXAS

In 1994 Bush challenged Democratic incumbent Ann Richards for the governorship of Texas. Bush won the election with 53 percent of the vote (compared with 46 percent for Richards), thus becoming the first child of a U.S. president to be elected a state governor.

As governor, Bush increased state spending on elementary and secondary education and made the salaries and promotions of teachers and administrators contingent on their students' performance on standardized tests. His administration increased the number of crimes for which juveniles could be sentenced to adult prisons following custody in juvenile detention and lowered to 14 the age at which children could be tried as adults. Throughout his tenure Bush received international attention for the brisk use of capital punishment in Texas relative to other states. Reelected in 1998 with nearly 70 percent of the vote, Bush became the first Texas governor to win consecutive four-year terms (in 1972 voters had approved a referendum that extended the governor's term from two years to four).

Bush formally announced his candidacy for the Republican presidential nomination in June 1999. He described his political philosophy as "compassionate conservatism," a view that combined traditional Republican economic policies with concern for the underprivileged. He won the Republican nomination, taking a strong lead in public opinion polls over Vice Pres. Al Gore, the

Democratic Party nominee; Ralph Nader, the Green Party candidate; and political journalist Patrick Buchanan, the nominee of the Reform Party. His running mate was Dick Cheney, former chief of staff for Pres. Gerald Ford and secretary of defense during the presidency of Bush's father.

As the general election campaign continued, the gap in the polls between Bush and Gore narrowed to the closest in any election in the previous 40 years. On election day the presidency hinged on the 25 electoral votes of Florida, where Bush led Gore by fewer than 1,000 popular votes after a mandatory statewide machine recount. After the Gore campaign asked for manual recounts in four heavily Democratic counties, the Bush campaign filed suit in federal court to stop them. For five weeks the election remained unresolved as Florida state courts and federal courts heard numerous legal challenges by both campaigns. Eventually the Florida Supreme Court decided (4–3) to order a statewide manual recount of the approximately 45,000 "undervotes"—ballots that machines recorded as not clearly expressing a presidential vote. The Bush campaign quickly filed an appeal with the U.S. Supreme Court, asking it to delay the recounts until it could hear the case; a stay was issued by the court on December 9. Three days later, concluding (7–2) that a fair statewide recount could not be performed in time to meet the December 18 deadline for certifying the state's electors, the court issued a controversial 5–4 decision to reverse the Florida Supreme Court's recount order, effectively awarding the presidency to Bush. By winning Florida, Bush narrowly won the electoral vote over Gore by 271 to 266—only 1 more than the required 270 (one Gore elector abstained).

With his inauguration, Bush became only the second son of a president to assume the nation's highest office; the other was John Quincy Adams (1825–29), the son of John Adams (1797–1801).

George W. Bush sitting at his desk in the Oval Office, with his father, George H.W. Bush, looking on, 2001. Eric Draper/The White House

PRESIDENCY

EARLY INITIATIVES

Bush was the first Republican president to enjoy a majority in both houses of Congress since Dwight D. Eisenhower in the 1950s. Taking advantage of his party's strength, Bush proposed a $1.6 trillion tax-cut bill in February 2001. A compromise measure worth $1.35 billion was passed by Congress in June, despite Democratic objections that it unfairly benefited the wealthy.

In foreign affairs, the Bush administration announced that the United States would not abide by the Kyoto Protocol on reducing the emission of gases responsible for global warming, which the United States had signed in the last days of the Bill Clinton administration, because the agreement did not impose emission limits on developing countries and because it could harm the U.S. economy. The administration also withdrew from the 1972 Anti-Ballistic Missile Treaty and attempted to secure commitments from various governments not to extradite U.S. citizens to the new International Criminal Court, whose jurisdiction it rejected.

THE SEPTEMBER 11 ATTACKS

On Sept. 11, 2001, Bush faced a crisis that would transform his presidency. That morning, four American commercial airplanes were hijacked by Islamic terrorists. Two of the planes were deliberately crashed into the twin towers of the World Trade Center in New York City, destroying both towers and collapsing or damaging many surrounding buildings. A third was used to destroy part of the Pentagon building outside Washington, D.C. The fourth plane crashed outside Pittsburgh, Pa., after passengers apparently attempted to retake it. The crashes—the worst terrorist incident on U.S. soil—killed some 3,000 people.

The Bush administration accused radical Islamist Osama bin Laden and his terrorist network, al-Qaeda (Arabic: "the Base"), of responsibility for the attacks and charged the Taliban government of Afghanistan with harbouring bin Laden and his followers (in a videotape in 2004, bin Laden acknowledged that he was responsible). After assembling an international military coalition, Bush ordered a massive bombing campaign against Afghanistan, which began on Oct. 7, 2001. U.S.-led forces quickly toppled the Taliban government and routed al-Qaeda fighters, though bin Laden himself remained elusive. In the wake of the September 11 attacks and during the war in Afghanistan, Bush's public-approval ratings were the highest of his presidency, reaching 90 percent in some polls.

Domestic Measures

Immediately after the September 11 attacks, domestic security and the threat of terrorism became the chief focus of the Bush administration and the top priority of government at every level. Declaring a global "war on terrorism," Bush announced that the country would not rest until "every terrorist group of global reach has been found, stopped, and defeated." To coordinate the government's domestic response, the administration formed a cabinet-level Department of Homeland Security, which began operating on Jan. 24, 2003.

In October 2001 the Bush administration introduced, and Congress quickly passed, the Uniting and Strengthening America by Providing Appropriate Tools Required to Intercept and Obstruct Terrorism Act (the USA PATRIOT Act), which significantly but temporarily expanded the search and surveillance powers of the Federal Bureau of Investigation and other law-enforcement agencies. (Most of the law's provisions were made permanent in 2006 by the USA PATRIOT Improvement and Reauthorization Act.)

In January 2002 Bush secretly authorized the National Security Agency (NSA) to monitor the international telephone calls and e-mail messages of American citizens and others in the United States without first obtaining an order from the Foreign Intelligence Surveillance Court, as required by the Foreign Intelligence Surveillance Act of 1978. After the program was revealed in news reports in December 2005, supporters of the administration in Congress attempted to provide a legal basis for the spying, but their efforts became mired in debate over whether telecommunications companies that cooperated with the NSA should be granted retroactive immunity against numerous civil lawsuits. Legislation granting immunity and expanding the NSA's surveillance powers was finally passed by Congress and signed by Bush in July 2008.

Treatment of Detainees

In January 2002, as the pacification of Afghanistan continued, the United States began transferring captured Taliban fighters and suspected al-Qaeda members from Afghanistan to a special prison at the country's permanent naval base in Guantánamo Bay, Cuba. Eventually hundreds of prisoners were held at the facility without charge and without the legal means to challenge their detentions. The administration argued that it was not obliged to grant basic constitutional protections to the prisoners, because the base was outside U.S. territory; nor was it required to observe the Geneva Conventions regarding the treatment of prisoners of war and civilians during wartime, because the conventions did not apply to "unlawful enemy combatants." It further maintained that the president had the authority to place any individual, including an American citizen, in indefinite military custody without charge by declaring him an enemy combatant.

The prison at Guantánamo became the focus of international controversy in June 2004, after a confidential report by the International Committee of the Red Cross found that significant numbers of prisoners had been interrogated by means of techniques that were "tantamount to torture." (The Bush administration had frequently and vigorously denied that the United States practiced torture.)

The leak of the report came just two months after the publication of photographs of abusive treatment of prisoners by American soldiers at the Abu Ghraib prison in Iraq. In response to the Abu Ghraib revelations, Congress eventually passed the Detainee Treatment Act, which banned the "cruel, inhuman, or degrading" treatment of prisoners in U.S. military custody. Although the measure became law with Bush's signature in December 2005, he added a "signing statement" in which he reserved the right to set aside the law's restrictions if he deemed them inconsistent with his constitutional powers as commander in chief.

In separate programs run by the Central Intelligence Agency (CIA), dozens of individuals suspected of involvement in terrorism were abducted outside the United States and held in secret prisons in eastern Europe and elsewhere or transferred for interrogation to countries that routinely practiced torture. Although such extrajudicial transfers, or "extraordinary renditions," had taken place during the Clinton administration, the Bush administration greatly expanded the practice after the September 11 attacks.

In February 2005 the CIA confirmed that some individuals in its custody had been subjected to "enhanced interrogation techniques," including waterboarding (simulated drowning), which was generally regarded as a form of torture under international law. The CIA's position that waterboarding did not constitute torture had been based on the legal opinions of the Justice Department and specifically on a secret memo issued in 2002 that adopted an unconventionally narrow and legally questionable definition of torture. After the memo was leaked to the press in June 2004, the Justice Department rescinded its opinion. In 2005, however, the department issued new secret memos declaring the legality of enhanced interrogation techniques, including waterboarding. After the new memos were revealed in news reports in 2007, Bush issued an executive order that prohibited the CIA from using torture or acts of cruel, inhuman, or degrading treatment, though the specific interrogation techniques it was allowed to use remained classified. In March 2008 Bush vetoed a bill directed specifically at the CIA that would have prevented the agency from using any interrogation technique, such as waterboarding, that was not included in the U.S. Army's field manual on interrogation.

THE IRAQ WAR

Road to War

In September 2002 the administration announced a new National Security Strategy of the United States of America. It was notable for its declaration that the United States would act "preemptively," using military force if necessary, to forestall or prevent threats to its security by terrorists or "rogue states" possessing biological, chemical, or nuclear weapons—so-called weapons of mass destruction. This policy soon came to be known as the Bush Doctrine.

Meanwhile, Bush and other high administration officials began to draw worldwide attention to Iraqi Pres. Ṣaddām Ḥussein and to suspicions that Iraq possessed or was attempting to develop weapons of mass destruction in violation of United Nations Security Council resolutions. In November 2002 the Bush administration successfully lobbied for a new Security Council resolution providing for the return of weapons inspectors to Iraq. Soon afterward Bush declared that Iraq had failed to comply fully with the new resolution and that the country continued to possess weapons of mass destruction. For several weeks, the United States and Britain tried without success to secure support from other Security Council members for a second resolution explicitly authorizing the use of force against Iraq (though administration officials insisted that earlier resolutions provided sufficient legal justification for military action). As part of the administration's diplomatic campaign, Bush and other officials frequently warned that Iraq possessed weapons of mass destruction, that it was attempting to acquire nuclear weapons, and that it had long-standing ties to al-Qaeda and other terrorist organizations.

Operation Iraqi Freedom

Finally, Bush announced the end of U.S. diplomacy. On March 17 he issued an ultimatum to Ṣaddām, giving him and his immediate family 48 hours to leave Iraq or face removal by force. Bush also indicated that, even if Ṣaddām relinquished power, U.S. military forces would enter the country to search for weapons of mass destruction and to stabilize the new government.

After Ṣaddām's public refusal to leave and as the 48-hour deadline approached, Bush ordered the invasion of Iraq, called Operation Iraqi Freedom, to begin on March 20 (local time). In the ground phase of the Iraq War, U.S. and British forces quickly overwhelmed the Iraqi army and irregular Iraqi fighters, and by mid-April they had entered Baghdad and all other major Iraqi cities and forced Ṣaddām's regime from power.

In the wake of the invasion, hundreds of sites suspected of producing or housing weapons of mass destruction within Iraq were investigated. As the search continued without success into the following year, Bush's critics accused the administration of having misled the country into war by exaggerating the threat posed by Iraq. Ṣaddām, who went into hiding during the invasion, was captured by U.S. forces in December 2003 and was executed by the new Iraqi government three years later.

Occupation and Insurgency

Although the Bush administration had planned for a short war, stabilizing the country after the invasion proved difficult. U.S. soldiers continued to be killed or wounded in guerrilla attacks by Iraqi insurgents; this, combined with the failure to uncover weapons of mass destruction, and the enormous cost to U.S. taxpayers (approximately $10 billion per month through 2007) gradually eroded public support for the war and damaged Bush's public-approval ratings.

While acknowledging that it had underestimated the tenacity of the Iraqi resistance, the Bush administration maintained that part of the blame for the continuing violence lay with Iran, which it accused of supplying weapons and money to Iraqi-based terrorist groups. In his State of the Union address in 2002, Bush had warned that Iran (along with Iraq and North Korea) was part of an "axis of evil" that threatened the world with its support of terrorism and its ambition to acquire nuclear weapons.

FOREIGN AID

In his State of the Union address in January 2003, Bush proposed an ambitious program to address the humanitarian crisis created by the HIV/AIDS pandemic in 15 countries in Africa and the Caribbean. With a budget of $15 billion over a five-year period, the President's Emergency Plan for AIDS Relief (PEPFAR) aimed to supply life-extending medications to 2 million victims of HIV/AIDS, to prevent 7 million new cases of the disease, and to provide care for 10 million AIDS sufferers and the orphaned children of AIDS victims. The program was widely praised in the United States, even by Bush's critics, and generated enormous goodwill toward the Bush administration in Africa. Medical professionals and public health officials welcomed the greater availability of retroviral drugs but generally objected to the program's requirement that one-third of prevention funds be spent on teaching sexual abstinence and marital fidelity.

In January 2004 the Bush administration established the Millennium Challenge Corporation to distribute development aid to poor countries that demonstrated a commitment to democracy, free enterprise, and transparent governance. The agency's innovative approach allowed recipient countries to design and manage their own multi-year programs to reduce poverty and promote economic growth. By 2008 the corporation had approved some $5 billion in grant requests, though relatively little of the money had been dispersed.

The Bush administration's foreign aid programs were designed to serve its declared foreign policy goal of promoting democracy abroad, especially in parts of the world plagued by poverty and war. In eastern Europe, Bush supported expanding the membership of the North Atlantic Treaty Organization (NATO) as a means of securing democracy and stability in war-ravaged or formerly communist countries. During his presidency NATO gained seven new members: Bulgaria, Estonia, Latvia, Lithuania, Romania, Slovakia, and Slovenia.

DOMESTIC AFFAIRS

In December 2001 Bush successfully negotiated with the Democratic-controlled Senate legislation that provided federal funding to religious, or "faith-based," charities and social services. The measure, he argued, would end long-standing discrimination in federal funding against churches and other religious groups that provided needed social services in poor communities. The bill was passed by the Senate despite objections from many Democratic senators that it violated the constitutional separation of church and state. A White House Office of Faith-Based and Community Initiatives was created in January 2001.

In 2002 the U.S. economy continued to perform poorly, despite having recovered from a recession the previous November. Widespread corporate accounting scandals, some of the largest corporate bankruptcies in U.S. history, and fears over war and terrorism all contributed to consumer uncertainty and a prolonged downturn in the financial markets. Despite the economic turmoil, Bush's personal popularity enabled the Republicans to regain a majority in the Senate in midterm elections in November 2002 (though the party also lost three state governorships). With both houses of Congress under Republican control, Bush secured passage of a second tax cut of $350 billion in May 2003.

Education

In January 2002 Bush signed into law the No Child Left Behind Act, which introduced significant changes in the curriculum of the country's public elementary, middle, and high schools and dramatically increased federal regulation of state school systems. Under the law, states were required to administer yearly tests of the reading and mathematics skills of public school students and to demonstrate adequate progress toward raising the scores of all students to a level defined as "proficient" or higher. Teachers were also required to meet higher standards for certification. Schools that failed to meet their goals would be subject to gradually increasing sanctions, eventually including replacement of staff or closure.

In the first years of the program, supporters pointed to its success in increasing the test scores of minority students, who historically performed at lower levels than white students. Indeed, in the 2000 presidential campaign Bush had touted the proposed law as a remedy for what he called "the soft bigotry of low expectations" faced by the children of minorities. Critics, however, complained that the federal government was not providing enough funding to implement the program's requirements and that the law had usurped the states's traditional control of education as provided for in the Constitution. Others objected that the law was actually eroding the quality of education by forcing schools to "teach to the test" while neglecting other parts of the curriculum, such as history, social science, and art.

Medicare

In December 2003 Bush won Congressional approval of the Medicare Modernization Act (MMA), a reform of the federally sponsored health insurance program for elderly Americans. Widely recognized as the most far-reaching overhaul of Medicare to date, the MMA enabled Medicare enrollees to obtain prescription drug coverage from Medicare through private insurance companies, which then received a government subsidy; it also vastly increased the number of private insurance plans through which enrollees could receive medical benefits. Although many members of Congress from both parties criticized the MMA as needlessly complex and expensive (its cost was estimated in January 2004 at $534 billion over 10 years), a bipartisan majority accepted the measure as an imperfect but necessary compromise that would bring a much-needed insurance benefit to senior citizens. Some conservative Republicans, however, rejected the MMA on both fiscal and philosophical grounds, and many Democrats objected to a provision in the plan that prevented Medicare administrators from negotiating with pharmaceutical companies for lower drug prices.

Reelection

In 2004 Bush focused his energies on his campaign for reelection against his Democratic challenger, U.S. Sen. John Kerry. Bush's key campaign platform was his conduct of the war on terrorism, which he linked with the war in Iraq. Kerry countered that the Iraq War had been poorly planned and executed and that Bush had neglected domestic priorities. Bush defeated Kerry with a slim majority of the electoral and popular vote, and the Republicans increased their majorities in both the House and the Senate.

Social Security and Immigration

The major domestic initiative of Bush's second term was his proposal to replace Social Security (the country's system of government-managed retirement insurance) with private retirement savings accounts. The measure attracted little support, however, mainly because it would have required significant cuts in retirement benefits and heavy borrowing during the transition to the private system.

Bush also proposed a reform of immigration laws that would have allowed most of the estimated 12 million people living in the country illegally to remain temporarily as "guest workers" and to apply for U.S. citizenship after returning to their home countries and paying a fine (though citizenship would not be guaranteed). Although the proposal was supported by some prominent Democrats, including Sen. Edward M. Kennedy of Massachusetts, most other Democrats and many members of Bush's own party remained wary of the idea. More than two years of debate produced no reform legislation, though Bush did sign a measure that authorized the construction of a 700-mile (1,127-km) fence along the U.S.-Mexican border.

Environmental and Science Policy

After the Supreme Court ruled in April 2007 that greenhouse gas emissions by automobiles constitute a form of air pollution under the Clean Air Act, Bush signed energy legislation that imposed increases in automobile fuel economy standards by the year 2020. In December, however, the Environmental Protection Agency blocked a proposal by California and 16 other states to issue regulations that would have required fuel economies greater than those called for in the new federal law.

The Bush administration was frequently accused of politically motivated interference in government scientific research. Critics charged that political appointees at various agencies, many of whom had little or no relevant expertise, altered or suppressed scientific reports that were incompatible with administration policies, restricted the ability of government experts to speak publicly on certain scientific issues, and limited access to scientific information by policy makers and the public. In most cases the administration claimed that the interventions were an appropriate attempt to ensure scientific objectivity or simply a benign exercise of the authority of political appointees.

LATER DEVELOPMENTS AND ASSESSMENT

2006 Elections

The continued lack of progress in the Iraq War, a series of corruption scandals involving prominent Republican politicians, and the administration's poor response to the devastation caused by Hurricane Katrina in New Orleans and surrounding areas in August 2005 helped the Democrats win control of both houses of Congress in the midterm elections of November 2006. The new Congress soon began investigations of the NSA spying program undertaken in 2002 and of allegedly improper political influence in the dismissals of several United States attorneys in December 2006. In the latter investigation the testimony of Alberto R. Gonzales, Bush's attorney general since 2005, was viewed with skepticism by both parties and reinforced the impression that the Justice Department under his leadership was not sufficiently independent of the White House. Gonzales resigned in August 2007 and was replaced in November with Michael Mukasey.

The Plame Affair

In March 2007 Cheney's chief of staff, I. Lewis ("Scooter") Libby, was convicted on charges of perjury and obstruction of justice in connection with an investigation into the leak of the identity of a covert CIA agent in 2003. The agent, Valerie Plame, was the wife of Joseph C. Wilson, a retired foreign service officer who had traveled to Africa in early 2002 at the request of the CIA to help determine whether Iraq had attempted to purchase enriched uranium from Niger. Wilson reported that there was no evidence of an attempted purchase, and in July 2003 he publicly speculated that the administration had ignored or distorted intelligence reports such as his to justify a military invasion of Iraq. Libby allegedly identified Plame as a CIA agent to journalists to discredit Wilson by suggesting that his selection for the CIA mission was the result of nepotism. In testimony before a grand jury and agents of the Federal Bureau of Investigation, Libby falsely claimed that he had not discussed Plame's identity with journalists. Bush commuted Libby's 30-month prison sentence in July 2007.

During his second term Bush appointed two Supreme Court justices: John G. Roberts, Jr. (confirmed as chief justice in 2005), and Samuel A. Alito, Jr. (confirmed in 2006). The appointments increased to four the number of solidly conservative justices on the nine-member Supreme Court.

BARACK OBAMA

(b. Aug. 4, 1961, Honolulu, Hawaii)

Barack Obama, the 44th president of the United States (2009–), is the first African American to hold the office. Before winning the presidency, Obama represented Illinois in the U.S. Senate (2005–08). He was the third African American to be elected to that body since the end of Reconstruction (1877). In 2009 he was awarded the Nobel Peace Prize "for his extraordinary efforts to strengthen international diplomacy and cooperation between peoples."

EARLY LIFE

Obama's father, Barack Obama, Sr., was a teenage goat-herd in rural Kenya; he won a scholarship to study in the United States and eventually became a senior economist in the Kenyan government. Obama's mother, S. Ann Dunham, grew up in Kansas, Texas, and Washington State before her family settled in Honolulu. In 1961 she and Barack Sr. met in a Russian language class at the University of Hawaii and married less than a year later.

When Obama was two, Barack Sr. left to study at Harvard University; shortly thereafter, in 1964, Ann and Barack Sr. divorced. (Obama saw his father only one more time, during a brief visit when Obama was 10.) Later Ann remarried, this time to another foreign student, Lolo Soetoro from Indonesia, with whom she had a second child, Maya. Obama lived for several years in Jakarta with his half sister, mother, and stepfather. While there, Obama attended both a government-run school where he received some instruction in Islam and a Catholic private school where he took part in Christian schooling.

He returned to Hawaii in 1971 and lived in a modest apartment, sometimes with his grandparents and some-times with his mother (she remained for a time in Indonesia, returned to Hawaii, and then went abroad again—partly to pursue work on a Ph.D.—before divorcing Soetoro in 1980). For a brief period his mother was aided by government food stamps, but the family mostly lived a middle-class existence. In 1979 Obama graduated from Punahou School, an elite college preparatory academy in Honolulu.

Obama attended Occidental College in suburban Los Angeles for two years and then transferred to Columbia University in New York City, where in 1983 he received a bachelor's degree in political science. Influenced by professors who pushed him to take his studies more seriously, Obama experienced great intellectual growth during college and for a couple of years thereafter. He led a rather ascetic life and read works of literature and philosophy by William Shakespeare, Friedrich Nietzsche, Toni Morrison, and others. After serving for a couple of years as a writer and editor for Business International Corp., a research, publishing, and consulting firm in Manhattan, he took a position in 1985 as a community organizer on Chicago's largely impoverished Far South Side. He returned to school three years later and graduated magna cum laude in 1991 from Harvard University's law school, where he was the first African American to serve as president of the *Harvard Law Review*. While a summer associate in 1989 at the Chicago law firm of Sidley Austin, Obama had met Chicago native Michelle Robinson, a young lawyer at the firm. The two married in 1992.

After receiving his law degree, Obama moved to Chicago and became active in the Democratic Party. He organized Project Vote, a drive that registered tens of thousands of African Americans on voting rolls and that is credited with helping Democrat Bill Clinton win Illinois and capture the presidency in 1992. The effort also helped make Carol Moseley Braun, an Illinois state legislator, the first African American woman elected to the U.S. Senate. During this period, Obama had his first book published. The memoir, *Dreams from My Father* (1995), is the story of Obama's search for his biracial identity by tracing the lives of his now-deceased father and his extended family in Kenya. Obama lectured on constitutional law at the University of Chicago and worked as an attorney on civil rights issues.

POLITICS AND THE PRESIDENCY

In 1996 Obama was elected to the Illinois Senate, where, most notably, he helped pass legislation that tightened campaign finance regulations, expanded health care to poor families, and reformed criminal justice and welfare laws. In 2004 he was elected to the U.S. Senate, defeating Republican Alan Keyes in the first U.S. Senate race in which the two leading candidates were African Americans. While campaigning for the U.S. Senate, Obama gained national recognition by delivering the keynote address at the Democratic National Convention in July 2004. The speech wove a personal narrative of Obama's biography with the theme that all Americans are connected in ways that transcend political, cultural, and geographical differences. The address lifted Obama's once obscure memoir onto bestseller lists, and, after taking office the following year, Obama quickly became a major figure in his party. A trip to visit his father's home in Kenya in August 2006 gained international media attention, and Obama's star continued ascending. His second book, *The Audacity of Hope* (2006), a mainstream polemic on his vision for the United States, was published weeks later, instantly becoming a major best seller. In February 2007 he announced at the Old State Capitol in Springfield, Ill., where Abraham Lincoln had served as a state legislator, that he would seek the Democratic Party's presidential nomination in 2008.

Obama's personal charisma, stirring oratory, and campaign promise to bring change to the established political system resonated with many Democrats, especially young and minority voters. On Jan. 3, 2008, Obama won a surprise victory in the first major nominating contest, the Iowa caucus, over Sen. Hillary Clinton, who was the overwhelming favourite to win the nomination. Five days later, however, Obama finished second to Clinton in the New Hampshire primary, and a bruising—and sometimes bitter—primary race ensued. Obama won more than a dozen states—including Illinois, his home state, and Missouri, a traditional political bellwether—on Super Tuesday, February 5. No

Barack Obama. Courtesy of the Office of U.S. Senator Barack Obama

clear front-runner for the nomination emerged, however, as Clinton won many states with large populations, such as California and New York. Obama produced an impressive string of victories later in the month, handily winning the 11 primaries and caucuses that immediately followed Super Tuesday, which gave him a significant lead in pledged delegates. His momentum slowed in early March when Clinton won significant victories in Ohio and Texas. Though still maintaining his edge in delegates, Obama lost the key Pennsylvania primary on April 22. Two weeks later he lost a close contest in Indiana but won the North Carolina primary by a large margin, widening his delegate lead over Clinton. She initially had a big lead in so-called superdelegates (Democratic Party officials allocated votes at the convention that were unaffiliated with state primary results), but, with Obama winning more states and actual delegates, many peeled away from her and went to Obama. On June 3, following the final primaries in Montana and South Dakota, the number of delegates pledged to Obama surpassed the total necessary to claim the Democratic nomination.

On August 27 Obama became the first African American to be nominated for the presidency by either major party and went on to challenge Republican Sen. John McCain for the country's highest office. McCain criticized Obama, still a first-term senator, as being too inexperienced for the job. To counter, Obama selected

Joe Biden, a veteran senator from Delaware who had a long resume of foreign policy expertise, to be his vice presidential running mate. Obama and McCain waged a fierce and expensive contest. Obama, still bolstered by a fever of popular support, eschewed federal financing of his campaign and raised hundreds of millions of dollars, much of it coming in small donations and over the Internet from a record number of donors. Obama's fund-raising advantage helped him buy massive amounts of television advertising and organize deep grassroots organizations in key battleground states and in states that had voted Republican in previous presidential cycles.

Memorabilia from Barack Obama's presidential campaign. Obama for America

The two candidates offered a stark ideological choice for voters. Obama called for a swift withdrawal of most combat forces from Iraq and a restructuring of tax policy that would bring more relief to lower- and middle-class voters, while McCain said the United States must wait for full victory in Iraq and charged that Obama's rhetoric was long on eloquence but short on substance. Just weeks before election day, Obama's campaign seized on the economic meltdown that had resulted from the catastrophic failure of U.S. banks and financial institutions in September, calling it a result of the Republican free-market-driven policies of the eight-year administration of George W. Bush.

Obama won the election, capturing nearly 53 percent of the popular vote and 365 electoral votes. Not only did he

PRIMARY DOCUMENT: BARACK OBAMA: INAUGURAL ADDRESS

My fellow citizens:

I stand here today humbled by the task before us, grateful for the trust you have bestowed, mindful of the sacrifices borne by our ancestors.

That we are in the midst of crisis is now well understood. Our nation is at war, against a far-reaching network of violence and hatred. Our economy is badly weakened, a consequence of greed and irresponsibility on the part of some, but also our collective failure to make hard choices and prepare the nation for a new age.

Today I say to you that the challenges we face are real. They are serious and they are many. They will not be met easily or in a short span of time. But know this, America—they will be met.

We remain the most prosperous, powerful nation on Earth. But our time of standing pat, of protecting narrow interests and putting off unpleasant decisions—that time has surely passed. Starting today, we must pick ourselves up, dust ourselves off, and begin again the work of remaking America.

Now, there are some who question the scale of our ambitions—who suggest that our system cannot tolerate too many big plans. Their memories are short. For they have forgotten what this country has already done; what free men and women can achieve when imagination is joined to common purpose, and necessity to courage.

As for our common defense, we reject as false the choice between our safety and our ideals. Our Founding Fathers, faced with perils we can scarcely imagine, drafted a charter to assure the rule of law and the rights of man, a charter expanded by the blood of generations. Those ideals still light the world, and we will not give them up for expedience's sake.

Guided by these principles once more, we can meet those new threats that demand even greater effort. We will not apologize for our way of life, nor will we waver in its defense, and for those who seek to advance their aims by inducing terror and slaughtering innocents, we say to you now that our spirit is stronger and cannot be broken; you cannot outlast us, and we will defeat you.

To the Muslim world, we seek a new way forward, based on mutual interest and mutual respect. To those leaders around the globe

who seek to sow conflict, or blame their society's ills on the West—
know that your people will judge you on what you can build, not what
you destroy.

Let it be said by our children's children that when we were tested
we refused to let this journey end, that we did not turn back nor
did we falter; and with eyes fixed on the horizon and God's grace upon
us, we carried forth that great gift of freedom and delivered it safely
to future generations.

hold all the states that John Kerry had won in the 2004 election, but also captured a number of states (e.g., Colorado, Florida, Nevada, Ohio, and Virginia) that the Republicans had carried in the previous two presidential elections. On election night tens of thousands gathered in Chicago's Grant Park to see Obama claim victory. Shortly after his win, Obama resigned from the Senate. On Jan. 20, 2009, hundreds of thousands turned out in Washington, D.C., to witness him taking the oath of office as president.

On only his second day in office Obama issued executive orders banning the "harsh interrogation techniques" that had become notorious during the George W. Bush administration, closing the secret prisons run by the Central Intelligence Agency, and directing the closure of the U.S. military's detention facility at Guantánamo Bay, Cuba, within one year. To the disappointment of some of his supporters, however, he opposed the creation of a national commission to investigate the treatment of detainees at Guantánamo and in military prisons in Iraq. In February 2009 Obama announced that the United States would withdraw all combat forces from Iraq by August 2010 (though 50,000 troops would remain in the country beyond that date). To address the country's economic crisis, Obama introduced a $825 billion stimulus package (later trimmed to $787 billion), which Congress

*Barack Obama—with his wife, Michelle—being sworn in as the 44th
president of the United States, Jan. 20, 2009.* MSgt Cecilio Ricardo,
U.S. Air Force/U.S. Department of Defense

passed in early February with only three Republican votes
in the Senate and none in the House. Later that month
Obama appointed an auto industry task force to negotiate
the terms of continued federal assistance to the auto
makers General Motors and Chrysler, and in March his
administration presented a plan to purchase mortgage-
backed securities and other "toxic" assets from troubled
banks using a combination of federal funds and subsidized
private investment. Obama also presented the outlines of
a plan to reform the country's health care system, one feature of which would be the creation of a public health
insurance plan to compete with private insurance companies. In May Obama nominated Sonia Sotomayor to the
Supreme Court to fill the seat to be vacated in June by
the retiring justice David Souter. After confirmation
hearings in July, Sotomayor became the first Hispanic
Supreme Court Justice.

Appendix:
Tables

PRESIDENTS OF THE UNITED STATES				
NO.	PRESIDENT	BIRTH-PLACE	POLITICAL PARTY	TERM
1	George Washington	Va.	Federalist	1789–97
2	John Adams	Mass.	Federalist	1797–1801
3	Thomas Jefferson	Va.	Democratic-Republican	1801–09
4	James Madison	Va.	Democratic-Republican	1809–17
5	James Monroe	Va.	Democratic-Republican	1817–25
6	John Quincy Adams	Mass.	National Republican	1825–29
7	Andrew Jackson	S.C.	Democratic	1829–37
8	Martin Van Buren	N.Y.	Democratic	1837–41
9	William Henry Harrison	Va.	Whig	1841*
10	John Tyler	Va.	Whig	1841–45
11	James K. Polk	N.C.	Democratic	1845–49
12	Zachary Taylor	Va.	Whig	1849–50*
13	Millard Fillmore	N.Y.	Whig	1850–53
14	Franklin Pierce	N.H.	Democratic	1853–57
15	James Buchanan	Pa.	Democratic	1857–61
16	Abraham Lincoln	Ky.	Republican	1861–65*
17	Andrew Johnson	N.C.	Democratic (Union)	1865–69

NO.	PRESIDENT	BIRTH-PLACE	POLITICAL PARTY	TERM
18	Ulysses S. Grant	Ohio	Republican	1869–77
19	Rutherford B. Hayes	Ohio	Republican	1877–81
20	James A. Garfield	Ohio	Republican	1881*
21	Chester A. Arthur	Vt.	Republican	1881–85
22	Grover Cleveland	N.J.	Democratic	1885–89
23	Benjamin Harrison	Ohio	Republican	1889–93
24	Grover Cleveland	N.J.	Democratic	1893–97
25	William McKinley	Ohio	Republican	1897–1901*
26	Theodore Roosevelt	N.Y.	Republican	1901–09
27	William Howard Taft	Ohio	Republican	1909–13
28	Woodrow Wilson	Va.	Democratic	1913–21
29	Warren G. Harding	Ohio	Republican	1921–23*
30	Calvin Coolidge	Vt.	Republican	1923–29
31	Herbert Hoover	Iowa	Republican	1929–33
32	Franklin D. Roosevelt	N.Y.	Democratic	1933–45*
33	Harry S. Truman	Mo.	Democratic	1945–53
34	Dwight D. Eisenhower	Texas	Republican	1953–61
35	John F. Kennedy	Mass.	Democratic	1961–63*
36	Lyndon B. Johnson	Texas	Democratic	1963–69
37	Richard M. Nixon	Calif.	Republican	1969–74**
38	Gerald R. Ford	Neb.	Republican	1974–77
39	Jimmy Carter	Ga.	Democratic	1977–81
40	Ronald Reagan	Ill.	Republican	1981–89
41	George Bush	Mass.	Republican	1989–93
42	Bill Clinton	Ark.	Democratic	1993–2001
43	George W. Bush	Conn.	Republican	2001–09
44	Barack Obama	Hawaii	Democratic	2009–

*Died in office.
**Resigned from office.

VICE PRESIDENTS OF THE UNITED STATES				
NO.	VICE PRESIDENT	BIRTH-PLACE	TERM	PRESIDENTIAL ADMINISTRATION SERVED UNDER
1	John Adams	Mass.	1789–97	George Washington
2	Thomas Jefferson	Va.	1797–1801	John Adams
3	Aaron Burr	N.J.	1801–05	Thomas Jefferson
4	George Clinton	N.Y.	1805–09	Thomas Jefferson
	George Clinton	N.Y.	1809–12*	James Madison
5	Elbridge Gerry	Mass.	1813–14*	James Madison
6	Daniel D. Tompkins	N.Y.	1817–25	James Monroe
7	John C. Calhoun	S.C.	1825–29	John Quincy Adams
	John C. Calhoun	S.C.	1829–32**	Andrew Jackson
8	Martin Van Buren	N.Y.	1833–37	Andrew Jackson
9	Richard M. Johnson	Ky.	1837–41	Martin Van Buren
10	John Tyler	Va.	1841	William Henry Harrison
11	George Mifflin Dallas	Pa.	1845–49	James K. Polk
12	Millard Fillmore	N.Y.	1849–50	Zachary Taylor
13	William Rufus de Vane King	N.C.	1853*	Franklin Pierce
14	John C. Breckinridge	Ky.	1857–61	James Buchanan
15	Hannibal Hamlin	Maine	1861–65	Abraham Lincoln
16	Andrew Johnson	N.C.	1865	Abraham Lincoln
17	Schuyler Colfax	N.Y.	1869–73	Ulysses S. Grant
18	Henry Wilson	N.H.	1873–75*	Ulysses S. Grant
19	William A. Wheeler	N.Y.	1877–81	Rutherford B. Hayes
20	Chester A. Arthur	Vt.	1881	James A. Garfield

NO.	VICE PRESIDENT	BIRTH-PLACE	TERM	PRESIDENTIAL ADMINISTRATION SERVED UNDER
21	Thomas A. Hendricks	Ohio	1885*	Grover Cleveland
22	Levi Morton	Vt.	1889–93	Benjamin Harrison
23	Adlai E. Stevenson	Ky.	1893–97	Grover Cleveland
24	Garret A. Hobart	N.J.	1897–99*	William McKinley
25	Theodore Roosevelt	N.Y.	1901	William McKinley
26	Charles Warren Fairbanks	Ohio	1905–09	Theodore Roosevelt
27	James Sherman	N.Y.	1909–12*	William Howard Taft
28	Thomas R. Marshall	Ind.	1913–21	Woodrow Wilson
29	Calvin Coolidge	Vt.	1921–23	Warren G. Harding
30	Charles G. Dawes	Ohio	1925–29	Calvin Coolidge
31	Charles Curtis	Kan.	1929–33	Herbert Hoover
32	John Nance Garner	Texas	1933–41	Franklin D. Roosevelt
33	Henry A. Wallace	Iowa	1941–45	Franklin D. Roosevelt
34	Harry S. Truman	Mo.	1945	Franklin D. Roosevelt
35	Alben W. Barkley	Ky.	1949–53	Harry S. Truman
36	Richard M. Nixon	Calif.	1953–61	Dwight D. Eisenhower
37	Lyndon B. Johnson	Texas	1961–63	John F. Kennedy
38	Hubert H. Humphrey	S.D.	1965–69	Lyndon B. Johnson
39	Spiro T. Agnew	Md.	1969–73**	Richard M. Nixon
40	Gerald R. Ford	Neb.	1973–74	Richard M. Nixon

NO.	VICE PRESIDENT	BIRTH-PLACE	TERM	PRESIDENTIAL ADMINISTRATION SERVED UNDER
41	Nelson A. Rockefeller	Maine	1974–77	Gerald R. Ford
42	Walter F. Mondale	Minn.	1977–81	Jimmy Carter
43	George Bush	Mass.	1981–89	Ronald Reagan
44	Dan Quayle	Ind.	1989–93	George Bush
45	Albert Gore	Wash., D.C.	1993–2001	Bill Clinton
46	Dick Cheney	Neb.	2001–09	George W. Bush
47	Joe Biden	Pa.	2009–	Barack Obama

*Died in office.
**Resigned from office.

FIRST LADIES OF THE UNITED STATES

FIRST LADY	PRESIDENT
Abigail Adams	John Adams
Louisa Adams	John Quincy Adams
Ellen Arthur	Chester A. Arthur
Barbara Bush	George Bush
Laura Welch Bush	George W. Bush
Rosalynn Carter	Jimmy Carter
Frances Cleveland	Grover Cleveland
Hillary Rodham Clinton	Bill Clinton
Grace Coolidge	Calvin Coolidge
Mamie Eisenhower	Dwight D. Eisenhower
Abigail Fillmore	Millard Fillmore
Betty Ford	Gerald R. Ford
Lucretia Garfield	James A. Garfield
Julia Grant	Ulysses S. Grant
Florence Harding	Warren G. Harding
Anna Harrison	William Henry Harrison
Caroline Harrison	Benjamin Harrison
Lucy Hayes	Rutherford B. Hayes
Lou Hoover	Herbert Hoover
Rachel Jackson	Andrew Jackson
Martha Jefferson	Thomas Jefferson
Eliza Johnson	Andrew Johnson
Lady Bird Johnson	Lyndon B. Johnson
Harriet Lane	James Buchanan
Mary Todd Lincoln	Abraham Lincoln
Dolley Madison	James Madison
Ida McKinley	William McKinley
Elizabeth Monroe	James Monroe
Pat Nixon	Richard M. Nixon

FIRST LADY	PRESIDENT
Michelle Obama	Barack Obama
Jacqueline Kennedy Onassis	John F. Kennedy
Jane Pierce	Franklin Pierce
Sarah Polk	James K. Polk
Nancy Reagan	Ronald Reagan
Edith Roosevelt	Theodore Roosevelt
Eleanor Roosevelt	Franklin D. Roosevelt
Helen Taft	William Howard Taft
Margaret Taylor	Zachary Taylor
Bess Truman	Harry S. Truman
Julia Tyler	John Tyler
Letitia Tyler	John Tyler
Hannah Van Buren	Martin Van Buren
Martha Washington	George Washington
Edith Wilson	Woodrow Wilson
Ellen Wilson	Woodrow Wilson

U.S. PRESIDENTIAL ELECTION RESULTS

CANDIDATE	POLITICAL PARTY	ELECTORAL VOTES[1]	POPULAR VOTES[2]	POPULAR PERCENT- AGE[3]
1789				
George Washington[4]	no formally organized parties	69[5]		
John Adams		34		
John Jay		9		
R.H. Harrison		6		
John Rutledge		6		
John Hancock		4		
George Clinton		3		
Samuel Huntington		2		
John Milton		2		
James Armstrong		1		
Benjamin Lincoln		1		
Edward Telfair		1		
(not voted)		44		
1792				
George Washington[4]	Federalist	132		
John Adams	Federalist	77		
George Clinton	Democratic-Republican	50		
Thomas Jefferson		4		
Aaron Burr		1		
1796				
John Adams	Federalist	71		
Thomas Jefferson	Democratic-Republican	68		
Thomas Pinckney	Federalist	59		

CANDIDATE	POLITICAL PARTY	ELECTORAL VOTES[1]	POPULAR VOTES[2]	POPULAR PERCENT-AGE
1796 (continued)				
Aaron Burr	Antifederalist	30		
Samuel Adams	Democratic-Republican	15		
Oliver Ellsworth	Federalist	11		
George Clinton	Democratic-Republican	7		
John Jay	Independent-Federalist	5		
James Iredell	Federalist	3		
George Washington	Federalist	2		
John Henry	Independent	2		
S. Johnston	Independent-Federalist	2		
Charles Cotesworth Pinckney	Independent-Federalist	1		
1800				
Thomas Jefferson	Democratic-Republican	73[6]		
Aaron Burr	Democratic-Republican	73[6]		
John Adams	Federalist	65		
Charles Cotesworth Pinckney	Federalist	64		
John Jay	Federalist	1		
1804				
Thomas Jefferson	Democratic-Republican	162		
Charles Cotesworth Pinckney	Federalist	14		

CANDIDATE	POLITICAL PARTY	ELECTORAL VOTES[1]	POPULAR VOTES[2]	POPULAR PERCENTAGE
1808				
James Madison	Democratic-Republican	122		
Charles Cotesworth Pinckney	Federalist	47		
George Clinton	Independent-Republican	6		
(not voted)		1		
1812				
James Madison	Democratic-Republican	128		
DeWitt Clinton	Fusion	89		
(not voted)		1		
1816				
James Monroe	Democratic-Republican	183		
Rufus King	Federalist	34		
(not voted)		4		
1820				
James Monroe	Democratic-Republican	231		
John Quincy Adams	Independent-Republican	1		
(not voted)		3		
1824				
John Quincy Adams	no distinct party designations	84[7]	108,740	30.9
Andrew Jackson		99	153,544	41.3
Henry Clay		37	47,531	13.0
William H. Crawford		41	40,856	11.2

CANDIDATE	POLITICAL PARTY	ELECTORAL VOTES[1]	POPULAR VOTES[2]	POPULAR PERCENT-AGE
1828				
Andrew Jackson	Democratic	178	647,286	56.0
John Quincy Adams	National Republican	83	508,064	43.6
1832				
Andrew Jackson	Democratic	219	687,502	54.2
Henry Clay	National Republican	49	530,189	37.4
William Wirt	Anti-Masonic	7	100,715	7.8
John Floyd	Nullifiers	11		
(not voted)		2		
1836				
Martin Van Buren	Democratic	170	762,678	50.8
William Henry Harrison	Whig	73	550,816	36.6
Hugh L. White	Whig	26	146,107	9.7
Daniel Webster	Whig	14	41,201	2.7
W.P. Mangum	Anti-Jackson	11		
1840				
William Henry Harrison	Whig	234	1,275,016	52.9
Martin Van Buren	Democratic	60	1,129,102	46.8
1844				
James K. Polk	Democratic	170	1,337,243	49.5
Henry Clay	Whig	105	1,299,062	48.1
James Gillespie Birney	Liberty		62,103	2.3
1848				
Zachary Taylor	Whig	163	1,360,099	47.3
Lewis Cass	Democratic	127	1,220,544	42.5
Martin Van Buren	Free Soil		291,501	10.1

CANDIDATE	POLITICAL PARTY	ELECTORAL VOTES[1]	POPULAR VOTES[2]	POPULAR PERCENT-AGE
1852				
Franklin Pierce	Democratic	254	1,601,274	50.8
Winfield Scott	Whig	42	1,386,580	43.9
John Parker Hale	Free Soil		155,210	4.9
1856				
James Buchanan	Democratic	174	1,838,169	45.3
John C. Frémont	Republican	114	1,341,264	33.1
Millard Fillmore	American (Know-Nothing)	8	873,053	21.5
1860				
Abraham Lincoln	Republican	180	1,866,452	39.9
John C. Breckinridge	Southern Democratic	72	847,953	18.1
Stephen A. Douglas	Democratic	12	1,380,202	29.5
John Bell	Constitutional Union	39	590,901	12.6
1864				
Abraham Lincoln	Republican	212	2,213,665	55.0
George B. McClellan	Democratic	21	1,805,237	45.0
(not voted)		81		
1868				
Ulysses S. Grant	Republican	214	3,012,833	52.7
Horatio Seymour	Democratic	80	2,703,249	47.3
(not voted)		23		
1872				
Ulysses S. Grant	Republican	286	3,597,132	55.6
Horace Greeley[8]	Democratic/ Liberal Republican		2,834,125	43.8

CANDIDATE	POLITICAL PARTY	ELECTORAL VOTES[1]	POPULAR VOTES[2]	POPULAR PERCENT-AGE
1872 (continued)				
Thomas A. Hendricks	Independent-Democratic	42		
B. Gratz Brown	Democratic	18		
Charles J. Jenkins	Democratic	2		
David Davis	Democratic	1		
(not voted)		17		
1876				
Rutherford B. Hayes	Republican	185	4,036,298	48.0
Samuel J. Tilden	Democratic	184	4,300,590	51.0
1880				
James A. Garfield	Republican	214	4,454,416	48.3
Winfield Scott Hancock	Democratic	155	4,444,952	48.2
James B. Weaver	Greenback		305,997	3.3
1884				
Grover Cleveland	Democratic	219	4,874,986	48.5
James G. Blaine	Republican	182	4,851,981	48.3
1888				
Benjamin Harrison	Republican	233	5,439,853	47.8
Grover Cleveland	Democratic	168	5,540,309	48.6
Clinton B. Fisk	Prohibition		249,819	2.2
1892				
Grover Cleveland	Democratic	277	5,556,918	46.1
Benjamin Harrison	Republican	145	5,176,108	43.0
James B. Weaver	People's (Populist)	22	1,027,329	8.5
John Bidwell	Prohibition		270,770	2.2

CANDIDATE	POLITICAL PARTY	ELECTORAL VOTES[1]	POPULAR VOTES[2]	POPULAR PERCENT-AGE
1896				
William McKinley	Republican	271	7,104,779	51.0
William Jennings Bryan	Democratic[9]	176	6,502,925	46.7
1900				
William McKinley	Republican	292	7,207,923	51.7
William Jennings Bryan	Democratic[9]	155	6,358,133	45.5
1904				
Theodore Roosevelt	Republican	336	7,623,486	56.4
Alton B. Parker	Democratic	140	5,077,911	37.6
Eugene V. Debs	Socialist		402,489	3.0
1908				
William Howard Taft	Republican	321	7,678,908	51.6
William Jennings Bryan	Democratic	162	6,409,104	43.0
Eugene V. Debs	Socialist		420,380	2.8
1912				
Woodrow Wilson	Democratic	435	6,293,454	41.8
Theodore Roosevelt	Progressive (Bull Moose)	88	4,119,207	27.4
William Howard Taft	Republican	8	3,483,922	23.2
Eugene V. Debs	Socialist		900,369	6.0
1916				
Woodrow Wilson	Democratic	277	9,129,606	49.2
Charles Evans Hughes	Republican	254	8,538,221	46.1
Allan L. Benson	Socialist		589,924	3.2

CANDIDATE	POLITICAL PARTY	ELECTORAL VOTES[1]	POPULAR VOTES[2]	POPULAR PERCENT-AGE
1920				
Warren G. Harding	Republican	404	16,147,249	60.3
James M. Cox	Democratic	127	9,140,864	34.1
Eugene V. Debs	Socialist		897,704	3.4
1924				
Calvin Coolidge	Republican	382	15,725,016	54.1
John W. Davis	Democratic	136	8,386,503	28.8
Robert M. La Follette	Progressive	13	4,822,856	16.6
1928				
Herbert Hoover	Republican	444	21,392,190	58.0
Alfred E. Smith	Democratic	87	15,016,443	40.7
1932				
Franklin D. Roosevelt	Democratic	472	22,821,857	57.3
Herbert Hoover	Republican	59	15,761,841	39.6
Norman Thomas	Socialist		884,781	2.2
1936				
Franklin D. Roosevelt	Democratic	523	27,476,673	60.2
Alfred M. Landon	Republican	8	16,679,583	36.5
1940				
Franklin D. Roosevelt	Democratic	449	27,243,466	54.7
Wendell L. Willkie	Republican	82	22,304,755	44.8
1944				
Franklin D. Roosevelt	Democratic	432	25,602,505	53.3
Thomas E. Dewey	Republican	99	22,006,278	45.8

CANDIDATE	POLITICAL PARTY	ELECTORAL VOTES[1]	POPULAR VOTES[2]	POPULAR PERCENT-AGE
1948				
Harry S. Truman	Democratic	303	24,105,695	49.4
Thomas E. Dewey	Republican	189	21,969,170	45.0
Strom Thurmond	States' Rights Democratic (Dixiecrat)	39	1,169,021	2.4
Henry A. Wallace	Progressive		1,156,103	2.4
1952				
Dwight D. Eisenhower	Republican	442	33,778,963	54.9
Adlai E. Stevenson	Democratic	89	27,314,992	44.4
1956				
Dwight D. Eisenhower	Republican	457	35,581,003	57.4
Adlai E. Stevenson	Democratic	73	25,738,765	42.0
Walter Jones	(not a candidate)	1		
1960				
John F. Kennedy	Democratic	303	34,227,096	49.7
Richard M. Nixon	Republican	219	34,107,646	49.5
Harry F. Byrd	(not a candidate)	15		
1964				
Lyndon B. Johnson	Democratic	486	42,825,463	61.1
Barry M. Goldwater	Republican	52	27,146,969	38.5
1968				
Richard M. Nixon	Republican	301	31,710,470	43.4
Hubert H. Humphrey	Democratic	191	30,898,055	42.7
George C. Wallace	American Independent	46	9,906,473	13.5
1972				
Richard M. Nixon	Republican	520	46,740,323	60.7
George S. McGovern	Democratic	17	28,901,598	37.5
John Hospers	Libertarian	1	3,673	<0.1

CANDIDATE	POLITICAL PARTY	ELECTORAL VOTES[1]	POPULAR VOTES[2]	POPULAR PERCENTAGE
1976				
Jimmy Carter	Democratic	297	40,825,839	50.0
Gerald R. Ford	Republican	240	39,147,770	48.0
Ronald W. Reagan	(not a candidate)	1		
1980				
Ronald W. Reagan	Republican	489	43,642,639	50.4
Jimmy Carter	Democratic	49	35,480,948	41.0
John B. Anderson	Independent		5,719,437	6.6
1984				
Ronald W. Reagan	Republican	525	54,455,075	58.8
Walter F. Mondale	Democratic	13	37,577,185	40.6
1988				
George Bush	Republican	426	48,886,097	53.4
Michael S. Dukakis	Democratic	111	41,809,074	45.7
Lloyd Bentsen	(not a candidate)	1		
1992				
Bill Clinton	Democratic	370	44,909,889	43.0
George Bush	Republican	168	39,104,545	37.4
Ross Perot	Independent		19,742,267	18.9
1996				
Bill Clinton	Democratic	379	47,402,357	49.2
Bob Dole	Republican	159	39,198,755	40.7
Ross Perot	Reform		8,085,402	8.4
2000				
George W. Bush	Republican	271	50,456,002	47.9
Al Gore	Democratic	266[10]	50,999,897	48.4
Ralph Nader	Green		2,882,955	2.7

CANDIDATE	POLITICAL PARTY	ELECTORAL VOTES[1]	POPULAR VOTES[2]	POPULAR PERCENTAGE
2004				
George W. Bush	Republican	286	62,028,285	50.7
John Kerry	Democratic	251	59,028,109	48.3
John Edwards	(not a candidate)	1		
2008				
Barack Obama	Democratic	365	69,456,000	52.9
John McCain	Republican	173	59,934,000	45.7

1 In elections from 1789 to 1804, each elector voted for two individuals without indicating which was to be president and which vice president.

2 In early elections, electors were chosen by legislatures, not by popular vote, in many states.

3 Candidates winning no electoral votes and less than 2 percent of the popular vote are excluded; percentages may not add up to 100 percent because of rounding.

4 Washington was unopposed for president in 1789 and 1792.

5 Because the two houses of the New York legislature could not agree on electors, the state did not cast its electoral vote. North Carolina and Rhode Island had not yet ratified the Constitution.

6 As both Jefferson and Burr received the same number of electoral votes, the decision was referred to the House of Representatives. The Twelfth Amendment (1804) provided that electors cast separate ballots for president and vice president.

7 As no candidate received a majority of the electoral votes, the decision was made by the House of Representatives.

8 Greeley died shortly after the election in November. Three electors pledged to Greeley cast their votes for him, but they were not counted; the others cast their votes for the other candidates listed.

9 Includes a variety of joint tickets with People's Party electors committed to Bryan.

10 One Gore elector from Washington, D.C., abstained from casting an electoral vote.

Sources: Electoral and popular vote totals based on data from the Office of the Clerk of the U.S. House of Representatives; the United States Office of the Federal Register; the Federal Election Commission; and Congressional Quarterly's Guide to U.S. Elections, 4th ed. (2001); and the official certified state vote totals.

CABINETS OF THE PRESIDENTS OF THE UNITED STATES

CABINET OF PRESIDENT GEORGE WASHINGTON

April 30, 1789–March 3, 1793 (Term 1)

State	Thomas Jefferson
Treasury	Alexander Hamilton
War	Henry Knox
Attorney General	Edmund Jennings Randolph

March 4, 1793–March 3, 1797 (Term 2)

State	Thomas Jefferson
	Edmund Jennings Randolph (from January 2, 1794)
	Timothy Pickering (from August 20, 1795)
Treasury	Alexander Hamilton
	Oliver Wolcott, Jr. (from February 2, 1795)
War	Henry Knox
	Timothy Pickering (from January 2, 1795)
	James McHenry (from February 6, 1796)
Attorney General	Edmund Jennings Randolph
	William Bradford (from January 29, 1794)
	Charles Lee (from December 10, 1795)

CABINET OF PRESIDENT JOHN ADAMS

March 4, 1797–March 3, 1801

State	Timothy Pickering
	John Marshall (from June 6, 1800)
Treasury	Oliver Wolcott, Jr.
	Samuel Dexter (from January 1, 1801)
War	James McHenry
	Samuel Dexter (from June 12, 1800)
Navy*	Benjamin Stoddert (from June 18, 1798)
Attorney General	Charles Lee

*Newly created department.

CABINET OF PRESIDENT THOMAS JEFFERSON	
March 4, 1801–March 3, 1805 (Term 1)	
State	James Madison
Treasury	Samuel Dexter
	Albert Gallatin (from May 14, 1801)
War	Henry Dearborn
Navy	Benjamin Stoddert
	Robert Smith (from July 27, 1801)
Attorney General	Levi Lincoln
March 4, 1805–March 3, 1809 (Term 2)	
State	James Madison
Treasury	Albert Gallatin
War	Henry Dearborn
Navy	Robert Smith
Attorney General	John Breckinridge
	Caesar Augustus Rodney (from January 20, 1807)

CABINET OF PRESIDENT JAMES MADISON	
March 4, 1809–March 3, 1813 (Term 1)	
State	Robert Smith
Treasury	Albert Gallatin
War	John Smith
	William Eustis (from April 8, 1809)
	John Armstrong (from February 5, 1813)
Navy	Robert Smith
	Paul Hamilton (from May 15, 1809)
	William Jones (from January 19, 1813)
Attorney General	Caesar Augustus Rodney
	William Pinkney (from January 6, 1812)
March 4, 1813–March 3, 1817 (Term 2)	
State	James Monroe
Treasury	Albert Gallatin

Treasury (continued)	George Washington Campbell (from February 9, 1814)
	Alexander James Dallas (from October 14, 1814)
	William H. Crawford (from October 22, 1816)
War	John Armstrong
	James Monroe (from October 1, 1814)
	William H. Crawford (from August 8, 1815)
Navy	William Jones
	Benjamin Williams Crowninshield (from January 16, 1815)
Attorney General	William Pinkney
	Richard Rush (from February 11, 1814)

CABINET OF PRESIDENT JAMES MONROE	
March 4, 1817–March 3, 1821 (Term 1)	
State	John Quincy Adams
Treasury	William H. Crawford
War	John C. Calhoun
Navy	Benjamin Williams Crowninshield
	Smith Thompson (from January 1, 1819)
Attorney General	Richard Rush
	William Wirt (from November 15, 1817)
March 4, 1821–March 3, 1825 (Term 2)	
State	John Quincy Adams
Treasury	William H. Crawford
War	John C. Calhoun
Navy	Smith Thompson
	Samuel Lewis Southard (from September 16, 1823)
Attorney General	William Wirt

CABINET OF PRESIDENT JOHN QUINCY ADAMS

March 4, 1825–March 3, 1829

State	Henry Clay
Treasury	Richard Rush
War	James Barbour
	Peter Buell Porter (from June 21, 1828)
Navy	Samuel Lewis Southard
Attorney General	William Wirt

CABINET OF PRESIDENT ANDREW JACKSON

March 4, 1829–March 3, 1833 (Term 1)

State	Martin Van Buren
	Edward Livingston (from May 24, 1831)
Treasury	Samuel Delucenna Ingham
	Louis McLane (from August 8, 1831)
War	John Henry Eaton
	Lewis Cass (from August 8, 1831)
Navy	John Branch
	Levi Woodbury (from May 23, 1831)
Attorney General	John Macpherson Berrien
	Roger Brooke Taney (from July 20, 1831)

March 4, 1833–March 3, 1837 (Term 2)

State	Edward Livingston
	Louis McLane (from May 29, 1833)
	John Forsyth (from July 1, 1834)
Treasury	Louis McLane
	William John Duane (from June 1, 1833)
	Roger Brooke Taney (from September 23, 1833)
	Levi Woodbury (from July 1, 1834)
War	Lewis Cass
Navy	Levi Woodbury
	Mahlon Dickerson (from June 30, 1834)

Attorney General	Roger Brooke Taney
	Benjamin Franklin Butler (from November 18, 1833)

CABINET OF PRESIDENT MARTIN VAN BUREN	
March 4, 1837–March 3, 1841	
State	John Forsyth
Treasury	Levi Woodbury
War	Joel Roberts Poinsett
Navy	Mahlon Dickerson
	James Kirke Paulding (from July 1, 1838)
Attorney General	Benjamin Franklin Butler
	Felix Grundy (from September 1, 1838)
	Henry Dilworth Gilpin (from January 11, 1840)

CABINET OF PRESIDENT WILLIAM HENRY HARRISON	
March 4, 1841–April 4, 1841	
State	Daniel Webster
Treasury	Thomas Ewing
War	John Bell
Navy	George Edmund Badger
Attorney General	John Jordan Crittenden

CABINET OF PRESIDENT JOHN TYLER	
April 6, 1841–March 3, 1845	
State	Daniel Webster
	Abel Parker Upshur (from July 24, 1843)
	John C. Calhoun (from April 1, 1844)
Treasury	Thomas Ewing
	Walter Forward (from September 13, 1841)
	John Canfield Spencer (from March 8, 1843)
	George Mortimer Bibb (from July 4, 1844)
War	John Bell

War (continued)	John Canfield Spencer (from October 12, 1841)
	James Madison Porter (from March 8, 1843)
	William Wilkins (from February 20, 1844)
Navy	George Edmund Badger
	Abel Parker Upshur (from October 11, 1841)
	David Henshaw (from July 24, 1843)
	Thomas Walker Gilmer (from February 19, 1844)
	John Young Mason (from March 26, 1844)
Attorney General	John Jordan Crittenden
	Hugh Swinton Legaré (from September 20, 1841)
	John Nelson (from July 1, 1843)

CABINET OF PRESIDENT JAMES K. POLK	
March 4, 1845–March 3, 1849	
State	James Buchanan
Treasury	Robert J. Walker
War	William Learned Marcy
Navy	George Bancroft
	John Young Mason (from September 9, 1846)
Attorney General	John Young Mason
	Nathan Clifford (from October 17, 1846)
	Isaac Toucey (from June 29, 1848)

CABINET OF PRESIDENT ZACHARY TAYLOR	
March 4, 1849–July 9, 1850	
State	John Middleton Clayton
Treasury	William Morris Meredith
War	George Washington Crawford
Navy	William Ballard Preston
Attorney General	Reverdy Johnson
Interior	Thomas Ewing (from March 8, 1849)

CABINET OF PRESIDENT MILLARD FILLMORE

July 10, 1850–March 3, 1853

State	Daniel Webster
	Edward Everett (from November 6, 1852)
Treasury	Thomas Corwin
War	George Washington Crawford
	Charles Magill Conrad (from August 15, 1850)
Navy	William Alexander Graham
	John P. Kennedy (from July 26, 1852)
Attorney General	Reverdy Johnson
	John Jordan Crittenden (from August 14, 1850)
Interior	Thomas Ewing
	Thomas McKean Thompson McKennan (from August 15, 1850)
	Alexander Hugh Holmes Stuart (from September 16, 1850)

CABINET OF PRESIDENT FRANKLIN PIERCE

March 4, 1853–March 3, 1857

State	William Learned Marcy
Treasury	James Guthrie
War	Jefferson Davis
Navy	James Cochran Dobbin
Attorney General	Caleb Cushing
Interior	Robert McClelland

CABINET OF PRESIDENT JAMES BUCHANAN

March 4, 1857–March 3, 1861

State	Lewis Cass
	Jeremiah Sullivan Black (from December 17, 1860)
Treasury	Howell Cobb
	Philip Francis Thomas (from December 12, 1860)

Treasury (continued)	John Adams Dix (from January 15, 1861)
War	John Buchanan Floyd
Navy	Isaac Toucey
Attorney General	Jeremiah Sullivan Black
	Edwin McMasters Stanton (from December 22, 1860)
Interior	Jacob Thompson

CABINET OF PRESIDENT ABRAHAM LINCOLN	
March 4, 1861–March 3, 1865 (Term 1)	
State	William Henry Seward
Treasury	Salmon P. Chase
	William Pitt Fessenden (from July 5, 1864)
War	Simon Cameron
	Edwin McMasters Stanton (from June 20, 1862)
Navy	Gideon Welles
Attorney General	Edward Bates
	James Speed (from December 5, 1864)
Interior	Caleb Blood Smith
	John Palmer Usher (from January 8, 1863)
March 4, 1865–April 15, 1865 (Term 2)	
State	William Henry Seward
Treasury	Hugh McCulloch
War	Edwin McMasters Stanton
Navy	Gideon Welles
Attorney General	James Speed
Interior	John Palmer Usher

CABINET OF PRESIDENT ANDREW JOHNSON	
April 15, 1865–March 3, 1869	
State	William Henry Seward
Treasury	Hugh McCulloch
War	Edwin McMasters Stanton
	John McAllister Schofield (from June 1, 1868)

Navy	Gideon Welles
Attorney General	James Speed
	Henry Stanbery (from July 23, 1866)
	William Maxwell Evarts (from July 20, 1868)
Interior	John Palmer Usher
	James Harlan (from May 15, 1865)
	Orville Hickman Browning (from September 1, 1866)

CABINET OF PRESIDENT ULYSSES S. GRANT	
March 4, 1869–March 3, 1873 (Term 1)	
State	Elihu Benjamin Washburne
	Hamilton Fish (from March 17, 1869)
Treasury	George Sewall Boutwell
War	John Aaron Rawlins
	William Tecumseh Sherman (from September 11, 1869)
	William Worth Belknap (from November 1, 1869)
Navy	Adolph Edward Borie
	George Maxwell Robeson (from June 25, 1869)
Attorney General	Ebenezer R. Hoar
	Amos Tappan Akerman (from July 8, 1870)
	George Henry Williams (from January 10, 1872)
Interior	Jacob Dolson Cox
	Columbus Delano (from November 1, 1870)
March 4, 1873–March 3, 1877 (Term 2)	
State	Hamilton Fish
Treasury	William Adams Richardson
	Benjamin Helm Bristow (from June 4, 1874)
	Lot Myrick Morrill (from July 7, 1876)
War	William Worth Belknap
	Alphonso Taft (from March 11, 1876)
	James Donald Cameron (from June 1, 1876)

Navy	George Maxwell Robeson
Attorney General	George Henry Williams
	Edward Pierrepont (May 15, 1875)
	Alphonso Taft (from June 1, 1876)
Interior	Columbus Delano
	Zachariah Chandler (October 19, 1875)

CABINET OF PRESIDENT RUTHERFORD B. HAYES	
March 4, 1877–March 3, 1881	
State	William Maxwell Evarts
Treasury	John Sherman
War	George Washington McCrary
	Alexander Ramsey (from December 12, 1879)
Navy	Richard Wigginton Thompson
	Nathan Goff, Jr. (from January 6, 1881)
Attorney General	Charles Devens
Interior	Carl Schurz

CABINET OF PRESIDENT JAMES A. GARFIELD	
March 4, 1881–September 19, 1881	
State	James G. Blaine
Treasury	William Windom
War	Robert Todd Lincoln
Attorney General	Wayne MacVeagh
Navy	William Henry Hunt
Interior	Samuel Jordan Kirkwood

CABINET OF PRESIDENT CHESTER A. ARTHUR	
September 20, 1881–March 3, 1885	
State	James G. Blaine
	Frederick Theodore Frelinghuysen (from December 19, 1881)
Treasury	William Windom

Treasury (continued)	Charles James Folger (from November 14, 1881)
	Walter Quintin Gresham (from September 24, 1884)
	Hugh McCulloch (from October 31, 1884)
War	Robert Todd Lincoln
Navy	William Henry Hunt
	William Eaton Chandler (from April 17, 1882)
Attorney General	Wayne MacVeagh
	Benjamin Harris Brewster (from January 3, 1882)
Interior	Samuel Jordan Kirkwood
	Henry Moore Teller (from April 17, 1882)

CABINET OF PRESIDENT GROVER CLEVELAND	
March 4, 1885–March 3, 1889 (Term 1)	
State	Thomas Francis Bayard
Treasury	Daniel Manning
	Charles Stebbins Fairchild (from April 1, 1887)
War	William Crowninshield Endicott
Navy	William C. Whitney
Attorney General	Augustus Hill Garland
Interior	Lucius Q.C. Lamar
	William F. Vilas (from January 16, 1888)
Agriculture*	Norman Jay Colman (from February 3, 1889)
March 4, 1893–March 3, 1897 (Term 2)	
State	Walter Quintin Gresham
	Richard Olney (from June 10, 1895)
Treasury	John Griffin Carlisle
War	Daniel Scott Lamont
Navy	Hilary Abner Herbert
Attorney General	Richard Olney
	Judson Harmon (from June 11, 1895)
Interior	Hoke Smith

Interior (continued)	David Rowland Francis (from September 4, 1896)
Agriculture	J. Sterling Morton

*Newly created department.

CABINET OF PRESIDENT WILLIAM MCKINLEY	
March 4, 1897–March 3, 1901 (Term 1)	
State	John Sherman
	William R. Day (from April 28, 1898)
	John Hay (from September 30, 1898)
Treasury	Lyman Judson
War	Russell Alexander Alger
	Elihu Root (from August 1, 1899)
Navy	John Davis Long
Attorney General	Joseph McKenna
	John William Griggs (from February 1, 1898)
Interior	Cornelius Newton Bliss
	Ethan Allen Hitchcock (from February 20, 1899)
Agriculture	James Wilson
March 4, 1901–September 14, 1901 (Term 2)	
State	John Hay
Treasury	Lyman Judson Gage
War	Elihu Root
Navy	John Davis Long
Attorney General	John William Griggs
	Philander Chase Knox (from April 10, 1901)
Interior	Ethan Allen Hitchcock
Agriculture	James Wilson

CABINET OF PRESIDENT THEODORE ROOSEVELT	
September 14, 1901–March 3, 1905 (Term 1)	
State	John Hay
Treasury	Lyman Judson Gage
	Leslie Mortier Shaw (from February 1, 1902)

War	Elihu Root
	William Howard Taft (from February 1, 1904)
Navy	John Davis Long
	William Moody (from May 1, 1902)
	Paul Morton (from July 1, 1904)
Attorney General	Philander Chase Knox
	William Moody (from July 1, 1904)
Interior	Ethan Allen Hitchcock
Agriculture	James Wilson
Commerce and Labor*	George Bruce Cortelyou (from February 16, 1903)
	Victor Howard Metcalf (from July 1, 1904)
March 4, 1905–March 3, 1909 (Term 2)	
State	John Hay
	Elihu Root (from July 19, 1905)
	Robert Bacon (from January 27, 1909)
Treasury	Leslie Mortier Shaw
	George Bruce Cortelyou (from March 4, 1907)
War	William Howard Taft
	Luke Edward Wright (from July 1, 1908)
Navy	Paul Morton
	Charles Joseph Bonaparte (from July 1, 1905)
	Victor Howard Metcalf (from December 17, 1906)
	Truman Handy Newberry (from December 1, 1908)
Attorney General	William Moody
	Charles Joseph Bonaparte (from December 17, 1906)
Interior	Ethan Allen Hitchcock
	James Rudolph Garfield (from March 4, 1907)
Agriculture	James Wilson

Commerce and Labor	Victor Howard Metcalf
	Oscar Solomon Straus (from December 17, 1906)

*Newly created department.

CABINET OF PRESIDENT WILLIAM HOWARD TAFT	
March 4, 1909–March 3, 1913	
State	Philander Chase Knox
Treasury	Franklin MacVeagh
War	Jacob McGavock Dickinson
	Henry Lewis Stimson (from May 22, 1911)
Navy	George von Lengerke Meyer
Attorney General	George Woodward Wickersham
Interior	Richard Achilles Ballinger
	Walter Lowrie Fisher (from March 7, 1911)
Agriculture	James Wilson
Commerce and Labor	Charles Nagel

CABINET OF PRESIDENT WOODROW WILSON	
March 4, 1913–March 3, 1917 (Term 1)	
State	William Jennings Bryan
	Robert Lansing (from June 23, 1915)
Treasury	William Gibbs McAdoo
War	Lindley Miller Garrison
	Newton Diehl Baker (from March 9, 1916)
Navy	Josephus Daniels
Attorney General	James McReynolds
	Thomas Watt Gregory (from September 3, 1914)
Interior	Franklin Knight Lane
Agriculture	David Franklin Houston
Commerce*	William Cox Redfield
Labor*	William Bauchop Wilson

March 4, 1917–March 3, 1921 (Term 2)	
State	Robert Lansing
	Bainbridge Colby (from March 23, 1920)
Treasury	William Gibbs McAdoo
	Carter Glass (from December 16, 1918)
	David Franklin Houston (from February 2, 1920)
War	Newton Diehl Baker
Navy	Josephus Daniels
Attorney General	Thomas Watt Gregory
	A. Mitchell Palmer (from March 5, 1919)
Interior	Franklin Knight Lane
	John Barton Payne (from March 13, 1920)
Agriculture	David Franklin Houston
	Edwin Thomas Meredith (from February 2, 1920)
Commerce	William Cox Redfield
	Joshua Willis Alexander (from December 16, 1919)
Labor	William Bauchop Wilson

*Department of Commerce and Labor reorganized into separate departments.

CABINET OF PRESIDENT WARREN G. HARDING	
March 4, 1921–August 2, 1923	
State	Charles Evans Hughes
Treasury	Andrew W. Mellon
War	John Wingate Weeks
Navy	Edwin Denby
Attorney General	Harry Micajah Daugherty
Interior	Albert Bacon Fall
	Hubert Work (from March 5, 1923)
Agriculture	Henry Cantwell Wallace

Commerce	Herbert Hoover
Labor	James John Davis

CABINET OF PRESIDENT CALVIN COOLIDGE	
August 3, 1923–March 3, 1925 (Term 1)	
State	Charles Evans Hughes
Treasury	Andrew W. Mellon
War	John Wingate Weeks
Navy	Edwin Denby
	Curtis Dwight Wilbur (from March 18, 1924)
Attorney General	Harry Micajah Daugherty
	Harlan Fiske Stone (from April 9, 1924)
Interior	Hubert Work
Agriculture	Henry Cantwell Wallace
	Howard Mason Gore (from November 21, 1924)
Commerce	Herbert Hoover
Labor	James John Davis
March 4, 1925–March 3, 1929 (Term 2)	
State	Frank B. Kellogg
Treasury	Andrew W. Mellon
War	John Wingate Weeks
	Dwight F. Davis (from October 14, 1925)
Navy	Curtis Dwight Wilbur
Attorney General	John Garibaldi Sargent
Interior	Hubert Work
	Roy Owen West (from January 21, 1929)
Agriculture	William Marion Jardine
Commerce	Herbert Hoover
	William Fairfield Whiting (from December 11, 1928)
Labor	James John Davis

CABINET OF PRESIDENT HERBERT HOOVER	
March 4, 1929–March 3, 1933	
State	Henry Lewis Stimson
Treasury	Andrew W. Mellon
	Ogden Livingston Mills (from February 13, 1932)
War	James William Good
	Patrick Jay Hurley (from December 9, 1929)
Navy	Charles Francis Adams
Attorney General	William De Witt Mitchell
Interior	Ray Lyman Wilbur
Agriculture	Arthur Mastick Hyde
Commerce	Robert Patterson Lamont
	Roy Dikeman Chapin (from December 14, 1932)
Labor	James John Davis
	William Nuckles Doak (from December 9, 1930)

CABINET OF PRESIDENT FRANKLIN D. ROOSEVELT	
March 4, 1933–January 20, 1937 (Term 1)	
State	Cordell Hull
Treasury	William Hartman Woodin
	Henry Morgenthau, Jr. (from January 8, 1934)
War	George Henry Dern
Navy	Claude Augustus Swanson
Attorney General	Homer Stille Cummings
Interior	Harold L. Ickes
Agriculture	Henry A. Wallace
Commerce	Daniel Calhoun Roper
Labor	Frances Perkins
January 20, 1937–January 20, 1941 (Term 2)	
State	Cordell Hull
Treasury	Henry Morgenthau, Jr.

War	Harry Hines Woodring
	Henry Lewis Stimson (from July 10, 1940)
Attorney General	Homer Stille Cummings
	Frank Murphy (from January 17, 1939)
	Robert Houghwout Jackson (from January 18, 1940)
Navy	Claude Augustus Swanson
	Charles Edison (from January 11, 1940)
	Frank Knox (from July 10, 1940)
Interior	Harold L. Ickes
Agriculture	Henry A. Wallace
	Claude Raymond Wickard (from September 5, 1940)
Commerce	Daniel Calhoun Roper
	Harry Lloyd Hopkins (from January 23, 1939)
	Jesse Holman Jones (from September 19, 1940)
Labor	Frances Perkins
January 20, 1941–January 20, 1945 (Term 3)	
State	Cordell Hull
	Edward Reilly Stettinius (from December 1, 1944)
Treasury	Henry Morgenthau, Jr.
War	Henry Lewis Stimson
Navy	Frank Knox
	James Vincent Forrestal (from May 18, 1944)
Attorney General	Robert Houghwout Jackson
	Francis Biddle (from September 5, 1941)
Interior	Harold L. Ickes
Agriculture	Claude Raymond Wickard
Commerce	Jesse Holman Jones
	Frances Perkins

January 20, 1945–April 12, 1945 (Term 4)	
State	Edward Reilly Stettinius
Treasury	Henry Morgenthau, Jr.
War	Henry Lewis Stimson
Navy	James Vincent Forrestal
Attorney General	Francis Biddle
Interior	Harold L. Ickes
Agriculture	Claude Raymond Wickard
Commerce	Jesse Holman Jones
	Henry A. Wallace (from March 2, 1945)
Labor	Frances Perkins

CABINET OF PRESIDENT HARRY S. TRUMAN	
April 12, 1945–January 20, 1949 (Term 1)	
State	Edward Reilly Stettinius
	James F. Byrnes (from July 3, 1945)
	George C. Marshall (from January 21, 1947)
Treasury	Henry Morgenthau, Jr.
	Frederick Moore (from July 23, 1945)
	John Wesley Snyder (from June 25, 1946)
War	Henry Lewis Stimson
	Robert Porter Patterson (from September 27, 1945)
	Kenneth Clairborne Royall (from July 25, 1947)
Defense*	James Vincent Forrestal (from September 17, 1947)
Navy	James Vincent Forrestal
Attorney General	Francis Biddle
	Tom C. Clark (from July 1, 1945)
Interior	Harold L. Ickes
	Julius Albert Krug (from March 18, 1946)

Agriculture	Claude Raymond Wickard
	Clinton Presba Anderson (from June 30, 1945)
	Charles Franklin Brannan (from June 2, 1948)
Commerce	Henry A. Wallace
	W. Averell Harriman (from January 28, 1947)
	Charles Sawyer (from May 6, 1948)
Labor	Frances Perkins
	Lewis Baxter Schwellenbach (from July 1, 1945)
January 20, 1949–January 20, 1953 (Term 2)	
State	Dean Acheson
Treasury	John Wesley Snyder
Defense	James Vincent Forrestal
	Louis Arthur Johnson (from March 28, 1949)
	George C. Marshall (from September 21, 1950)
	Robert Abercrombie Lovett (from September 17, 1951)
Attorney General	Tom C. Clark
	James Howard McGrath (from August 24, 1949)
Interior	Julius Albert Krug
	Oscar Littleton Chapman (from January 19, 1950)
Agriculture	Charles Franklin Brannan
Commerce	Charles Sawyer
Labor	Maurice Joseph Tobin

*Newly created department, subsuming the Departments of War and the Navy.

CABINET OF PRESIDENT DWIGHT D. EISENHOWER	
January 20, 1953–January 20, 1957 (Term 1)	
State	John Foster Dulles
Treasury	George Magoffin Humphrey
Defense	Charles Erwin Wilson

Attorney General	Herbert Brownell
Interior	Douglas McKay
	Frederick Andrew Seaton (from June 8, 1956)
Agriculture	Ezra Taft Benson
Commerce	Sinclair Weeks
Labor	Martin Patrick Durkin
	James Paul Mitchell (from October 9, 1953)
Health, Education, and Welfare*	Oveta Culp Hobby (from April 11, 1953)
	Marion Bayard Folson (from August 1, 1955)
January 20, 1957–January 20, 1961 (Term 2)	
State	John Foster Dulles
	Christian Archibald Herter (from April 22, 1959)
Treasury	George Magoffin Humphrey
	Robert Bernerd Anderson (from July 29, 1957)
Defense	Charles Erwin Wilson
	Neil Hosler McElroy (from October 9, 1957)
	Thomas Sovereign Gates, Jr. (from December 2, 1959)
Attorney General	Herbert Brownell, Jr.
	William Pierce Rogers (from January 27, 1958)
Interior	Frederick Andrew Seaton
Agriculture	Ezra Taft Benson
Commerce	Sinclair Weeks
	Frederick Henry Mueller (from August 10, 1959)
Labor	James Paul Mitchell
Health, Education, and Welfare	Marion Bayard Folsom
	Arthur Sherwood Flemming (from August 1, 1958)

*Newly created department.

CABINET OF PRESIDENT JOHN F. KENNEDY	
January 20, 1961–November 22, 1963	
State	Dean Rusk
Treasury	C. (Clarence) Douglas Dillon
Defense	Robert S. McNamara
Attorney General	Robert F. Kennedy
Interior	Stewart Lee Udall
Agriculture	Orville Lothrop Freeman
Commerce	Luther Hartwell Hodges
Labor	Arthur Joseph Goldberg
	W. (William) Willard Wirtz (from September 25, 1962)
Health, Education, and Welfare	Abraham Alexander Ribicoff
	Anthony Joseph Celebrezze (from July 31, 1962)

CABINET OF PRESIDENT LYNDON B. JOHNSON	
November 22, 1963–January 20, 1965 (Term 1)	
State	Dean Rusk
Treasury	C. (Clarence) Douglas Dillon
Defense	Robert S. McNamara
Attorney General	Robert F. Kennedy
Interior	Stewart Lee Udall
Agriculture	Orville Lothrop Freeman
Commerce	Luther Hartwell Hodges
Labor	W. (William) Willard Wirtz
Health, Education, and Welfare	Anthony Joseph Celebrezze
January 20, 1965–January 20, 1969 (Term 2)	
State	Dean Rusk
Treasury	C. (Clarence) Douglas Dillon
	Henry Hamill Fowler (from April 1, 1965)
	Joseph Walker Barr (from December 23, 1968)

Defense	Robert S. McNamara
	Clark M. Clifford (from March 1, 1968)
Attorney General	Nicholas deBelleville Katzenbach
	William Ramsey Clark (from March 10, 1967)
Interior	Stewart Lee Udall
Agriculture	Orville Lothrop Freeman
Commerce	John Thomas Connor
	Alexander Buel Trowbridge (from June 14, 1967)
	Cyrus Rowlett Smith (from March 6, 1968)
Labor	W. (William) Willard Wirtz
Health, Education, and Welfare	Anthony Joseph Celebrezze
	John William Gardner (from August 18, 1965)
	Wilbur Joseph Cohen (from May 9, 1968)
Housing and Urban Development*	Robert C. Weaver (from January 18, 1966)
	Robert Coldwell Wood (from January 7, 1969)
Transportation*	Alan Stephenson Boyd (from January 16, 1967)

*Newly created department.

CABINET OF PRESIDENT RICHARD M. NIXON	
January 20, 1969–January 20, 1973 (Term 1)	
State	William Pierce Rogers
Treasury	David Matthew Kennedy
	John Bowden Connally, Jr. (from February 11, 1971)
	George Pratt Shultz (from June 12, 1972)
Defense	Melvin Robert Laird
Attorney General	John Newton Mitchell
	Richard Gordon Kleindienst (from June 12, 1972)
Interior	Walter Joseph Hickel
	Rogers Clark Ballard Morton (from January 29, 1971)

Agriculture	Clifford Morris Hardin
	Earl Lauer Butz (from December 2, 1971)
Commerce	Maurice Hubert Stans
	Peter George Peterson (from February 21, 1972)
Labor	George Pratt Shultz
	James Day Hodgson (from July 2, 1970)
Health, Education, and Welfare	Robert Hutchinson Finch
	Elliot Lee Richardson (from June 24, 1970)
Housing and Urban Development	George Wilcken Romney
Transportation	John Anthony Volpe
January 20, 1973–August 9, 1974 (Term 2)	
State	William Pierce Rogers
	Henry A. Kissinger (from September 22, 1973)
Treasury	George Pratt Shultz
	William Edward Simon (from May 8, 1974)
Defense	Elliot Lee Richardson
	James Rodney Schlesinger (from July 2, 1973)
Attorney General	Richard Gordon Kleindienst
	Elliot Lee Richardson (from May 25, 1973)
	William Bart Saxbe (from January 4, 1974)
Interior	Rogers Clark Ballard Morton
Agriculture	Earl Lauer Butz
Commerce	Frederick Baily Dent
Labor	Peter Joseph Brennan
Health, Education, and Welfare	Caspar Willard Weinberger
Housing and Urban Development	James Thomas Lynn
Transportation	Claude Stout Brinegar

CABINET OF PRESIDENT GERALD R. FORD

August 9, 1974–January 20, 1977

State	Henry A. Kissinger
Treasury	William Edward Simon
Defense	James Rodney Schlesinger
	Donald Henry Rumsfeld (from November 20, 1975)
Attorney General	William Bart Saxbe
	Edward Hirsch Levi (from February 7, 1975)
Interior	Rogers Clark Ballard Morton, Jr.
	Stanley Knapp Hathaway (from June 13, 1975)
	Thomas Savig Kleppe (from October 17, 1975)
Agriculture	Earl Lauer Butz
	John Albert Knebel (from November 4, 1976)
Commerce	Frederick Baily Dent
	Rogers Clark Ballard Morton, Jr. (from May 1, 1975)
	Elliot Lee Richardson (from February 2, 1976)
Labor	Peter Joseph Brennan
	John Thomas Dunlop (from March 18, 1975)
	Willie Julian Usery, Jr. (from February 10, 1976)
Health, Education, and Welfare	Caspar Willard Weinberger
	Forrest David Matthews (from August 8, 1975)
Housing and Urban Development	James Thomas Lynn
	Carla Anderson Hills (from March 10, 1975)
Transportation	Claude Stout Brinegar
	William Thaddeus Coleman, Jr. (from March 7, 1975)

CABINET OF PRESIDENT JIMMY CARTER	
January 20, 1977–January 20, 1981	
State	Cyrus Vance
	Edmund Sixtus Muskie (from May 8, 1980)
Treasury	Werner Michael Blumenthal
	George William Miller (from August 6, 1979)
Defense	Harold Brown
Attorney General	Griffin Boyette Bell
	Benjamin Richard Civiletti (from August 16, 1979)
Interior	Cecil Dale Andrus
Agriculture	Robert Selmer Bergland
Commerce	Juanita Morris Kreps
	Philip Morris Klutznick (from January 9, 1980)
Labor	Fred Ray Marshall
Health, Education, and Welfare*	Joseph Anthony Califano, Jr.
	Patricia Roberts Harris (from August 3, 1979)
Health and Human Services*	Patricia Roberts Harris (from September 27, 1979)
Housing and Urban Development	Patricia Roberts Harris
	Moon Landrieu (from September 24, 1979)
Transportation	Brockman Adams
	Neil Edward Goldschmidt (from September 24, 1979)
Energy**	James Rodney Schlesinger (from October 1, 1977)
	Charles William Duncan, Jr. (from August 24, 1979)
Education*	Shirley Mount Hufstedler (from December 6, 1979)

*Department of Health, Education, and Welfare reorganized into
Departments of Health and Human Services and Education.
**Newly created department.

CABINET OF PRESIDENT RONALD REAGAN	
January 20, 1981–January 20, 1985 (Term 1)	
State	Alexander Meigs Haig, Jr.
	George Pratt Shultz (from July 16, 1982)
Treasury	Donald Thomas Regan
Defense	Caspar Willard Weinberger
Attorney General	William French Smith
Interior	James Gaius Watt
	William Patrick Clark (from November 21, 1983)
Agriculture	John Rusling Block
Commerce	Malcolm Baldrige
Labor	Raymond Joseph Donovan
Health and Human Services	Richard Schultz Schweiker
	Margaret Mary O'Shaughnessy Heckler (from March 9, 1983)
Housing and Urban Development	Samuel Riley Pierce, Jr.
Transportation	Drew (Andrew) Lindsay Lewis, Jr.
	Elizabeth Hanford Dole (from February 7, 1983)
Energy	James Burrows Edwards
	Donald Paul Hodel (from December 8, 1982)
Education	Terrel Howard Bell
January 20, 1985–January 20, 1989 (Term 2)	
State	George Pratt Shultz
Treasury	Donald Thomas Regan
	James Addison Baker III (from February 25, 1985)
	Nicholas Frederick Brady (from August 18, 1988)
Defense	Caspar Willard Weinberger
	Frank Charles Carlucci III (from November 21, 1987)
Attorney General	William French Smith
	Edwin Meese III (from February 25, 1985)

Attorney General (continued)	Richard Lewis (Dick) Thornburgh (from August 11, 1988)
Interior	Donald Paul Hodel
Agriculture	John Rusling Block
	Richard Edmund Lyng (from March 7, 1986)
Commerce	Malcolm Baldrige
	Calvin William Verity, Jr. (from October 19, 1987)
Labor	Raymond James Donovan
	William Emerson (Bill) Brock III (from April 29, 1985)
	Ann Dore McLaughlin (from December 17, 1987)
Health and Human Services	Margaret Mary O'Shaughnessy Heckler
	Otis Ray Bowen (from December 13, 1985)
Housing and Urban Development	Samuel Riley Pierce, Jr.
Transportation	Elizabeth Hanford Dole
	James Horace Burnley IV (from December 3, 1987)
Energy	John Stewart Herrington
Education	Terrel Howard Bell
	William John Bennett (from February 7, 1985)
	Lauro Fred Cavazos, Jr. (from September 20, 1988)

CABINET OF PRESIDENT GEORGE BUSH	
January 20, 1989–January 20, 1993	
State	James Addison Baker III
Treasury	Nicholas Frederick Brady
Attorney General	Richard Lewis (Dick) Thornburgh
	William P. Barr (from November 20, 1991)
Interior	Manuel Lujan, Jr.

Agriculture	Clayton Keith Yeutter
	Edward Madigan (from March 7, 1991)
Commerce	Robert Adam Mosbacher
Labor	Elizabeth Hanford Dole
Defense	Dick Cheney
Health and Human Services	Louis Wade Sullivan
Housing and Urban Development	Jack Kemp
Transportation	Samuel K. Skinner
	Andrew H. Card (from January 22, 1992)
Energy	James David Watkins
Education	Lauro Fred Cavazos, Jr.
	Lamar Alexander (from March 14, 1991)
Veterans Affairs*	Edward Joseph Derwinski (from March 15, 1989)

*Newly created department.

CABINET OF PRESIDENT BILL CLINTON	
January 20, 1993–January 20, 1997 (Term 1)	
State	Warren M. Christopher
Treasury	Lloyd Bentsen, Jr.
	Robert E. Rubin (from January 10, 1995)
Attorney General	Janet Reno
Interior	Bruce Babbitt
Agriculture	Mike Espy
	Dan Glickman (from March 30, 1995)
Commerce	Ronald H. Brown
	Mickey Kantor (from April 12, 1996)
Labor	Robert B. Reich
Defense	Les Aspin
	William J. Perry (from February 3, 1994)
Health and Human Services	Donna E. Shalala

Housing and Urban Development	Henry G. Cisneros
Transportation	Federico Peña
Energy	Hazel R. O'Leary
Education	Richard W. Riley
Veterans Affairs	Jesse Brown
January 20, 1997–January 20, 2001 (Term 2)	
State	Madeleine Albright
Treasury	Robert E. Rubin
	Lawrence H. Summers (from July 2, 1999)
Attorney General	Janet Reno
Interior	Bruce Babbitt
Agriculture	Dan Glickman
Commerce	William M. Daley
	Norman Mineta (from July 21, 2000)
Labor	Alexis M. Herman
Defense	William Cohen
Health and Human Services	Donna E. Shalala
Housing and Urban Development	Andrew M. Cuomo
Transportation	Rodney Slater
Energy	Federico Peña
	Bill Richardson (from August 18, 1998)
Education	Richard W. Riley
Veterans Affairs	Togo D. West, Jr.
	Hershel W. Gober (from July 25, 2000)

CABINET OF PRESIDENT GEORGE W. BUSH	
January 20, 2001–January 20, 2005 (Term 1)	
State	Colin Powell
Treasury	Paul O'Neill
	John Snow (from February 3, 2003)
Attorney General	John Ashcroft

Interior	Gale Norton
Agriculture	Ann M. Veneman
Commerce	Don Evans
Labor	Elaine Chao
Defense	Donald Rumsfeld
Health and Human Services	Tommy Thompson
Housing and Urban Development	Mel Martinez
	Alphonso Jackson (from April 1, 2004)
Transportation	Norman Mineta
Energy	Spencer Abraham
Education	Rod Paige
Veterans Affairs	Anthony Principi
Homeland Security*	Tom Ridge (from October 8, 2001)
January 20, 2005– January 20, 2009 (Term 2)	
State	Colin Powell
	Condoleezza Rice (from January 26, 2005)
Treasury	John Snow
	Henry M. Paulson, Jr. (from July 10, 2006)
Attorney General	John Ashcroft
	Alberto Gonzales (from February 3, 2005)
	Michael B. Mukasey (from November 9, 2007)
Interior	Gale Norton
	Dirk Kempthorne (from May 26, 2006)
Agriculture	Ann M. Veneman
	Mike Johanns (from January 21, 2005)
Commerce	Don Evans
	Carlos Gutierrez (from February 7, 2005)
Labor	Elaine Chao
Defense	Donald Rumsfeld
	Robert Gates (from December 18, 2006)

Health and Human Services	Tommy Thompson
	Michael O. Leavitt (from January 26, 2005)
Housing and Urban Development	Alphonso Jackson
Transportation	Norman Mineta
Energy	Spencer Abraham
	Samuel W. Bodman (from February 1, 2005)
Education	Margaret Spellings
Veterans Affairs	Anthony Principi
	Jim Nicholson (from February 1, 2005)
Homeland Security	Tom Ridge
	Michael Chertoff (from February 15, 2005)

*Newly created department.

CABINET OF PRESIDENT BARACK OBAMA	
January 20, 2009–	
State	Hillary Clinton
Treasury	Tim Geithner
Defense	Robert Gates
Attorney General	Eric Holder
Interior	Ken Salazar
Agriculture	Tom Vilsack
Commerce	Gary Locke
Labor	Hilda Solis
Health and Human Services	Kathleen Sebelius
Housing and Urban Development	Shaun Donovan
Transportation	Ray LaHood
Energy	Steven Chu
Education	Arne Duncan
Veterans Affairs	Eric Shinseki
Homeland Security	Janet Napolitano

Glossary

abrogate Abolish; annul by an authoritative act.

amalgam A mixture or combination.

Anti-Masons A group created in avowed opposition to Freemasonry.

arteriosclerosis Degenerative disorder characterized by thickening of blood vessel walls leading to decreased blood flow.

bicameral A legislative body that has two branches, chambers, or houses.

bootleg To traffic in something (especially liquor) illegally.

brevet A commission promoting an officer to a higher rank without a pay increase, often granted as an honour.

captious Apt to notice or make much of trivial faults or defects; difficult to please.

colonnade A series of columns placed at regular intervals.

epileptoid Related to epilepsy and its symptoms.

Freemasons Originating with the guilds of medieval stonemasons, the organization became an honorary society in the 17th and 18th century, adopting the rites and trappings of ancient religious orders and chivalric brotherhoods. The Freemasons are the world's largest secret society.

gerrymander The dividing of an area into election districts that benefit one political party.

Hessians German mercenaries used by the British during the American Revolution.

ileitis Inflammation of the lowest portion of the small intestine.

imbroglio A misunderstanding or complication causing bitterness between persons or nations.

impenitent Unrepentant; not sorry.

impressment The act or policy of seizing private property for public use or forcing individuals into public (usually military) service.

indenture To contractually bind the service of one to another.

ineluctable Incapable of being evaded.

lame duck Period for an officeholder or governing body between the time of failure to win an election and the inauguration of a successor.

malaise A vague or unfocused feeling of uneasiness or physical illness.

meum and tuum Latin words meaning "mine" (meum) and "thine," or "yours" (tuum).

piedmont A district lying along the foot of a mountain range.

plenipotentiary A person invested with the authority to transact business on behalf of another.

portico An outdoor space with a column-supported roof.

rawboned Having little flesh on a large-boned frame; gaunt.

rectitude Correctness in principle or conduct.

regent An officer at a university who exercises general supervision over the conduct and welfare of the students.

remunerative Profitable.

salus populi Latin phrase meaning "the welfare of the people should be the supreme law."

salutatorian Second-highest-ranking student in a graduating class.

sedulously Accomplished with diligent perseverance.

sexton Church official in charge of taking care of the church building and organization.

Shogunate In pre-1867 Japan, the government of one of a line of hereditary military governors ruling that country.

sinecure A position requiring little or no actual work, but that provides an income.

squire A title applied to a justice of the peace or other local dignitary of a small town or rural district.

sue for peace The initiation of a peace process wherein the terms are more favourable to the initiator than unconditional surrender.

taciturn Markedly reserved and incommunicative.

For Further Reading

Aberbach, Joel D., and Mark A. Peterson. *Institutions of American Democracy: The Executive Branch*. New York, NY: Oxford University Press, 2006.

Adams, Abigail, and John Adams. Margaret A. Hogan and C. James Taylor, eds. *My Dearest Friend: Letters of Abigail and John Adams*. Cambridge, MA: Belknap Press of Harvard University Press, 2007.

Amar, Akhil Reed. *America's Constitution: A Biography*. New York, NY: Random House, 2005.

Angelo, Bonnie. *First Families: The Impact of the White House on Their Lives*. New York, NY: Harper, 2007.

Bausum, Ann. *Our Country's Presidents: All You Need to Know About the Presidents from George Washington to Barack Obama*. Washington, DC: National Geographic, 2009.

Beeman, Richard R. *Plain, Honest Men: The Making of the American Constitution*. New York, NY: Random House, 2009.

Boller, Paul, Jr. *Presidential Campaigns: From George Washington to George W. Bush*. New York, NY: Oxford University Press, 2004.

Cronin, Thomas E., and Michael A. Genovese. *The Paradoxes of the American Presidency*. New York, NY: Oxford University Press, 2009.

Dyer, Davis, and Alan Brinkley, eds. *The American Presidency*. New York: Mariner Books, 2004.

Foner, Eric. *The Story of American Freedom*. New York, NY: W. W. Norton, 1999.

Giddens-White, Bryon. *The President and the Executive Branch*. Chicago, IL: Heinemenn Library, 2006.

Grace, Catherine O. *The White House: An Illustrated History*. New York, NY: Scholastic, 2003.

Hennessey, Jonathan. *The United States Constitution: A Graphic Adaptation*. New York, NY: Hill and Wang, 2008.

Kettl, Donald F. *The Next Government of the United States: Why Our Institutions Fail Us and How to Fix Them*. New York, NY: W. W. Norton, 2009.

Lott, Jeremy. *The Warm Bucket Brigade: The Story of the American Vice Presidency*. Nashville, TN: Thomas Nelson, 2008.

Mayhew, David R. *Parties and Policies: How the American Government Works*. New Haven, CT: Yale University Press, 2008.

McPherson, James M. *To the Best of My Ability*. New York, NY: DK Adult, 2004.

Obama, Barack. *The Audacity of Hope: Thoughts on Reclaiming the American Dream*. New York, NY: Vintage, 2008.

Roberts, Cokie. *Ladies of Liberty: The Women Who Shaped Our Nation*. New York, NY: William Morrow, 2008.

Ross, Tara. *Enlightened Democracy: The Case for the Electoral College*. Dallas, TX: Colonial Press, 2005.

Shambaugh, George. *The Art of Policy Making: Tools, Techniques, and Processes in the Modern Executive Branch*. New York, NY: Longman, 2003.

Index